*How Jews and Christians
Interpret Their Sacred Texts*

How Jews and Christians Interpret Their Sacred Texts
A Study in Transvaluation

Charles David Isbell

RESOURCE Publications · Eugene, Oregon

HOW JEWS AND CHRISTIANS INTERPRET THEIR SACRED TEXTS
A Study in Transvaluation

Copyright © 2014 Charles David Isbell. All rights reserved. Except for brief quotations in critical publications or reviews, no part of this book may be reproduced in any manner without prior written permission from the publisher. Write: Permissions. Wipf and Stock Publishers, 199 W. 8th Ave., Suite 3, Eugene, OR 97401.

Resource Publications
An Imprint of Wipf and Stock Publishers
199 W. 8th Ave., Suite 3
Eugene, OR 97401

www.wipfandstock.com

ISBN 13: 978-1-61097-519-3

Manufactured in the U.S.A.   08/18/2014

For Leslie, my hero

Contents

Preface | ix
List of Abbreviations | xiii
Introduction | xvii

1. The Sacred Texts of Judaism and Rabbinic Instruction | 1
2. The Sacred Texts of Christianity: Early Authors | 36
3. Early Jewish Principles of Interpretation | 55
4. Hermeneutics of the New Testament, the Early Church, and Beyond | 102
5. Jewish Transvaluation | 145
6. New Testament and Early Christian Transvaluation | 173

   Conclusion: Future Directions | 200

Bibliography | 209
Scripture and Other Sources Index | 213
Names Index | 227
Subject Index | 233

Preface

IN THE FLOOD OF books and articles that have appeared in the twenty-first century about Judaism and Christianity, a starting point for many analysts has been the belief that radical or fundamentalist adherents of each system are dedicated to a literal reading of the holy books of their faith. I believe that such an assumption is demonstrably false.

Some recent books about Christianity have focused on distinctions between Christianity and radical Islam, typically without proper understanding of the latter. Others have denounced the failures of the Christian faith to achieve its own goals in the world; of course these "goals" vary widely depending upon the viewpoint of the author enumerating them.[1] Christianity has been divided over a wide array of issues: abortion, gay marriage, and a myriad of other political and social questions. Both sides of these internal Christian debates accept the assumption that the "fundamentalist" or "conservative" Christians are the ones who take the Bible literally. To be sure, this is a perception that fundamentalist Christians prefer to advance about themselves, often in ignorance of the fact that proponents of many different perspectives within Christianity remain convinced that a simple reading of the Bible supports *their* cause. Indeed, one of the fastest growing branches of Christianity witnessed by the new century has been the explosion of non-denominational congregations, with loyalties only to their own local group. The common way such groups describe themselves is, "we believe exactly [and only] what the Bible says."

Current Jewish scholarship has seen a great number of books discussing anti-Semitism and the Shoah, Jewish history around the world, a

---

1. On fundamentalist expressions of goals for America, see Chris Hedges, *American Fascists*.

political and religious perspective of modern Israel, and of course biblical and rabbinic exegesis. Orthodox Jews also seem anxious at every turn to presume that their positions are self-evidently *the* one true Judaism, and even liberal or non-practicing Jews often seem content to assume that Orthodox Jews are correct in announcing that their views of the Bible and the Talmud are somehow more Jewish than the stances of Conservative, Reform, or Reconstructionist Jews.

No book of which I am aware has tackled the question that forms the central focus of my work here, for no author has attempted to explain the *methodology* of interpreters who offer their nostrums to the world in the name of one sacred book or another. Always the focus is upon *what* is being taught rather than on the methodological route traveled to arrive at those teachings. Believing their sacred texts are inerrant and bear only a single meaning, such writers are invariably led to the specific interpretation that conforms in the most consistent fashion to the teachings of their particular group. However, when methodology is examined, it becomes clear that so-called literal readings are not literal at all, but are personal interpretations based upon the political or theological agendas of their authors and the communities they represent. Accordingly, this book is my attempt to illustrate the classical rules of interpretation that allowed both Jews and Christians to move beyond the literal meaning of their respective sacred texts in search of interpretations that supported the social and political needs of their co-religionists two millennia ago. This is an issue that commentators have addressed only tangentially if at all.

To describe this process of appropriation, it is necessary to distinguish between literal interpretation and *inerrancy*,[2] the presumption that a sacred text contains no error of any kind—historical, scientific, moral, or political. This view often presumes that there must be one and only one correct meaning for the Bible, in the process ignoring the wide-ranging interpretations that began to appear even within the pages of the biblical text itself.[3]

---

2. Those who believe in inerrancy argue that while no one can deny the presence of errors in the texts we now possess, the original manuscripts (autographs) were inerrant. I fail to see how it solves the problem to argue that God originally gave humanity an inerrant text that no one has ever seen and thus cannot be read or studied.

3. To cite only a few examples, the biblical narratives offer creation occurring in two different sequences, fail to agree on the number of animals taken into the ark by Noah, and even offer two different ideas about when the sacred name of YHWH (Yahweh) first began to be used among the early Israelites.

But there are differences between what a biblical text *meant* in its original context and what it has come to *mean* in the hands of post-biblical, and now modern interpreters. To describe the process by which these differences occur, I have chosen to speak of *transvaluation*, by which I mean attempts to retain the core *values* of classical sacred texts that are bound to specific times and *Sitze im Leben*, while seeking to extrapolate from those ancient texts teachings believed relevant to faith and praxis in the lifetime of the interpreters. Transvaluation presupposes the necessity of re-interpreting perceived *timeless* teachings in light of historical, sociological, theological, and political developments that occurred long after the composition of the text itself. Another way to say this is that religious *symbol*s, sacred texts in this case, remain constant, retaining a fixed literary form over centuries of time. However, the *interpretations* (plural!) of the text/symbol shifted in response to new knowledge learned from other, often non-religious spheres of life. It is thus especially significant to demonstrate exactly how classical *faith* texts are being used by post-classical interpreters, and then by modern-day adherents, themselves often quite ignorant of the original context and historical roots of the faith they espouse, as support for a particular social or political agenda.

I believe that scholars of religion will benefit from this work as will lay members of both faiths who need to examine the methodological assumptions that operate in the minds of those who write their textbooks and sermons, their manuals and their devotional literature. I believe further that departments of religion in public institutions will utilize the material I have assembled, even when their instructors disagree with my conclusions. Rabbinical colleges and Christian seminaries will be able to use this work to supplement their courses on inter-faith dialogue, as well as in more general course work in hermeneutics.

I have worked from the primary sources in every case, taking my examples from the Hebrew Bible, the Hebrew and Aramaic Talmud, and the Greek New Testament. In a large number of cases I have worked from the original languages of the secondary literature as well, whether the Hebrew of the post-Talmudic rabbis or the Greek and Latin of the church fathers. The translations throughout are my own, except where indicated, and I have also noted places where original sources were not available to me.

I have tried to read current scholarly analyses, but my purpose is not to deal with current secondary literature so much as to allow the classical texts to speak for themselves as the basis for my argument that their voices are not, and never were, unchallenged, literal sources for Jewish or Christian theology. Because contextual and political needs have informed the interpretations given to classical texts from the outset, modern interpreters should understand that they have at their disposal acceptable historical models that allow for tolerance and respect even in the face of apparently rigid and unbending formulations found in their respective sacred texts.

Abbreviations

ABD   *Anchor Bible Dictionary*. 6 vols. Edited by David Noel Freedman. New York: Doubleday, 1992.

ANET   J. B. Pritchard, editor, *Ancient Near Eastern Texts Relating to the Old Testament*, Third Edition with Supplement. Princeton: Princeton University Press, 1969.

Arndt & Gingrich   *A Greek-English Lexicon of the New Testament and Other Early Christian Literature*. Chicago: University of Chicago Press, 1979.

BAR   *Biblical Archaeology Review*

BCE   Before the Common Era

CBQ   *Catholic Biblical Quarterly*

CCAR   *Central Conference of American Rabbis*

CE   Common Era

EJ   *Encyclopedia Judaica*

HTR   *Harvard Theological Review*

IDB   *Interpreter's Dictionary of the Bible*. 4 vols. Edited by George Arthur Buttrick. Nashville: Abingdon, 1962.

IDBSup   *Interpreter's Dictionary of the Bible. Supplementary Volume*. Edited by Keith Crim. Nashville: Abingdon, 1976.

ISBE	*International Standard Bible Encyclopedia.* 4 vols. Edited by Geoffrey W. Bromiley et al. Grand Rapids: Eerdmans, 1979–88.
JBL	*Journal of Biblical Literature*
JBQ	*Jewish Biblical Quarterly*
JPS	*Jewish Publication Society*
JSOT	*Journal for the Study of the Old Testament*
LXX	The Septuagint
MT	The Massoretic Text
TB	*Babylonian Talmud*
TJ	*Jerusalem Talmud*
TDNT	*Theological Dictionary of the New Testament.* 10 vols. Edited by Gerhard Kittel and Gerhard Friedrich. Translated by Geoffrey W. Bromiley. Grand Rapids: Eerdmans, 1964–76.
TDOT	*Theological Dictionary of the Old Testament.* 14 vols. Edited by G. Johannes Botterweck and Helmer Ringgren. Translated by Geoffrey W. Bromiley et al. Grand Rapids: Eerdmans, 1974–2004.
WAB	*D. Martin Luthers Werke Briefwechsel,* edited by K. Burdach et al. Weimar, Germany: 1930.

Old Testament

Gen	Genesis
Ex	Exodus
Lev	Leviticus
Num	Numbers
Deut	Deuteronomy
Josh	Joshua
Judg	Judges
1 Sam	First Samuel
2 Sam	Second Samuel
1 Kgs	First Kings
2 Kgs	Second Kings
Isa	Isaiah
Jer	Jeremiah
Ezek	Ezekiel
Hos	Hosea
Joel	Joel
Amos	Amos
Obad	Obadiah
Jonah	Jonah
Micah	Micah
Nah	Nahum
Hab	Habakkuk
Zeph	Zephaniah
Hag	Haggai
Zech	Zechariah
Mal	Malachi
Pss	Psalms
Prov	Proverbs
Ruth	Ruth
Song	Song of Songs
Eccl	Ecclesiastes
Lam	Lamentations
Esth	Esther
Dan	Daniel
Ezra	Ezra
Neh	Nehemiah
1 Chron	First Chronicles
2 Chron	Second Chronicles

New Testament

Matt	Matthew
Mark	Mark
Luke	Luke
John	John
Acts	Acts
Rom	Romans
1 Cor	First Corinthians
2 Cor	Second Corinthians
Gal	Galatians
Eph	Ephesians
Phil	Philippians
Col	Colossians
1 Thess	First Thessalonians
2 Thess	Second Thessalonians
1 Tim	First Timothy
2 Tim	Second Timothy
Titus	Titus
Phlm	Philemon
Heb	Hebrews
Jas	James
1 Pet	First Peter
2 Pet	Second Peter
1 John	First John
2 John	Second John
3 John	Third John
Jude	Jude
Rev	Revelation

Talmudic, Tractates, and Rabbinic Sources

Ar.	Arakhin	Oh.	Ohalot
A.Z.	Avodah Zarah	Or.	Orlah
B. Bat.	Baba Batra	Parah	Parah
Bek.	Berakhot	Peah	Peah
Ber.	Bekhorot	Pes.	Pesahim
Bik.	Bikkurim	Qidd.	Qiddushin
B.M.	Baba Metzia	Qinnim	Qinnim
B.M.R.	Ba-Midbar Rabbah	R.H.	Rosh ha-Shanah
B.Q.	Baba Qamma (or B.K. – Baba Kamma)	S.A.	Shulhan Arukh
		Sanh.	Sanhedrin
		S.H.	Sefer ha-Hinnuch
Ed.	Eduyyot	Shab.	Shabbat
E.R.	Ecclesiaster Rabbah	Shav.	Shavu'ot
Erub.	Erubin	Shev.	Shevi'it
Gem.	Gemara	Sheq.	Sheqalim
Git.	Gittin	Sifra	Sifra
Hag.	Hagigah	Sotah	Sotah
Hal.	Hallah	S.S.	Sifrei Shoftim
Hor.	Horayot	Sukkah	Sukkah
Hul.	Hullin	Tamid	Tamid
Kel.	Kelim	TB	Babylonian Talmud
Ker.	Keritot	Tem.	Temurah
Ket.	Ketubot	Ter.	Terumot
Kil.	Kilayim	TJ	Palestinian (Jerusalem) Talmud
Mak.	Makkot		
Makh.	Makhshirin	Tos.	Tosephta
M.R.	Midrash Rabbah	Toh.	Tohorot
Meg.	Megillah	Yad.	Yadayim
Menah.	Menahot	Yal.	Yalqut
Miq.	Miqvaot	Yebam.	Yebamot
Naz.	Nazir	Yoma	Yoma
Ned.	Nedarim	Zabim	Zabim
Neg.	Negaim	Zev.	Zevahim
Nid.	Niddah		

Introduction

THIS MANUSCRIPT IS AN exploration of the ways in which rabbinic Judaism and early Christianity perceived and interpreted their sacred books. When I began my research, I assumed that the early interpreters of these two faith systems must have employed radically different methods of exegesis in order to arrive at conclusions that were so different as to be mutually exclusive. This attitude is exemplified in the theological treatment of Judaism and Christianity by virtually all scholars, and is articulated most sharply by Professor Hartmut Gese of Tübingen. Gese argues that the Old and New Testaments of the *Christian* Bible form a single closed corpus or continuum of tradition, the New Testament forming the completion of the process of divine revelation begun in the Old. In *Judaism*, Gese maintains, the Pharisees enacted a "reduction" of the available written traditions by excluding numerous works[4] from the third major section of the Hebrew Scriptures (*Ketuvim*). In short, for Gese, as also for other Christian theologians, Judaism and Christianity treated their common tradition in radically different ways. Judaism reduced the "old" tradition and initiated a "new" one that contrasted sharply with all that had preceded it. Christianity completed the ancient stream of tradition and, despite the name of its own sacred works, contributed nothing "new" methodologically, simply continuing the flow of ideas that issue from the Old Testament.

Another aspect of this scholarly view is the lip service given by almost everyone who authors a work of "Old Testament Theology" to the necessity of establishing a straight line link with the New Testament. That

---

4. Gese mentions books like Tobit, Judith, the "Wisdom of Solomon," the Testament of the Twelve Patriarchs, the books of Maccabees, ben Sira, and Enoch. His argument is spelled out in detail in *Vom Sinai zum Zion, 11–30.*

such a link is often strained and in fact virtually impossible from the starting point of responsible exegesis is a point well made by Professor James Barr.[5] Yet the perception remains that the New Testament treatment of the Old Testament is so fundamentally different from the rabbinic reformulation of the same text that two competing methods of interpretation must be assumed. It was this assumption that led ultimately to the views of Gese, that the New Testament continued the theological traditions of the Old Testament, while the early rabbis broke with it entirely in order to create a totally different system.

At the beginning of my research, I began almost immediately to sense that this assumption is far too simplistic. Conclusions are one thing, but the methodology employed to reach those conclusions is something else entirely. Thus in the course of examining the methods of the early rabbis and then the New Testament and other early Christian authors, it became clear that the two faith systems had spoken from the outset a common hermeneutical language despite the radically different conclusions that began to shape the religious beliefs and practices in the two great faith traditions in the first- and second-century CE. Consequently, for later interpreters, the differing conclusions of the two systems served to obscure the similarities of method that had existed from the outset.

One shortcoming common to both Judaism[6] and developing Christianity has been the failure to define the difference between *principle* and *practice*. That is, the ways in which individual Jews or Christians have appropriated the interpretations of their respective classical scholars have often become radically different from what the models of their own faith systems indicate they *should* do. In principle, both religions teach "peace" and "love." But because adherents of Judaism and Christianity throughout the centuries have often been ill-informed not only about their sister faith, but also about their own, the temptation has been always to judge one's own religion by appeal to its *principles* while condemning the faith of the "other" by citing the poor *practices* of some of its followers.

I do not wish to offer another in a long line of saccharine assurances that "Judaism teaches social justice" or that "Christianity is a religion of love." I am concerned about the ways in which scholars of the two sister faiths operated from earliest times with stunning freedom to reach theological positions that suited their own social, religious, and political

---

5. *The Concept of Biblical Theology* (Minneapolis: Fortress Press, 1999), *passim*.
6. As distinct from the early Yahwism of the Bible or the Judaism of a later era.

needs. And I am fascinated by the fact that this freedom always tied itself to canonical sacred literature no matter how ill-suited the ligatures might appear retrospectively to the modern mind. In the coming chapters, I will demonstrate the connections made between the Hebrew Scriptures, sacred to both Judaism and Christianity, by the Talmud and the New Testament, which became respectively the bases for all modern systems of the two faiths. Similar developments exegetically are attested in each case. First, a core canon of literature developed over time and was then proclaimed to be authoritative. Second, an equally authoritative corpus of interpretive reformulations was produced, either proclaiming itself (as the rabbis did) or being subsequently ratified (as was the case of the Church and the New Testament) as authentic explication of the initial core canon. Third, complicated interpretations of these original reformulations were produced by commentators whose backgrounds within the faith varied and whose conclusions were tied to regional or their own current cultural customs and practices. Finally, despite seemingly irreconcilable differences, and despite obvious interpretative movement well outside the sphere of the literal or plain sense of an original, sacred text, commentators in both faith systems continued to hold doggedly to the position that their conclusions were not only based firmly upon the initial authoritative text but were in fact a natural extension and continuation of it.

One important question is whether extreme passages from the canonical texts of the two religions can be wrenched from historical context and forged into an excuse for exclusionary social agendas or even violent actions. I will argue that it is not a simplistic and literal reading of literature that permits a particular sacred text to be forged into such uses. To the contrary, such reshaping occurs only by the implementation of long-standing and sophisticated interpretative methods. As stated in the *Preface*, to describe these classical and early post-classical appropriations, I have chosen to speak of the *transvaluation* of a text. My former Professor of Bible at Brandeis University, the esteemed Nahum M. Sarna, used the term "Transformations."[7]

While it is absolutely essential to condemn the extremist interpreters of such texts, regardless of which faith system is represented, it is inappropriate to issue a blanket condemnation of an entire faith system merely by citing some of its texts that the civilized world now believes to be offensive.

7. See his "The Authority and Interpretation of Scripture in Jewish Tradition," C. Thoma and M. Wyschogrod, eds., *Understanding Scripture*, 9-20.

Furthermore, it is crucial that modern interpreters be required to recognize and acknowledge their own processes. They may indeed claim, and perhaps sincerely believe, that they are simply reading the "plain sense" of the Bible or the New Testament, but ideological agendas are easily detectable just below the surface. The issue is not that no one ever claims to be reading their own holy books literally, only that no one actually does so. I believe my research will illustrate that such readings not only are impossible in our modern era but that such has always been the case. In short, interpreters from the earliest moments of their engagement with the text recognized the need, and exercised the freedom, to go beyond a simplistic, literalistic understanding of sacred literature.

In the light of our examination of the interpretation methods used over the centuries by sages within the two faith systems, we can see also the unavoidable consequences that have always flowed, not from literal readings of the difficult pre-modern sacred texts that are present in all religions, but from the wide-ranging freedom each system allows methodologically. The use of physical violence ("terror") or political blackmail to achieve political agendas is one of the most pressing religio-political issues of the twenty-first century, and the history of both faiths has much to teach the world about terror founded upon a sacred text. Both Judaism and Christianity had to learn by sober experience the consequences of reading their own texts monolithically as an excuse for exclusion, hatred, and violence.

Extremist Jews started an unwinnable war against Rome in 67 CE, a conflict that led to the destruction of Jerusalem, the slaughter of scores of thousands of Jews, the expulsion of Jews from their own holy city and its sacred sites, and a 1900-year forced exile from the land of Israel. Extremist Christians witnessed the sending forth of children on crusades to free the holy land from the "infidels." Many of these children died and many others were enslaved in Muslim-controlled lands. Christianity also witnessed the results of numerous acts of murder and destruction against Jews who were officially regarded as their precursors in the faith, but who were tagged by literalist interpreters of Christian sacred texts as the killers of god. The final insanity of the *Shoah* ("holocaust") so shook the Christian world that major theological changes have been issued from Rome and several Protestant bodies; despite the fact that Christian anti-Jewish feelings still exist, it is no longer defensible openly to espouse the killing or persecution of Jews on the supposed basis of a Christian canonical text.

Two-thousand years ago, the soul searching forced upon Judaism and Christianity alike by the fall of the Second Temple, and the unquestioned hegemony of pagan Rome, required both rabbis and early Christian authors to admit that their own sacred text (and it was the *same* text!) simply did not work literally in all situations and in every context. A fair reading of the interpretative history of Judaism and Christianity attests that the earliest scholars in both faiths knew this from the beginning, and the record of their earliest attempts to appropriate biblical truth for their day quickly sounded the death knell to all attempts at understanding them monolithically. To have insisted in the first century CE upon a literalistic hermeneutic by failure (or refusal) to acknowledge the time-bound and event-specific nature of biblical literature would have meant that both Judaism and Christianity would have failed to act responsibly to the realities of the changing world in which they lived and to which they declared their beliefs. Had they failed at this point, both faith systems might have died aborning.

Signs of hope for mutual respect and honest dialogue, not merely some vanilla form of "tolerance," must be generated internally by each faith system. And in both Judaism and Christianity, such internal generation is apparent historically. Judaism witnessed the *Haskalah*, the teaching of Mordecai Kaplan, and a now 250-year-old "Reform" movement, all beamed in the direction of modernity. Christianity contributed to and benefited from the enlightenment that swept over Europe, inheriting rigorous new methods of textual and literary analysis as well as a fresh breeze of openness to critical thought. Yet to be decided is whether Judaism and Christianity facing new issues in our era will acknowledge the methodological openness exemplified by their earliest interpreters, who reformulated Scripture rigorously in light of their own times.

1

The Sacred Texts of Judaism and Rabbinic Instruction

As stated in the Introduction, this book is an examination of hermeneutical methods employed to interpret the Bible by the early rabbis, the authors of the New Testament, and early post-New Testament Christian scholars. Because their work involved texts they believed were sacred and authoritative, it is necessary at the outset to describe what those texts were and how they developed into the written forms that Jews and Christians came to venerate as canonical before we proceed to describe the processes by which they went about the business of interpretation.

The Bible

TORAH	PROPHETS	WRITINGS
Genesis	Joshua	Psalms
Exodus	Judges	Proverbs
Leviticus	Samuel	Job
Numbers	Kings	Song of Songs
Deuteronomy	Isaiah	Ruth

TORAH	PROPHETS	WRITINGS
	Jeremiah	Lamentations
	Ezekiel	Ecclesiastes
	"The Twelve"	Esther
		Daniel
		Ezra-Nehemiah
		Chronicles

The Hebrew Bible is the basic holy book of Judaism. But the term "book" is misleading. As shown in the chart above, the Bible of Judaism includes three major divisions consisting of five, eight, and eleven smaller units, a total of twenty-four.[1] The first of these divisions is known by various names. In Hebrew it may be called the *Ḥumash* (*ḥûmaš*) meaning "five" or "fifths," or simply Torah, a broad term signifying "teaching" or "instruction." Its best-known English designation is Pentateuch, a compound word from two Greek terms meaning "five scrolls."

The second major division of the Bible is the Prophets (*nəvî'îm*), which includes two subdivisions: Former Prophets[2] and Latter Prophets.[3] Because its subject matter deals with historical events, initially with the conquest and subsequent division of the land and then with the careers of the kings and prophets of Israel and Judah (spanning roughly six hundred years), the first of these subdivisions is often called Historical Books, especially by non-Jewish scholars. Yet the Former Prophets cannot be considered history by any objective reading of the text itself.[4] These books present the prophetic *interpretation* of the religious significance

---

1. The Protestant English Bible counts thirty-nine by dividing Samuel, Kings, Ezra-Nehemiah, and Chronicles into two separate books and by counting as separate the twelve Minor Prophets. The Catholic Bible, to be discussed in the next chapter, numbers forty-six to fifty-four.

2. The books of Joshua, Judges, Samuel, and Kings.

3. The books of Isaiah, Jeremiah, Ezekiel, and the Twelve (minor prophets).

4. Isbell, "'History' and 'Writing.'" The rabbis also recognized quite early that biblical narratives are not "history" as we would define that term. Among the thirty-two hermeneutical principles of Rabbi Yose ben Elazar (second-century Galilean), followed in the rabbinic interpretation of the Torah itself, two are noteworthy here: "There is no early or late in the Torah" (*'eyn muqdam u-me'uḥar ba-torah*); "The pericopes of the Torah were not given in chronological order" (*lo' nitnu parshiyoteyha shel torah 'al ha-seder*).

or spiritual meaning of the period of Israelite history from the Conquest led by Joshua in the twelfth century BCE to the conquest of Jerusalem by the Babylonians in 587 BCE. What is more, the perspective of the work is unabashedly Judahite, slanted in favor of a Jerusalem capital, a Davidic king, and a national center of worship at the Temple in Jerusalem. Because of this Judahite preference, northern kings that were merely politically significant received only terse notice from the prophetic editors except in instances where their evil actions were chronicled in detail to explain a current political crisis, and great attention was given to kings whose spiritual deficiency created political problems. The best example of this lack of interest in matters that were merely political or military is found in the way that the career of Omri is treated. Omri was a significant monarch internationally,[5] who founded a ninth-century dynasty that still bore his name one hundred years after his death,[6] built an impressive new capital city at Samaria, and launched a series of successful military campaigns that brought significant territorial gains to the northern kingdom of Israel. But he was dismissed by the prophetic editors of Kings in a mere handful of verses in 1 Kings (16:16–28). On the other hand, kings like David and Solomon, Hezekiah, and Josiah, all of whom were perceived as spiritually significant leaders and all of whom were Judahite, received lavish praise and prophetic approval from the same editorial guild.

The other subdivision of the Prophets is known in Hebrew as the Latter Prophets, often referred to by scholars as the writing prophets. In this literature, the careers of prophetic giants are chronicled, some of their messages are set down in writing, probably by generations of students who studied in their wake,[7] and additional prophetic opinions about political events are recorded. In the past two hundred years, there has been a good deal of scholarly debate about the true authors of these books. Earlier ultra-conservative scholars routinely held that most if not all of the books were written by the prophet whose name they bear. However, the majority of modern scholars view each book as a composite work that has come to its present form from numerous individual hands

---

5. His military prowess is cited by the inscription of King Mesha of Moab (ninth century BCE).

6. Several eighth century Assyrian inscriptions list Jehu as the "son of Omri," and refer to the whole of the northern Kingdom of Israel as "the dynasty of Omri." See *ANET*, 280–81 and 284–85.

7. See Isbell, "The *Limmudim* in the Book of Isaiah," 99–109.

by a process of growth and development, sometimes lasting for several decades or more.

The third major division of the Hebrew Bible receives the name the Writings (*kətûvîm*), a designation that could also be taken to mean "miscellaneous."[8] This division includes literature ranging in subject matter from interpreted history to apocalyptic musings, from practical aphorisms (proverbs) to philosophical speculation about the true meaning of life and death.

From ancient times, the author of the entire Pentateuch was believed to have been a single individual, the great leader of the Exodus from Egypt named Moses. And yet, as early as one thousand years ago, a close reading of the text itself led some Jewish scholars to doubt such a simplistic explanation. First, throughout the Pentateuch, Moses is described in the third person, an awkward perspective for an author who is writing firsthand, especially if one tries to imagine such an author describing his own death in the past tense (Deut 34). Second, the entire work is in Hebrew, a language Moses almost surely did not know.[9] The narrative of his life[10] describes him as having been officially adopted and given a pure Egyptian name by the princess who found him floating on the Nile River. He was then reared in the Egyptian palace, where he would have received his education in the language of Egypt rather than in what would only later develop as a dialect (i.e., Hebrew) of Canaan, a place he never visited!

Third, some statements appear to have been written down much later than Moses could have lived. Statements like, "the Canaanites were in the land at that time" (Gen 12:6) obviously had to have been written at some time after the Canaanites were no longer in the land, and such a time was long after the death of Moses.

Fourth, Moses is described as "the most humble man on the face of the earth" (Num 12:3), a self-appraisal that a truly humble person could hardly have written about himself.

Fifth, parallel accounts (doublets) of numerous events contain differences in language and style, in important details, and even names by which God is known and addressed. Thus there are two versions of creation, the Flood, the conquest of the city of Shechem, the name by

---

8. Its Hebrew designation *ketuvim* means "written things."

9. Thus when Moses first confronts the Pharaoh in Exodus 5, they communicate directly without the need of an interpreter.

10. Exodus 2:1–10 describe his birth, naming, and subsequent legal adoption by an Egyptian princess.

which Abraham addressed God, the call of Moses to lead the Exodus, and many other events. Furthermore, differing names of God, technical terminology, and other details of language and style fall consistently into a particular group of these doublets.

Sixth, even more intriguing is the fact that various strata of the Pentateuch give evidence of different theological perspectives. In one creation story, God is like a kindly big brother who strolls around in the Garden of Eden chatting with Adam and Eve.[11] In the other, God is more formal and distant, with a clear chasm existing between the humans and the divine. These theological perspectives also fall consistently within groups characterized by divine names, terminology, etc.

Scholars thus conclude that the present biblical work known as the Pentateuch is an edited version of several shorter independent editions of earlier literature.[12] Some of it reflects a northern point of view, some of it is openly southern. Some passages appear to derive from the mind of a lay person who was a great storyteller, while other passages are tightly woven and concerned with the kinds of details that would interest religious professionals (e.g., priests). Some of the passages are in elegant poetic form, the earliest of which scholars now date to the twelfth century BCE, but other passages are in a narrative style that deals with issues of interest well into the sixth century. No single individual could have lived long enough to write this entire work.

But even if it is supposed that Moses himself had the ability, or the inclination, to write in what was a foreign language to him, to compose more than one version of the same story numerous times, to give advice about kings many years before there was a monarchy, and to serve as the founder of the guild of the prophets before such a guild may be documented, one fact remains. The Bible itself bears witness to the *human* authorship of this most basic holy text of Judaism. Of course, there are many students of the Bible who believe what "Moses" wrote was inspired by God, and spoken directly to him by God. But the biblical text does not portray Moses as merely a passive tool standing by dumbly while God spoke, serving only as a mechanical mouthpiece. To the contrary, the text has Moses debate with God, as had Abraham and others before his time.[13]

---

11. Cf. Gen 3:8ff.

12. For a convenient and useful summary of the evidence for multiple sources in the Pentateuch, see Friedman, "Torah (Pentateuch)." Note also the bibliography there.

13. See Genesis 18:22–33 and note Jacob's deal with God negotiated in Genesis 28:20–22.

And in one famous text Moses wins the debate, refusing to allow God to act out his stated intentions with respect to the disobedient Israelites![14]

The fact of human authorship is also beyond dispute with respect to the Prophets, even where scholars disagree about the identity of the author of a particular book or passage. And once again, the humans who are quoted and examined in this part of the Bible are anything but passive instruments in the presence of an overpowering God.[15] In fact, one of the major functions of a true prophet was to intercede with God on behalf of the population at large, an audience that was seldom receptive to the prophetic voice. It is also clear that prophetic truth was not considered some kind of a monolithic glob that always meant the same thing at all times and in every political situation.[16]

When we turn to the third major division of the Hebrew Bible, once again we discover a large number of human authors involved in the process that ultimately produced the final version of each book that entered into the sacred canon. Perhaps somewhat surprisingly, not all of the heroes and/or authors in this division were Israelites/Jews. The hero of the book of Job was from the unknown Land of Uz, and two unidentified non-Israelites, Agur and Lemuel, are cited as authors or sources of parts of the book of Proverbs. The hero of the book of Daniel is named after an international figure well known from Ugaritic (later Phoenician) sources some twelve hundred years before the composition of the biblical book that bears his name. Even the books ascribed to famous Israelites testify to a large number of authors or editors. Among these are David and Solomon, Moses as author of Psalm 90, notable religious leaders like Ezra or Jeremiah, and even secular leaders like Nehemiah.

This fact of multiple authors involved with all three divisions of the Hebrew Bible leads to a feature of biblical literature that is often overlooked. The works that now comprise the canonical Scriptures were not the only literature produced by ancient Israel. And that means someone had to make choices about which books, or stories, or versions of a story, should be included and which could be excluded without appreciable damage to the community that turned to them for religious guidance and inspiration. It is certain that many individual authors of these works were

---

14. See Exodus 32:9–14.

15. To cite only one example, the passionate Jeremiah openly accused God of having deceived him (20:7), and wished that he had not been required to do the work of a prophet.

16. We will examine this phenomenon more fully in chapter 5.

no longer living when such decisions were made. In other words, it is not enough merely to assert that the authors of the Bible were "inspired," whatever may be meant by the term. In order to have faith in the Bible, ancient Israel had to put its trust in an entire community of students, disciples, and other spiritual leaders who chose the texts that came to be viewed as essential for the people as a whole. Said another way, it is not enough to believe that God inspired a deeply spiritual collection of messages from a great prophet or wise man at a given point in time. Had no one in the community of the prophets recognized the value of his messages, had no one copied them for and taught them to future generations, had no one insisted upon their spiritual value for the community of faith, they could not possibly have been included among the most influential books in all of Judaism.

Again, however much we believe that the people making such choices about which books to copy and study and transmit to the future were guided by God, it is clear that we must come to grips with the human dimension of the process. And this is underscored by the language of the Bible itself. The Hebrew language of Scripture is not an artificial language spoken by God in heaven and otherwise unknown here on the earth. In fact, what we call Hebrew was actually a dialect of Canaanite that came to be written using the Aramaic alphabet.[17] It conforms to rules of grammar and syntax, and for the most part is startlingly pointed and clear. In other words, although it may be argued that the teachings of the Bible are extraordinary, these teachings come to us as ordinary human speech set forth in ordinary human written forms.[18]

When we examine the time frame required for the composition of these different kinds of literature dealing with so many historical epochs and subjects, we discover a period of roughly one thousand years between the earliest (poems like Exodus 15) and latest (the book of Daniel) passages in the Bible. This span of time accords well with what we know of the human involvement in the composition of biblical literature. Scores, perhaps even hundreds, of individual authors and editors worked for virtually an entire millennium in order to produce what Jews came to revere as "the Bible." Because of this long passage of time, and because people from different geographical regions were involved, the language of the Bible reflects more than a single dialect of Canaanite Hebrew. And this

---

17. Similar to the way in which English is written in the Latin alphabet.

18. As we will see in chapter 3, this fact was openly acknowledged by post-biblical Jewish interpreters.

information must also be factored into our understanding of the ways (plural!) in which the Bible came to be read and interpreted.

We must mention here another historical fact indicating the fluidity of approaches to reading the Bible among early Jews. As early as the third century BCE, Jewish scholars began to translate the Bible from Hebrew into Greek to allow Greek-speaking Jews living in Egypt to understand the holy books. In addition, and almost as early as the Greek translation, Jewish leaders of worship also began the practice of translating for their congregations the portions of the Bible that were being read in services of worship. This was done simultaneously and orally into Aramaic, the common language of most Jews in the holy land. These translations are of special importance in indicating that Jews of the era did not view the original Hebrew as the only medium through which divine truth could be transmitted to the worshipping community. Rather, it was the *ideas* of Scripture that were deemed to be more important than the language in which they had been written. In fact, the classical rabbinic idea was that as early as the era of Joshua, the Torah had been translated into seventy different languages to make its contents available to the entire world.[19] This does not mean Hebrew was considered unimportant, but merely that Jewish scholars wanted people to understand in their own language the foundational or core texts of the faith.

The Talmud

Oral Torah: The Mishnah
דברה תורה כלשון בני אדם[20]
(dibrah ha-torah bilshon benei 'adam)

While it is true that the Hebrew Bible was/is the foundational sacred text of Judaism, it is equally true that the Bible presented a challenge of critical proportions to its earliest interpreters, the men who would come to be known as the "rabbis."[21] Originally not a professional guild, "a rabbi could be a priest or a layman, rich or poor, of noble ancestry or a recent convert, but he had to be upright in character, searching for knowledge,

---

19. See *Sotah* 35b.
20. "The Torah spoke in the language of ordinary people" (*Berakhot* 31b).
21. See Kolatch, *Masters of the Word*, 73–78.

and dedicated to his task."[22] The problem facing these men was the need to square the biblical teaching that Israel was the beloved and specially chosen people of God with the cruel historical fact that Israel's history was marked by suffering, and repeated defeats at the hands of godless enemies. Responses to this gap between biblical rhetoric and historical reality actually began within the pages of the Bible itself, when the great prophets attempted to explain Israelite suffering and defeats at the hands of godless Assyria and Babylonia as justly deserved punishment for infidelity and disobedience.

A second option, given by early post-biblical (rabbinic) interpreters, was that God was testing Israel because he loved her. On this view, the suffering of Israel turned paradoxically into evidence that those who suffer the most are recipients of special divine attention. This view was never adopted widely in normative Judaism.

Yet a third view, hinted at in late biblical texts and more fully developed in post-biblical rabbinic texts, suggested that Jews would be rewarded in the world to come for their suffering endured in this present world.

When we begin to analyze the thinking that permitted the rabbis to offer different creative responses to biblical texts, the most important statement about the sacred literature of Judaism is given in the opening verse of *Pirkei 'Avot*:[23] "Moses received Torah from God at Sinai. He transmitted it to Joshua, Joshua to the Elders, the Elders to the Prophets, the Prophets to the members of the Great Assembly." This assertion occurs in one of the later portions of the eclectic literary work known as the Mishnah, and addresses both the origin and the continuing importance of torah. But in this statement, the word "torah" has acquired a new and broader meaning, for here it is referring not only to the first five books of the Bible, but also to post-biblical "teaching" or "instruction" designed to help Jews interpret that Bible.

It is impossible to understand the way in which Judaism views its sacred texts without tracing the path that led to the writing of the Mishnah. Allowing for minor additions, it seems likely that the first section of the Hebrew Bible, the Torah, was completed as early as the fifth century BCE, in conjunction with the return from Babylonian Exile of several groups of Jews, led by the religious leader Ezra and his secular/political counterpart, Nehemiah. Also by that time, although the canon of Scripture

---

22. Trepp, *Judaism*, 23
23. A division of the Mishnah in the section on torts.

would not be finalized until the first Christian century, major sections of the prophetic narratives were already in use, as well as numerous parts of the Writings.[24]

But another force was at work as well. Virtually all of the literature of the Bible presumes an independent country, a capital in Jerusalem, a Temple, a king, and active guilds of prophets and priests. Beginning with the Babylonian Exile in the sixth century BCE, all of these were lost or withdrawn by conquering powers (except for a brief period in the second and first centuries BCE). This meant that by the beginning of the early rabbinic era (ca. 100 BCE–100 CE), much of the Bible addressed situations that no longer pertained to the everyday life of Jews. Even though Jews had been permitted by the Persian Empire to return to Jerusalem, to rebuild their Temple, and to enjoy a modicum of political rights, the old Kingdom of Judah no longer existed. What had once been a proud and independent nation was now only a tiny province within the Persian Empire, and Jews no longer controlled their own destiny. As history advanced, the Persians were replaced in succession by the Greeks, then by successors of Alexander who vied for control over Judea,[25] and finally by the Romans in 63 BCE.

By the time Rome occupied the land, Jews as a people were scattered in numerous different nations, from Egypt to Babylonia and elsewhere, and even those who remained in the Roman province of Judea experienced daily life that was far different from the conditions that had existed during the time when biblical literature was composed and edited. Already in biblical times, Judahism[26] from the time of Ezra had undergone a radical paradigm switch, so that in late pre-Christian biblical religion, social, and theological issues were no longer heavily influenced by prophets. Instead, the written Torah assumed center stage as *the* authoritative source for Jews. But such a Torah demanded interpretation in light of the political changes that had been forced upon Jews, and a new group of scholars and sages stepped forward to provide these interpretations. It is to this era that we must trace the origins of Judaism as a faith system that could be practiced wherever people live, not merely as the religion of one

---

24. I have traced the development of this literature as it came to be the Bible among Jews in my book, *God's Scribes*.

25. Under whom there was a period of about one hundred years when Jews took back political control of their own land and destiny.

26. Judahism may be defined as the religion of Judah prior to the era of the reconstruction of biblical faith into normative rabbinic Judaism (ca. 440–100 BCE).

specific political entity with a king, a capital city, a sacred Temple, and a free population. To make this possible, the Bible could not be viewed in a mechanical and literal fashion, but began to be interpreted in new and creative ways.

Judean Jews of the Roman era were deeply divided about how to interpret their Bible. One wealthy and influential group, the Sadducees, chose quite a narrow and conservative position. For them, only the Torah, the Pentateuch, was authoritative. What is more, the method by which they chose to interpret the Torah was very similar to the method of literalism practiced among conservative religious groups in all eras. So, for example, "You shall not curse a deaf man, nor set a stumbling block before the blind," (Lev 19:14), had only one meaning for the Sadducees. As long as one did not actually utter a curse or physically set a blockade in the pathway of a blind person, the commandment was considered fully kept. There was no attempt to probe behind the text, to consider a metaphorical sense for its teaching, or to broaden its application to real life. While examples such as this one could be multiplied, it is of particular significance to notice the rejection of the idea of resurrection by the Sadducees, a teaching not found in the Pentateuch, and therefore left out of their doctrine as well.

But there was another reason for the Sadducees to accept only the Pentateuch as authoritative, this one purely political. In the first century BCE, the Sadducees had quickly become the partners of Rome in the administration of the province of Judea. Assuring the Romans that they could control the population and prevent uprisings or disorder of any kind, they were granted control over the Temple with its significant income derived from contributions sent by Jews in every country in which they lived. Because of their wealth, their power, and their political status backed by Roman military force, it is not hard to understand why the Sadducees had no interest in the interpretations of the ancient prophets. The prophets had preached many a sermon about justice and fair treatment for all people, and they had indicted not only Jewish kings but also rulers in other countries as well. To take their writings seriously would have been to sound the death knell to any Jewish group courting favor with Rome.[27]

---

27. This idea underpins a striking passage in the New Testament, where the Sadducees fear that the activities of Jesus, left unchecked, would bring the Roman army in force to punish Judea: "the Romans will come and take away both our status and our nation" (John 11:48).

The Sadducees were opposed by another party, the Pharisees, a group that was destined to outlast them. Perhaps the single most important difference between the two groups centered on their view of sacred texts. The Pharisees accepted as authoritative not only the Torah (Pentateuch), but also the Prophets and the Writings, that is, all three divisions of the Bible introduced earlier. Not only did they accept the authority of far more literature than did the Sadducees, but the Pharisees also employed radically different methods of interpretation. Said simply, the idea of the "rabbis," as they would come to be known, was that while the central *principles* of truth in the Torah, Prophets, and Writings (i.e., the Bible) remained unchanged, it was necessary to interpret or reconstruct the ways in which these principles could be put into *practice* in the post-biblical era so that they could accommodate the realities of life under occupation. For the Pharisees, Leviticus 19:14 meant far more than merely abstaining from cursing or setting up roadblocks for the handicapped. They engaged in a long discussion about the verse, concluding that speech behind someone's back, designed to harm his reputation, even though spoken technically outside the hearing of the target party, was also included in the commandment. Similarly, using one's legal education to write a contract that a lay person could not read, and using such a contract to cheat that person in court, was considered by the Pharisees to be as fully "sinful" as the literal act of putting a chair in the path of a blind person.

There were other Jewish sectarian groups as well. The Essenes decided that Temple worship was no longer being carried out properly and retreated to the desert to wait for divine intervention in a great cosmic war that would signal the end of history and the return of all Jews to political and spiritual freedom in Judea.

Yet a fourth group of Jews, the Zealots, decided to take matters into their own hands, and initiate a campaign of terror against Rome. Their belief was that if they were to start a war against Rome, the most powerful military machine in the entire world, the God of the Bible, of Exodus, of Conquest in Canaan, would miraculously appear to help them win. History, of course, witnessed quite a different result. When the Zealots murdered numerous leading Sadducees, whom they hated for their partnership with Rome, the Roman army came to Jerusalem in force, laid siege to the city in 67 CE, and almost totally destroyed it three years later. There would be one final hiccup of resistance in 135 CE, a desperate attempt that met with the same result from Rome. But in the end, the holy Temple lay in ruins, scores of thousands of Jews were killed, and all Jews were banned from entering the city limits of Jerusalem. In a final insult, the Romans renamed the territory of Judea after a hated ancient Jewish enemy that had not existed for over six centuries.[28]

The only groups of Jews that survived this first century catastrophe were the Pharisees and the followers of Jesus of Nazareth who came to be called "Christians" (see Acts 11:26), both of whom began the process of building new religious faith systems. It is well known that the early Christians embarked on a concerted effort to reinterpret the Jewish Bible in order to ground their new religion.[29] What needs to be understood is that Judaism was no less assiduous than Christianity in its own impulse to redefine and reinterpret the old Scriptures. Christian reconstruction would lead to a new faith system grounded in fresh ways of reading the Bible. Jewish reconstruction, developing in virtually the same time frame and political context, re-interpreted the same sacred texts in order to make possible a totally new framework of biblical faith: rabbinic Judaism.[30]

It is important to stress the fact that the rabbinic teachings that carried such weight in formative Judaism were not merely miscellaneous ideas of isolated rabbis who worked alone giving private opinions.[31] Rather, these rabbinic rulings represented a consensus that was reached in the wake of open and vigorous debate. The most important and widely accepted among these opinions circulated in oral form among numerous groups of scholars known as *Tanna'im*[32] and their students, until the dawn of the third century CE. During this period, these rabbinic opinions acquired the title of oral torah, literally "Torah that is in the mouth" (*torah še-bəʿal peh*). Because oral torah was believed to have existed long before their day,[33] *Tanna'itic* commitment to the necessity of two torahs (writ-

---

28. *Palaestina* is the Latin translation of "Philistine."

29. We will discuss this process in chapter 2.

30. In chapters 5 and 6, we will examine several specific examples of the reformulations of both groups.

31. One indication of the openness to differences among scholars comes from the era of the Zugot (ca. 100–30 BCE), pairs of scholars, one of whom served as president of the Sanhedrin while the other was the head of the rabbinic court. The last pair, Hillel (a liberal) and Shammai (a conservative), are an example of the diversity that was prized in the search for legal and theological opinions.

32. The Hebrew equivalent is שונים, "repeaters," from the same root that yields the word "Mishnah." Note that although the seven pairs of Zugot have a distinct name for their era, they are actually part of the *Tanna'im*.

33. Attested in biblical passages like Exodus 34:27 and 24:12. See *Gittin* 60b and *Berakhot* 5a.

ten in the Bible and the oral opinions that resulted from their debates) was a fundamental principle guiding their work. Doubtless because of the veneration felt for biblical texts that already existed in written form, these oral opinions remained unwritten until the third century CE, at which time they were codified, and edited into a series of tractates that we know today as the Mishnah. We shall soon learn that the publication of the Mishnah in written form did not mark the end of the process of debate and reformulation of Jewish ideals and beliefs.[34]

Seeds	Rules governing agriculture, planting of crops, portions to be preserved for the poor, rest for the land, etc., but also including a series of appropriate "blessings" to be recited, and tithes to be presented.
Set Feasts/Fasts	Rules regulating the calendar year of Judaism, especially as its relates to various religious holidays and celebrations: the Sabbath, Passover, Yom Kippur, etc.
Women	Rules for family life, including children, betrothal and marriage, adultery, divorce; centering often on rules for the woman who was given primary responsibility for day-to-day family affairs.
Damages	Rules aimed at regulating business and interpersonal relationships, including the payment of monetary damages for injuries, and rules for the rabbinic courts with legal authority to decide such matters.

---

34. Within one hundred years, a smaller collection of additional opinions by the same *Tanna'im* was published. These acquired the name *tosephta* (תוספתא), "additions."

Holy Things	Rules that govern worship in the Temple, no longer standing, yet envisioned as still the focus of hope for a future restoration. In anticipation of this restoration, procedure for various offerings and sacrifices are set.
Purities	Extension of the sanctity accorded to the Temple proper into all aspects of life, but especially the home and synagogue. Details for appropriate treatment of illnesses and wounds also appear in this section.

It is the authoritative character of the Mishnah that is most remarkable, for when we examine once again their statement from *Pirkei 'Avot* cited above, it is clear that its authors and editors believed deeply that both the written Bible *and* their treatment of it were authoritative. Students reading the Mishnah for the first time are often surprised at the small number of times that the rabbis actually quote a specific text from the Bible. This fact is a reflection of two separate ideas. First, the *Tanna'im* knew the text of the Bible virtually from memory, so that even seemingly obscure allusions to a biblical teaching were easily identified by those involved in the discussion. Second, a paucity of specific citations from Scripture indicates the confidence of the *Tanna'im* that their own opinions conformed to the spirit and intention of Scripture so critical for Jewish life in their era. In other words, they had so immersed themselves in Scripture that they felt no need to quote it to each other, confident that all in their number knew the Bible well enough to understand exactly what it had spoken to an earlier era, as well as the issues under discussion that clouded its clear meaning. But while they ingested the words of Scripture and made it their own, they were simultaneously transforming and being transformed by it. Thus they had no hesitation to say, in effect, that their current interpretations had equal status and validity for Jewish life alongside the very words of Moses himself! In fact, the word "Mishnah" means repetition; the authors of this work believed their modern interpretations were not different in principle from the original teachings of the Bible, but merely reformulations (transvaluations) of those biblical principles necessary to shape them into an instrument that could remain relevant in a world that was in constant flux politically and religiously.

They did not believe they were teaching anything new, but were merely updating and bringing to relevance what they perceived to be a very old and authoritative system of faith and praxis.

Examination of the Mishnah illustrates another important principle. It does not include only the majority opinions or the winning side of each issue. To the contrary, minority opinions are represented in the discussions of question after question, with no attempt to mask the depth of disagreement involved.[35] It is important here to understand why the scholars of the Mishnah declined to tell all Jews that there must be one and only one position even with respect to what they believed to be fundamentally important issues of life and faith. We get the impression that choosing only one position would have been considered inappropriate on at least two counts. On the one hand, to have published only one opinion would have forced the rabbis to pretend to unanimity of judgment among them that simply did not exist. Even a cursory reading of their discussions attests that their disagreements with each other were real, and they refused to mask them merely for appearance sake, or even for written publication. Their intellectual honesty demanded that substantive disagreements be recorded. But there is a second reason why the creators of the Mishnah were quite comfortable to present many differing points of view. Each opinion was championed by a prestigious scholar whose honesty and integrity were beyond question, and one does not simply ignore such men. This meant the masters of the Mishnah left numerous questions open for subsequent generations of scholars to address, thereby ensuring that no scholar living in and studying at a time subsequent to the Mishnaic period would be bound by a single point of view. Instead, all scholars in successive generations would be not only free, but obligated, to defend and explain why they agreed with one position or the other.

The period of the Zugot encompasses a significant phase in the development of rabbinic discussion and debate. During this period of almost two hundred years (174 BCE to 10 CE), five pairs (zugot) of rabbinic scholars are credited with having maintained the chain of oral torah down to the time of Yohanan ben Zakkai, (introduced below). The first member of each pair was elected head of the Sanhedrin (*nasi'*) and the second became the leader of the system of smaller courts (*'av bet din*);[36] Each pair consisted of one Tanna' whose rulings were liberal, and one

---

35. In chapter 3 we will examine several examples of this phenomenon.

36. Neither the exact significance of these two titles nor their precise function is clear from the sources.

whose rulings were more conservative, and their rulings illustrate the freedom allowed for the expression of alternative points of view.[37]

Despite such sharp differences of opinion, debate and disagreement was intended to take place within an appropriate context of respect and civility. Thus in a discussion involving the final and most famous pair of scholars, Hillel and Shammai, the consensus developed that the opinions of the Hillel school were generally preferable to those of Shammai and his followers not merely because they were exegetically superior, but also because the Hillelites, "were kindly and modest, and they studied both their own rulings and those of the Shammaites. What is more, they mentioned first the Shammaite rulings before their own."[38] In other words, students/successors were impressed as much by the Hillelite *attitude* of humility and respect for their opponents as by the legal/technical superiority of their *halakhic* rulings. Students were free to choose either the more lenient rulings of Hillel or the normally more stringent decisions of Shammai, as long as they refrained from the impulse to "rabbi shop," seeking a lenient ruling in one instance from one rabbi and a strict ruling in another instance from a different rabbi.[39]

Within these boundaries of civility, very sharp disagreements often arose as the rabbis struggled to help Judaism comprehend its history of loss and punishment at the hands of the Babylonians, the cruelty of Antiochus Epiphanes, and finally the loss of the Temple to the Romans in 70 CE. Without suppressing disagreement and minority opinions, their efforts managed to produce a recasting of the entire system of Jewish worship in at least four important ways:

1. The local meeting place, or synagogue, replaced the Temple as the center of religious life.
2. A well-developed system of prayer and study replaced the regimen of sacrifices that had been followed in the Temple.

---

37. The best example of the refusal to insist on a single point of view is found in the debate about whether it was necessary to lay hands on a sacrifice offered during a festival. In each of the five zugot, one member said yes, while the other said no, and no final decision was ever reached.

38. *Eruvin* 13b. Similarly, Matthew 23:3 appears to acknowledge the technical rulings of the Pharisees while at the same time issuing a harsh denunciation of their conduct in life.

39. This is argued persuasively in *Eruvin* 6b.

3. All of time and space were co-opted as universes to be conquered and made holy, replacing the holy of holies that had made the Temple the most important site in the world before its destruction.

4. The idea of political independence was pushed into the background. Although it was retained in Jewish liturgy as a future hope, it was forced by reality into a position of secondary importance in Jewish life. In particular, the politically sensitive word "king" was redefined to refer only to God rather than any human monarch whom Rome might perceive as a political threat.

None of these four interpretative steps could have been accomplished by a simple reading of the Hebrew Bible taken in its literal sense. Instead, the rabbis of the first Christian centuries embarked upon a measured campaign to demonstrate the viability of their Bible as a guide to faith and religious practice among people who had lost everything once believed necessary to worship God.

Oral Torah: Gemara

As hinted above, the publication of the Mishnah was not the end of the era of rabbinic debate, discussion and reformulation. Following the era of the Zugot, a succession of four generations of scholars living in Israel contributed to what ultimately became the Mishnah, each generation of which produced at least one famous teacher. In the first generation were Yohanan ben Zakkai and Shimon ben Gamliel I, followed by Gamliel II (a grandson of Hillel), who served as head of the academy. The second generation boasted rabbis Akiva, Ishmael, Tarfon, and others, whose opinions are frequently cited in the Mishnah. The leaders of the third generation included numerous students of Akiva, and they were the group who lived through the ravages of the bar Kokhba rebellion that ended in 135 CE. In the last half of the second century CE, the outstanding Tanna' was Yehudah ha-Nasi', who served as head of the Sanhedrin. To him fell the task of overseeing the final editing of the Mishnah for written publication (ca. 220 CE). Because of increased Roman persecution beginning at the dawn of the third century, large numbers of scholars moved from Israel to Babylonia, where the creation of the Gemara ensued.

Even as the Mishnah was being prepared for written publication, the process of argumentation and debate continued under the direction of a group of scholars who were known as the 'Amoraim.⁴⁰ Between 200 and 500 CE, these rabbinic teachers, now based in Babylonia,⁴¹ not only sought to continue the work of the *Tanna'im*, but to build upon that work in a most interesting way. Taking one ruling of the Mishnah at a time, these later scholars almost routinely opened their discussion of each Mishnaic opinion with a question: "How [in what manner] is this true?" And whereas the framers of the Mishnah had seldom bothered to cite the biblical texts upon which they based their opinions, the *'Amoraim* went to great lengths to justify the conclusions of their predecessors by tying them directly to biblical authority, seeking ligatures in specific verses, half-verses, or even single words of the biblical text. They did not seek to overturn the rulings of the *Tanna'im*, but endeavored to provide the framework of biblical texts which they believed supplemented and justified the biblical foundation of those rulings.

The Babylonian *'Amoraim* did their work orally over a period of three plus centuries, finally setting forth a written document called the *Gemara*, an Aramaic word that means "completion." This title attests to the fact that the *'Amoraim* perceived their work to be genetically connected to the Mishnah of the *Tanna'im*, which, as we have seen, the *'Amoraim* tied closely to the Bible. After a period of some three centuries during which they expanded their discussions about the viability of each Mishnaic teaching and sought also to provide the biblical framework and support for the Mishnah, a written edition of the Gemara was published in the sixth century CE. This published version was clearly understood as a commentary upon the Mishnah, and the combined work of Mishnah and Gemara earned the title Talmud ("teaching"). Although there is only one Mishnah, scholars in Palestine and Babylonia produced two different versions of the Gemara.⁴²

---

40. Taken together, the *Tanna'im* and the *'Amoraim* became known as the "Hazal" (*ḥakhamenû zikhrônam livrakhah*), "our wise [teachers], may their memory be a blessing."

41. Although many other scholars remained in Israel, producing a Jerusalem Gemara to the Mishnah in ca. 350 CE. See later.

42. The more frequently cited, better-known, and more widely studied version is the *Babylonian Talmud* (*TB*). Except where specifically noted, all references to Talmud are to it rather than to the Jerusalem version (*TJ*). Shortly after the completion of the *Jerusalem Talmud*, in the context of a Roman Empire that had become Christianized via the conversion of the Emperor Constantine in 313, life in Israel became so difficult that the influence of the Jewish centers of learning declined dramatically.

Noteworthy too was the commitment of the *'Amoraim* to continue one other practice begun in the Mishnah, for in their written document as well, they published not merely the majority opinion, or the winning side of each argument, but also numerous minority or dissenting points of view. Once again, those who studied their work would not have handed to them an authoritative single answer to problems. They possessed instead a *methodological* model that was intended to serve all scholars in later Judaism—total immersion in and respect for the basic text of the Bible accompanied by an awareness and openness to numerous alternate opinions on virtually every issue. In fact, the most appropriate way to describe both the Mishnah and the Gemara is as a series of case studies in methods of argumentation and debate. It is clear that the *process* of study and debate itself was of far greater importance than arrival at a unanimous point of view to which all good Jews would be required to adhere. Becoming and remaining involved in this lifelong process of study marked the scholarly Jew. There was no call for lock-step agreement with a single conclusion perceived to be *the* one and only truth.

Rabbinic Instruction

While the Mishnah and Gemara were being framed in oral form by the rabbis to serve as instruction for fellow rabbis and scholars, a parallel task fell to them as well: the education of Jewish children. This fact indicates that rabbinic scholarship was not carried out in isolation from the daily life of ordinary Jews. Rather, the first "laboratory" in which rabbinic interpretations and methods were tested was the classroom, and the importance of this involvement by the rabbis in education cannot be overstated. It might even be said that the work of the rabbis required some means by which to commend itself to the larger Jewish community, and this could be done through children better than by any other avenue.[43]

Talmudic Subjects of Inquiry

Through the years, various branches of Judaism, and most non-Jewish students of the Talmud, have assumed that the Talmud was intended as a rigid guide to every minute aspect of life. Because many subjects discussed

---

43. The importance of educating children is an important theme in the Bible as well, of course. See my "Deuteronomy's Definition of Jewish Learning," 109–16.

in the Talmud are mundane, this has led to a fundamental misconception of the *function* of the Talmud in Jewish life. It must be remembered that during the years spanning the composition of the Talmudim,[44] education among non-Jews was available only for the wealthy élite throughout the known world. Thus the first important aspect of Talmudic activity was its function as the educational backbone for Jews. At a time when illiteracy was high throughout the world, virtually all Jews learned to read at least the Bible, the *Siddur* (prayer book), and the Mishnah-Talmud.

A second issue was philosophical. As the Christian world wrestled with Greek philosophy, especially with epistemology, Jews were creating a philosophical system of their own that was not always intended to be strictly practical. Abstract ideas were prized, and great value was assigned to the ability to think clearly and then to articulate specific positions. As a result, many of the absurdly fine points of Talmudic disputation have no specific practical value, but are intended to teach students and scholars how to think, how to discriminate, how to draw out every single ounce of meaning in the consideration of a problem. In this sense, Talmudic reasoning is rather like the academic field of mathematics. The emphasis is on problem solving, rather than merely on the importance of the particular problem used as a case study.

This means, third, that no area of common life was excluded from the discussions of the rabbis. In particular, questions that vexed less well-educated Jews were often sent to the scholars for their opinions.

Many of the questions addressed by the rabbis involved a concept of great importance, signified by the word *halakhah*. *Halakhah* is often defined as "law," but this is far too simplified a designation. At the root of the noun *halakhah* is the verb that means "to walk, to travel" (*halakh*). *Halakhah* is thus the "walk" of life, the pathway chosen for the journey each person takes in the daily living out of earthly existence. And a *halakhic* life must be an examined life, a life aware of the conclusions reached through intense debate among the finest minds in all of Judaism, but a life that does not shrink from arduous study in search of a personal stance on important issues. Law is an important part of this walk, but it is merely a part and not the whole. And this is verified when the subjects covered by the Talmud are examined. There the observant Jew may find rabbinic instruction about how to slaughter an animal properly for food, how to light candles for Shabbat, how to offer a blessing, the correct order in

---

44. Mishnaic period ca. 100 BCE–200 CE; period of Gemara, 200–500 CE.

which to offer prayers in worship, and scores of other technical matters. But there too the reader will find equally intense discussions about such "secular" matters as the appropriate way to respond when one finds a lost object. How long and how hard does one seek to find the true owner? When and under what circumstances does the lost object become the property of the finder? What if two people claim ownership of the same object? In other words, all areas of living, the secular as well as the sacred, were to be covered by guidelines, *halakhah*.

While virtually the entire Mishnah is *halakhah* as taught by the *Tanna'im*,[45] most of the Gemarot (pl. of Gemara) of the *'Amoraim* are liberally sprinkled with a second significant genre of literature to which the term *haggadah*[46] may be applied. At the root of this noun is the verb that means "to tell" (*lehagîd*). A *haggadah* is thus a story, the most famous of which is the Passover Haggadah, the story of Passover. Sprinkled throughout the pages of the Gemara are hundreds of stories, most of which involved well-known teachers in a variety of social, theological, and even political situations. As good teachers, the rabbis realized that their actions could often speak louder than their words. Accordingly, they accepted the responsibility that comes with being a role model, because they knew that "in the presence of their disciples their action spelled out both a legal precedent and an inspiration in faith. Seen in this manner, the concern of these men is not a dwelling on trivialities and hairsplitting, but an act of guidance. No one ever knows how deep the impression of his actions may be on others, though they may appear insignificant to himself."[47]

But there are also stories about nameless characters, Jew and non-Jew alike. By reading and discussing these stories, Jews were learning by example. Rather than a "do this" in circumstance "A", Jews learned what rabbi X had done in a particular circumstance that might be parallel to a situation encountered often. This was teaching by example rather than by dictate. One of the more amusing of these *haggadic* examples concerns a tricky legal situation.

On a certain occasion the Egyptians brought a lawsuit against the Jews before Alexander of Macedon. They argued this way: "Is it not written, 'And the Lord gave the people favor in the sight of the Egyptians so

---

45. The chief exception is Tractate *Pirkei 'Avot*.
46. Also spelled *'Aggadah*.
47. Trepp, *Judaism*, 270.

that they lent them [gold and precious stones, etc.]?' So return to us the gold and silver that you took."

Then Gebiha the son of Pesisa said to the Sages:

> "Give me permission to go and argue against them before Alexander of Macedon. If they defeat me, just say, 'You have defeated an ignorant man among us'. But if I defeat them, say 'The Torah of Moses has defeated you.'" So they gave him permission, and he went and argued against them.
>
> "From where do you adduce your proof?" he asked.
>
> "From the Torah," they replied.
>
> So he said, "Then I too will bring proof only from the Torah. There it is written that 'the sojourning of the people of Israel who dwelled in Egypt was four hundred and thirty years.' Pay us for the work of six hundred thousand men whom you enslaved for four hundred and thirty years."
>
> Then King Alexander said to [the Egyptians], "Answer him."
>
> "Give us three days," they requested, and he allowed them a recess. They searched but found no answer. So they ran away.[48]

There are several important things to notice about this story. First, it does not propose to bring forward a rule of life for every day, because one does not get sued in a foreign court of law every day. It might be argued that the story surely implies that a Jew facing court action should defend himself or herself, but that would have been self-evident without this little tale. Thus there is a second and more important idea to be found in the identity of Gebiha the son of Pesisa. He was not a scholar, but a very ordinary man. As such, the picture of him using good common sense comes sharply into focus. The scholar who is learned in matters of law and procedure is not the only person who can succeed. Even the most humble Jew can stand up and be counted, and can make a difference for the whole community. But a third idea is most important of all, namely the idea that the Torah can be an important component in the life of even the most ordinary Jew. What Gebiha said in court was so basic that even a modestly educated Jew would have known it. Yet the power of the Torah is such that it equips people for those touchy situations in life where most of us long for direction and answers. In other words, Gebiha was correct. He did not win the case; the Torah did!

48. *Kiddushin* 20b.

Sometimes the Talmud uses a *haggadah* to make an important technical or legal point. For example, the single most important declaration of faith for Jews is the short utterance found in Deuteronomy 6:4, known by its first word as the *Shemaʿ*—"Hear [or "listen"], O Israel. YHWH is our God. YHWH is One." Observant Jews recite the *Shemaʿ* four times each day, and hope to face death with its words on their lips. Countless thousands of Jewish martyrs have faced a violent, premature death while reciting the *Shemaʿ*.[49] In terms of *halakhah*, the significance of the *Shemaʿ* is reflected by the fact that its recital came to stand as a symbol of someone willing to accept the full responsibility of being a Jew, to carry what the rabbis called, "the yoke of the kingdom of the heavens." As such, heartfelt recitation of the *Shemaʿ* was perceived to imply the acceptance of God as one's King along with the myriad of demands that King made on the life of the Jew. So it is not surprising that a well-known Mishnaic passage makes clear that, whenever he recites the *Shemaʿ*, the pious Jew both voluntarily takes upon himself the "yoke" of the kingdom of the heavens, and concordantly also accepts upon himself the obligation of a *halakhic* life. A short story told about Rabban Gamaliel serves as a *haggadic* reminder of this aspect of the *Shemaʿ* when readers learn that the pious Gamaliel was known to have recited the *Shemaʿ* even on the first night of his wedding. The object lesson of the story was to teach his students that the pious rabbi would not avoid "the yoke of the kingdom of the heavens even for a moment."[50]

Midrash is a third category of rabbinic literature. Derived from the verb "to investigate, inquire" (*daraš*), a Midrash may be either *halakhic* or *haggadic*, i.e., may be viewed as a source of law/life (a legal interpretation), or it may function basically as a vehicle that carries religious inspiration and moral exhortation, much like a modern sermon or homily. In both cases, a Midrash seeks to draw from a biblical passage something of value for the present day. And once again it should be noted that just as the *Tannaʾim* and the *ʾAmoraim* had differed in their interpretations of various issues, different Midrashim (plural of Midrash) frequently offered different interpretations of the Bible. As one modern rabbi has expressed it, such differences of opinion illustrate "that a reader understands a text in light of his own experiences."[51] But they illustrate another point as well.

---

49. The most famous of whom was Rabbi Akiva, a second-century sage tortured to death by Rome.

50. *Ber.* 2:2,4.

51. Telushkin, *Jewish Literacy*, 157.

Once again, as we learned with respect to the Mishnah and the Gemara, the variety of viewpoints found in various Midrashim bear witness to a community of scholars comfortable with the idea that a sacred text could be interpreted in more than one way.

The Organization of Education

Since one of the most important assignments given to the rabbis was the teaching of Jewish children, the variety of texts and literary genres to be studied required great skill from teachers and students alike. Teaching took place either in the home of the teacher or (more often) in the synagogue, in rooms set aside for this purpose. Girls received a basic education in some towns, but boys in all towns were sent to school beginning at age five or six. Normal class size was twenty to twenty-five students, the first level of education lasted about five years, and the majority of students had no additional education beyond this point. However, as noted above, virtually every Jewish child had this minimal level of education, so that all Jews could read the Bible and the *Siddur*, and could recite the common blessings and prayers of Jewish life and worship, a skill necessary to enable everyone to participate in the prayer services on Saturday morning and on the market days of Monday and Thursday, at which the weekly Torah portion was read and discussed. During this era, a short talk on the biblical passage was often given by a local scholar. In some locations, advanced students in training would sometimes give the sermon, to be followed by the main lecture from the town rabbi.

Children who proved to be gifted in learning were encouraged to continue their studies past elementary biblical studies to a second level during which the study of the Mishnah was central. During this second period of five or six years, most of the Mishnah was memorized and its content debated.

At the age of fifteen or sixteen, the brightest second level students were pushed to attend a local or regional Yeshivah, where they began the study of Gemara, either as a vocation or as an avocation that was designed to last for a lifetime. According to one rabbinic authority, "a thousand enter to study the Bible, a hundred to study Mishnah, ten to study Gemara, and one to teach,"[52] that is, only one out of one thousand students would become proficient enough to teach others. In a Yeshi-

---

52. Steinsaltz, *The Talmud*, 18.

vah, as distinct from the home of an individual teacher, the physical arrangement was established early on.

Set apart from the activities of the average students was a "house of the scholars," where senior scholars studied alone or in small groups, not following a rigid curriculum, but addressing issues of concern to a particular scholar or his group.

However, there was an officially structured curriculum of study for students enrolled at any of a number of regional academies that served as general teaching institutions. Whereas the rabbi preaching a sermon was expected to limit his message to reviews of widely accepted interpretations, the stated goal of these formal schools was to arrive at *halakhic* rulings that would be considered authoritative for the general community.[53] In these houses of study, a fixed class arrangement also became customary. The head of the Yeshivah sat at the front on a chair or cushion, with rows of students sitting opposite him. Academy teachers and senior scholars in the community occupied the front row, and here too sat the most advanced students of the Yeshivah head, who was also the most senior teacher at the institution. Each row of seats contained successively less advanced students, with beginners seated at the back. "As a student advanced in his studies, he would be brought closer to the head of the yeshivah."[54]

Everyone was expected to prepare in advance to discuss a particular tractate from the Gemara. After the head of the Yeshivah or another senior scholar had introduced the Mishnaic rulings and added explanatory words of his own, a "reciter"[55] who knew both the standard Mishnaic and numerous non-Mishnaic rabbinic opinions[56] by heart, was asked to provide citations of those opinions that were pertinent to the subject. From the introduction on, the students and other scholars present were expected to "raise a series of questions before the assembled gathering, questions of interpretation, halakhic questions, difficulties in various sources, or other problems of logical analysis."[57] All persons present were

---

53. But not binding! This is shown in the fact that whenever a community disagreed with a particular ruling, they were free to write to another Yeshivah and seek an alternative view.

54. Steinsaltz, *The Talmud*, 20.

55. Aramaic *Tanna'*, "repeater," is the singular of *Tanna'im*.

56. *Baraitot*, external opinions, not included in the official Mishnah, but still thought important.

57. Steinsaltz, *The Talmud*, 20.

not only allowed but encouraged to take part in the debate that ensued, a discussion that sought a consensus or lasted until it was agreed that no consensus was attainable, in which case, a letter to another academy might be composed to solicit their ideas on the problem.

Although this was the schedule for the entire year, very few were able to participate all year long. Two special months became designated as the "months of general (assembly)" because agricultural work was lighter during these two months.[58] When students attended school during these two special months, it was expected that they had studied the assigned lesson or tractate during the preceding five months, and students who asked questions that indicated a lack of preparation were rebuked sharply![59] Except for this proviso, however, everyone was expected to participate in the flurry of questions, debate, and discussion. Particularly prized was the ability to point out the flaw in an argument, or to offer a more pertinent or relevant source of authority to sustain one's own point of view. Often, asking a question that was not answered adequately by the theory being propounded was a sign of superior intellect.[60]

Students were not allowed to raise questions related only to their personal problems and issues, but were expected to leave the formal classroom with such questions in order to do private research, often with the assistance of a study partner (ḥaver). This meant that debates in the classroom revolved around issues of broad concern to the community at large, but "occasionally the discussions involved matters of a private nature, the actual problems of individual families and even political issues,"[61] which it was advantageous to keep from the ears of the secular authorities! In order to encourage frank participation, all discussions were secret, and a student would be expelled for publicizing remarks that had been made in the classroom. This was intended to allow greater freedom to express personal opinions, especially when all present realized that a question under discussion might have direct bearing on a family or group well known

---

58. Following a lunar calendar, 'Adar: February, and 'Elul: September.

59. Note the phrase "rebuking the students" by teachers who felt that certain questions were impertinent or off subject, or students had not prepared in advance for a class session. Steinsaltz, *The Talmud*, 21.

60. It is interesting that to the Gentile author Luke, the *answers* given by the young Jesus to older teachers were amazing (2:47). But it is significant that Luke also mentions the fact that the young man was not only listening to Jewish teachers in the Temple, but specifically "asking them questions" (2:46).

61. Steinsaltz, *The Talmud*, 21.

in the small and tightly knit community. Again, it must be remembered that these activities took place during the period before the formal editing and publication of either Talmud. These discussions, or at least those considered to be the most edifying among them, came to form the heart of the published Talmudim.

The Role of the Teacher

Even early in this era, during which Jews lacked a formal educational structure and institutions of formal learning were virtually unknown, leaders in each community tried to ensure that their town or village would have at least one schoolteacher, who taught the basic rudiments of reading (Bible, *Siddur*, Mishnah), and *halakhah*. All teachers were supervised by the local rabbinical court or by a committee of the scholars in the area. Financial support of the teacher was the responsibility of parents rather than the community at large.

Scholars were treated with great respect, because they were believed to be the link that tied a community to its sacred past and helped to define its path into the future. Teachers and their advanced students often received special benefits from the community, including exemption from certain taxes, but in reality they were an integral part of the community. Most worked at a trade or craft, or as manual laborers or herdsmen, and were unable to engage full time in scholarship. Only a few possessed inherited wealth, some were supported by their families, but those in the highest positions, particularly Yeshivah heads, received generous salaries and other benefits such as housing. Several of the larger communities initiated the practice of special housing for students who were unable to afford private accommodations.

But it was the relationship between teacher and student that evolved most sharply. In the early stages of their advanced studies, students would be instructed by one particular scholar, and the custom in Israel was for a student to remain with the same teacher virtually throughout his educational life. Accordingly, "both in their personal relations and also in the eyes of the Halakhah such students forged a very deep bond with their teacher, a relationship of great love and profound respect."[62] Such bonds were apparent early in the development of Judaism, and the biblical book of Proverbs attests several admonitions about practical wisdom

---

62. Ibid., 22.

addressed from father to son,[63] clearly describing more than a biological relationship. These statements about fathers and sons in Proverbs were interpreted by the *Tanna'im* as references to teachers and students as well, and the great medieval commentator Rashi explicitly stated that Deuteronomy 6:7 refers to one's students as well as to one's biological offspring.[64]

The rabbis also believed that because students were indeed the children of their teachers, their success was paramount. Rabbi Elʻazar ben Shamuʻa said it well: "Let the honor of your student be as dear to you as your own."[65] In other words, since students were the truest measure of a teacher, their level of achievement was the most meaningful product of all, and the rabbis accepted the idea that a teacher had not taught until a student had learned.[66]

Of course, not every student was a delight, and the *Tanna'im* noted that learners came in four types:[67] a sponge that absorbs everything; a funnel that takes in at one end and lets out at the other; a strainer that lets the wine flow through and retains the sediment; a sieve that allows the flour dust to pass through and retains the fine flour.

However, honor flowing from the teacher to the student was not taken to imply that teachers were at the mercy of their students no matter how poorly they prepared or learned. The other side of the coin was equally important. In addition to the biblical commandment to honor one's biological parents, both the Bible and the rabbinic writings are also sprinkled with numerous statements urging upon students the necessity of finding a good teacher,[68] and then of respect and honor for the teacher. The primary teacher of all was God, of course, but many biblical texts also

---

63. 1:8, 10, 15; 2:1; 3:1; 4:1, 10, 20; 5:1, etc.

64. "We find everywhere that students are called 'sons,' . . . and just as students are called 'sons,' the teacher is called 'father.'" I have written about some of the methods of instruction envisioned in the book of Deuteronomy in "Deuteronomy's Definition of Jewish Learning," 109–16.

65. *Pirkei 'Avot* 4:15.

66. Even today, if we want to know whether someone is a good teacher, regardless of how fervently he defends a favorite method or style of teaching, we meet his or her students.

67. *Pirkei 'Avot* 5:18.

68. "Get a teacher for yourself" (*Pirkei 'Avot* 1:6).

emphasized the role of the faithful human teacher,[69] and render severe condemnation of false teachers.[70]

Finally, we should note the significance of study partners (*haverîm*). The rabbis knew that students would not always understand the explanation of a teacher, and might respond more favorably to the comments and tutelage of someone closer to their own age and circumstances. Quite often a simplified explanation given by a student reached certain members of the class more directly than the complicated way in which an experienced teacher may have phrased the same principle. The rabbis not only knew that students were helping each other by studying together, they encouraged it, as the following statement indicates: "Whoever learns from a partner[71] one chapter, one *halakhah*, one verse, one [Torah] statement, or even a single letter–must treat him with respect/honor."[72]

The Role of the Synagogue

We have already noted that the synagogue frequently served as the central meeting place for teachers and students. In Israel and in Babylonia, synagogues existed wherever there was a Jewish community, and in larger communities, there were often several synagogues, some attended by members of a particular profession, others by people who shared a common country of origin. Many synagogues were built in the country in order to involve more than one smaller community in their building and maintenance costs. Often such buildings did not contain a fixed "holy ark" in the main sanctuary, but kept one or more Torah scrolls in a separate room that could be locked. The reading of the Torah was the highlight of each Shabbat service. But here too, education became an integral part of the ceremony.

The Torah reading in the synagogue was not only a ceremonial matter but also served a practical educational purpose. For many generations it was customary to translate the weekly portion as it was recited aloud, generally verse by verse, into Aramaic. Usually the translators used a well-known Aramaic translation of the Torah, such as that of Onkelos. In Eretz Israel at the end of the Amoraic period the translators often added

---

69. See 2 Chron 17:7–9.
70. E.g., Isa 9:15; Micah 3:11; Malachi 2:7.
71. Note a חבר (*haver*), a "study partner," not a teacher!
72. *Pirkei 'Avot* 6:3.

explanations and Aggadic material, and these served as the basis for the Jerusalem Targum (translation) of the Torah, erroneously called "Targum Yonatan."[73]

The rabbinic sermon to which we alluded earlier was called a *Sidra*, and could touch upon a wide variety of subjects. Although the main purpose of a Sidra was to allow the rabbi opportunity to explain in detail a matter of *halakhic* importance, *haggadic* material also began to be used in these sermons early on as an aid to capturing the interest of the congregation. During festival occasions, the custom was for the rabbi to preach about the theme and special rules that applied for the specific holiday, sometimes beginning several weeks in advance. In the middle of the second century CE, many of these sermons, or at least the more interesting stories and illustrations they contained, were compiled into collections, and these *haggadic* Midrashim served as important commentaries on the last four of the Pentateuchal books. Early in the following century, a Midrashic commentary on Genesis was published as well. Only slightly later the large collection known as Midrash Rabbah ("The Great Midrash") appeared, which covers the Pentateuch plus the five short scrolls of Ruth, Esther, Song of Songs, Qohelet (Ecclesiastes), and Lamentations.

After the Talmud: Authoritative but not "Sacred"

This rather lengthy discussion of rabbinic instruction has been necessary to highlight two significant points in the development of sacred literature within Judaism. First, it is clear that the sacred texts of Judaism were prized for their practical value as textbooks for learning and sources of examples for young students to follow in their pursuit of an authentically Jewish way of life. *How* to think was emphasized more than merely *what* one must think. Second, just as the publication of the Mishnah did not mark the end of rabbinic discussion and debate, so the publication of the Gemara failed to halt that tide as well. Following the publication of the complete Talmud, Jews in numerous countries around the world continued to raise questions that were answered in neither sacred corpus of texts available in writing, the Bible or the Talmud. Once again, in much the same fashion they had been doing for more than five hundred years, rabbinic scholars set themselves to the task of addressing

---

73. Steinsaltz, *The Talmud*, 18 (emphasis added).

new and current questions that arose with the changing of the times, and the early post-Talmudic era witnessed its own flurry of scholarly activity. As great centers of learning were founded, particularly in Babylonia and in Palestine, teachers at minor institutions, or teachers who lacked internationally recognized reputations, began to send written questions by letter to the great academies, asking for specific rulings from the best-known teachers. These rulings, known as *responsa*,[74] were framed much as Mishnaic and Gemaric rulings had been. They were not merely the opinion of a single rabbi working in isolation somewhere, but were the result of a cooperative effort that included public debate and scholarly disputation. Once again we notice the phenomenon encountered earlier, for these early *responsa* made no attempt to mask differences of opinion, but contained something of the history of discussion leading to a majority opinion as well as the majority opinion itself. Again it was clear that no single correct opinion was recognized by all Jews. Instead, the weight of a particular opinion was tied directly to the reputation of the scholar(s) who penned it.[75]

As Jews became more and more dispersed in different countries, the gap between professional scholars and ordinary Jews grew. By far a majority of Jews were simply unable to understand the Talmud, much less to formulate intelligent opinions about its complicated discussions. By the dawn of the new millennium, a number of gifted scholars arose to lend their talents to Talmudic studies. The greatest of these men was a towering intellectual named Moses ben Maimon (Maimonides, 1135–1204).[76] He was born in Spain, home to the largest Jewish population in the world at the time, and a country that had been a haven for Jewish intellectuals, especially physicians, scientists, poets, and men of letters, since its occupation by liberal Muslim rulers in the eighth century. Maimonides moved to Egypt as a young man, where he became chief physician to the court of Saladin. But he also maintained close contact with Muslim and

---

74. Volumes of "responsa" are still being published today by committees of scholars within the various branches of Judaism.

75. In fact, as noted above, a warning continued to be repeated against the temptation to "rabbi shop," i.e., to seek an opinion from a conservative authority on one issue but a liberal rabbi on another issue, so as to frame answers to suit individual preferences. Jews were enjoined to search for a series of opinions that had some sense of internal consistency, whether liberal, conservative, or moderate.

76. See Davidson, *Moses Maimonides*.

Christian thinkers of his era, and published an astonishing number of scholarly works in the field of Talmudic thought.

The first of the three most influential works of Maimonides was a commentary on the Mishnah, an effort to harmonize the ethics of Aristotle with Jewish tradition.[77] The second major work of Maimonides was *Repetition of the Torah*, designed as a compendium of Talmudic teaching arranged in a logical style that was more easily grasped by the non-scholar than the seemingly haphazard presentation of subjects in the Talmud. In his short introduction to the work, Maimonides, ever the physician, argued for sound hygiene on the ground that a healthy body enhances one's ability to observe Jewish patterns of life. But his chief purpose was to state clearly the philosophical, ethical, and moral ideals that undergird Jewish life. So Maimonides turned his attention to magic and superstition. As children of their era, the rabbis of the Talmud had accepted conventional wisdom about magic, astrology, and necromancy, etc., viewing them as dangers to be feared because they were commonly seen as linked to, and deriving power from, malevolent forces like devils, demons, ghosts, evil spirits, etc.[78] Maimonides, to the contrary, argued that all beliefs centered on such things are sheer nonsense, and have no power either for good or for ill. In taking this enlightened position, Maimonides argued from the fact that the Bible had outlawed magical practices not because they were real, but because the biblical writers realized that their readers who feared demonic powers *perceived* them to be real and were likely to be influenced by them. He concluded that the Torah's perspective on such things had been an accommodation to simple people who might easily be led astray. In like fashion, he argued that sacrifices had no intrinsic value, and urged Jews to forget about the hope that Temple rituals might be restored at some bright future date. Sacrifices, he believed, had been another accommodation to the times of the Bible, when people universally believed that the killing of an animal might somehow placate an angry deity. Reading Maimonides today, we are struck with the modernity of his thought on many points, but even more with the fact that he felt free to restate biblical teachings in light of his own scientific education and knowledge.

77. We will have more to say about his method of fusion in chapter 4.

78. In fact, an entire corpus of literature attests the development of this folkloristic aspect of Judaism among non-scholars at the same time that the Talmudic masters were creating the Mishnah-Tosefta-Gemara. See Isbell, *Corpus of the Aramaic Magical Incantation Bowls*.

On one additional topic, Maimonides deserves a modern hearing. His view of Christianity and Islam was extremely open and tolerant. Both of these faiths, he argued, contain revealed (divine) truth, and both have rescued numerous persons from the degradation of raw paganism. And he believed both religions would continue to contribute to the education of humanity, which when complete, would usher in a new era of peace, understanding among peoples of different backgrounds, and harmonious co-existence.

The third and most famous work of Maimonides boasts an amusing title, *A Teacher for the Confused*, for a deadly serious subject. In it he attempts to explain Talmudic teachings for the common person, simplifying the structure of Talmudic literature and grouping material together according to subject matter.[79]

It should not be surprising that the work of Maimonides was not universally accepted among Jewish scholars. In fact, he became for many Jews a pioneer in the conflict that would bedevil not only Judaism but church and mosque as well, the struggle between science and religion.[80]

One other major work deserves mention. Even today, Orthodox rabbis turn first to the *Shulḥan Arukh* ("The Prepared Table") when asked to rule on matters of *halakhic* and legal importance. Written by Joseph Karo (1488–1575), the *Shulḥan Arukh* was a compendium of Jewish legal rulings dealing with virtually every aspect of daily life. Karo, born in Spain and reared in Turkey, was a mystic who believed that the Mishnah spoke to him in almost personal terms. Guided by an angelic voice, Karo emigrated to the Holy Land and concluded that the commandments of the Bible and the Talmud were a bond that could unite Jews who were dispersed throughout the world. Because he was Sephardic,[81] as was Maimonides, several important additions to the *Shulḥan Arukh* were believed necessary by the Ashkenazic rabbi, Moses Isserles of Poland. As a result, the *Shulḥan Arukh* came to be published with Karo's rulings listed first, followed by the dissents and additions of Isserles printed in italics.

It is only fair to note that neither the works of Maimonides nor the *Shulḥan Arukh* stand on a par with the Bible or the Talmud in the hierarchy of Jewish sacred literature. But it is also necessary to note that these

---

79. We will return to the guide in chapter 4.

80. The fall (1997) *CCAR Journal* includes articles on Maimonides sketching some of the controversy that still surrounds his ideas. See Sonsino, "Shabbetay Zevi."

81. Jews whose families came from Spain or the Arab world. Jews whose families came from central and eastern Europe are known as "Askenazic."

works are the constant companion of many modern Jewish rabbis whose task it is to interpret both Bible and Talmud. As such they carried and carry great weight of authority.

2

The Sacred Texts of Christianity: Early Authors

The Christian Scriptures

UNLIKE MOST NEW RELIGIONS, Christianity came into existence with a canon of sacred Scripture already in its possession, the Greek translation of the Hebrew Scriptures known as the Septuagint (LXX), to which reference was made in chapter 1. Also important to an understanding of the LXX is the fact that it included books that fell outside the sacred twenty-four of the Hebrew Bible. Some of these extra-canonical additions were separate books: Judith, Tobit, 1 and 2 Maccabees, the Wisdom of Solomon, Baruch, Ecclesiasticus, the Letter of Jeremiah.[1] Others were additions to the standard Hebrew texts: the book of Esther, the book of Daniel, and the book of Psalms.

Before turning to the literary and methodological analysis of the sacred texts adopted by Christianity, it must be noted that there were distinctive differences between the ways in which the rabbis and the early Christians developed their respective faith systems in the first century CE. First, while the rabbis substituted study and prayer to replace the system of sacrifices that had been centered in the Jerusalem Temple,

---

1. These books are known as Apocrypha ("hidden") because their authors are not always identified. There are a total of fourteen such books, but the Catholic (Roman) tradition and other Christian traditions (especially the Slavonic Bible of eastern orthodoxy) contain different text choices among the fourteen. See Harrington, *Invitation to the Apocrypha*.

Christians argued that the universal sacrifice of the divine Jesus had made animal sacrifices unnecessary for all time. Second, Jewish worship and study took place in small groups meeting in synagogues, while Christians held cellular meetings for worship in private homes. Third, the center of rabbinic Judaism was Jerusalem, while the centers of early Christianity quickly moved first to Antioch and then to Rome. Fourth, while the rabbis studied and taught from the Hebrew Scriptures accompanied by oral translations of the weekly Torah portions into Aramaic, early Christians focused their attention on the oral repetition of gospel stories describing the teachings and activities of Jesus. Although Jesus had spoken in Aramaic, the collections of his teachings were published in Greek in order to reach a wider audience. Fifth, the rabbis ordained pairs (*zugot*) of teachers to explain both the written and the oral Torah, while Christians dispatched pairs of missionaries to explain the life and ministry of Jesus as a prelude to conversion into Christianity. Sixth, the avowed purpose of the radical rabbinic reconstruction of biblical literature into Judaism was the sanctification of all of time and space in an effort to provide a form of worship structure for Jews who had lost the pillar of biblical religion, the Temple. In sharp contrast, the avowed purpose of the original Christian missionaries was to conquer the known political and social world of the Roman Empire by changing the religious convictions of all people in an effort to convert them to Christianity.

Because the first Christians were Jews, it is understandable that they would accord great authority to the Jewish Scriptures. But succeeding generations of Christians entered the faith from non-Jewish backgrounds and lacked a prior respect for the Bible of the Jews. So marked was this difference between Jewish and non-Jewish early Christians, that the first attempt within Christianity to set forth a fixed authoritative canon of Scripture vehemently rejected the Hebrew Scriptures, even in their Greek translation, as unworthy of the new faith. Early in the second century, a radical ascetic theologian from northeast Asia Minor named Marcion argued that Jesus had revealed a deity previously unknown to the world. For Marcion, the deity of the NT was not the god of the Hebrew Bible whom he perceived as vengeful and unpredictable, but a divinity of love who was the Father of Jesus. As a consequence of his *di-theism*, Marcion made the first attempt to articulate a canon of Christian literature, accepting only a shortened version of the Gospel of Luke, ten letters written by

Paul,[2] and a literary work of his own titled *Antitheses*, essentially a listing of contradictions between the teachings of Jesus and the Old Testament.

The bold suggestion of Marcion impacted the new faith sharply enough to require a response, and the reaction of mainstream proto-orthodox Christianity was to reject the excisions demanded by Marcion. While Marcion would simply have discarded the Hebrew Bible in its entirety, proto-orthodoxy wanted to retain the authority of that sacred work as the foundation for its own existence. However, left to their apparent literal meanings, many passages in the Hebrew Scriptures did indeed describe a deity of wrath and vengeance. In order to function as the Bible of Christianity, the Hebrew Scriptures of the rabbis needed to be interpreted and transvalued in at least three significant ways.

First, many early Christian interpreters believed it could be shown that the Hebrew Bible itself had spoken of Jesus in a predictive manner, anticipating his birth, life, death, resurrection, and many of his basic teachings. While it was believed that the rabbis had overlooked or even rejected the true meaning of such texts, expositors of the new religion believed they could see the deeper truths of the (Jewish) Bible through the lens of faith provided by the life and teachings of Jesus.

Second, the apparently straightforward teaching of many biblical stories could be viewed as "types" of the reality soon to be ushered into the world via Jesus. In this, the early church was heavily influenced by the philosophy of neo-Platonism.

Third, early Christian authors believed that many biblical teachings operated on multiple levels. In addition to the "plain sense," one looking with the eyes of faith could discern a deeper or allegorical truth, again pointing clearly to the future era of Jesus. In chapter 6 we will examine several specific examples of all three of these exegetical responses to the Bible by the New Testament and the early church.

A second challenge for Christianity issued forth from the Phrygian (west central Asia Minor) scholar Montanus, who claimed to experience fresh personal revelations from God via his reception of prophetic gifts directly from the divine spirit, which he combined with strict ascetic discipline. This idea of new and continuing personal revelations influenced the church to fall back on the authority of antiquity,[3] and argue that Jew-

---

2. Marcion excluded from his list of accepted works the Pastorals and the book of Hebrews, also believed by the early church to have been Pauline.

3. Akenson has described this phonemenon as "the grammar of antiquity" in *Surpassing Wonder*.

ish biblical and apostolic connections were a prerequisite for Christian authority. In other words, new or innovative theological ideas could not continue unchecked past the time of Jesus, whose work was the ultimate and final revelation of God to man. But once again, if the past were to serve as authority for the present, it was essential for that past to be redefined and reformulated in a manner that would establish the meaningful and acceptable links between the past and the present. As we saw with the work of the rabbis, so now we observe a similar action by early Christian scholars who sought to show the relevance of the "old" book (the Bible) to the new faith, and to state the earliest possible provenance for the authority of the "new" book (the New Testament), whose official canonization was still a long way into the future (the fourth century CE). The important point here is the fact that a beginning step along the path to full canonization was the formulation of the principle that authority in Christianity did not derive from new or "modern" personal inventions. It was portrayed as coming from the Bible itself (i.e., the Jewish Scriptures/Old Testament), as it had been reformulated by Jesus and his closest companions who had lived and studied with him, the apostles.

The year 180 CE marks a watershed in the development of the NT canon. In that year Irenaeus, the Bishop of Lyons, published a major work, *Against Heresies*, in which he acknowledged the authority of the Old Testament (LXX) and added a New Testament consisting of Christian writings. Interestingly, Irenaeus lists or cites all of the books that were ultimately to become the official New Testament except James, Jude, 2 Peter, and Hebrews. The rationale for the choices of Irenaeus may be seen to rest on two pillars. The first presumed "the great early Christian project of *rereading* the scriptures that the church inherited from Judaism,"[4] into a Christian Bible. This is exactly what we are calling the *transvaluation* of the Old Testament. As a result of their rereading or transvaluation, "the church came to insist that the God of Israel was the God of Jesus Christ and also that the significance of the Hebrew Scriptures lay in the testimony they bore to Christ."[5] The second pillar revolved around the question "as to which Christian writings could be considered the apostolic witness to Christ . . . really a decision that these books interpreted Christ correctly from a theological point of view."[6] The types of literature

---

4. O'Keefe and Reno, *Sanctified Vision*, 41 (emphasis added).
5. Kugel and Greer, *Early Biblical Interpretation*, 111.
6. Ibid.

included by Irenaeus were of four genres: records of the teachings and miracles of Jesus (gospels), a history of the early church (Acts), letters (of Paul, John, Peter), and one Apocalypse.[7]

The first of these literary genres has acquired the name "gospel" and the story of gospel composition and acceptance is a compelling one. As eyewitnesses to the miracles and sermons of Jesus began to die, it was deemed necessary to set forth a written record to preserve the account of his life. As new non-Jewish members of the faith became the majority, the expediency of composing literature in the widely used Greek language also became apparent. But the appearance of written gospels did not signal the end of the era of oral accounts of the teachings of Jesus. Thus an early church historian named Eusebius quotes Papias, a bishop in Asia Minor ca. 175 CE, on two points. First, he noted that Papias expressed his preference for "a living voice" over a book. Second, Eusebius cited the following opinion of Papias: "Matthew compiled the prophetic oracles in the Hebrew dialect, and each one interpreted them as best he was able."[8]

Now the Greek word used by Eusebius for "compile" (*syntaxo*) also means "to arrange." Papias recognized that there were numerous teachers, each one interpreting the stories circulating about Jesus, who found this arrangement by Matthew a helpful resource. But Papias does not use the word "gospel." He refers to the compilations of Matthew as "prophetic oracles," in testimony to the belief that Jesus was in fact a prophet in the ancient sense of the term as one who speaks forth for God. In the NT itself, the Greek word used to describe the four canonical gospels is *evangelion*,[9] a noun formed from the verb *evangelizein*, "to announce, to bring good news." The English word "gospel" is the modern form of an Anglo-Saxon term "god-spell," referring to a story that derives from or teaches about a deity/god.

In this context, the question, "What is a gospel?" arises with respect to the manner in which the term is used with reference to the first four books of the Christian NT. Each NT gospel contains elements that might be called biography, yet, except for one story in Luke about Jesus at age twelve, details about the life of Jesus that would be sought by any competent biographer are omitted, including the entire period of his life from birth until the beginning of his public career. Elements of legend

---

7. For a slightly different treatment of this period, see Ehrman, *Lost Christianities*, 229–46.

8. Eusebius, *Ecclesiastical History*, 39.

9. Used in Mark 1:1; Matthew 4:23; numerous times by Paul.

are also found in the gospels: Jesus walking on top of a body of water or materializing inside a locked door. But the gospels are united in their insistence that Jesus was not merely a human hero with legendary feats to his credit. Likewise, the gospels may be described as classical "myths," stories about a god rather than a human hero. Gods on earth could be perceived anthropomorphically, as Jesus was when he wept at the loss of a human friend, became hungry, thirsty, sleepy, or angry, or exhibited understandable human fear in the face of adversity. But the picture of God (!) traveling through the birth canal of a human mother proved to be a major source of contention for early Christianity.

A far more fruitful line of inquiry would point to the connection between the gospel treatments of the significance of the life and teaching of Jesus and the way in which the narrators of the Hebrew Bible searched for the significance of what Israelite and Judahite kings did. As we noted in chapter 1, the biblical books dealing with the reigns of the kings of Israel and Judah are not "history," but prophetic interpretations of the theological *meaning* of the life and policies of each king. That NT authors envisioned a similar interpretative task is shown by the referential field established by their use of *evangelion*. Thus we find expressions like "the *mystery* of the gospel" (Eph 6:19); "the *truth* of the gospel" (Gal 2:5, 14); "the *hope* of the gospel" (Col 1:23); "the *faith* of the gospel" (Phil 1:27); "the gospel of the *kingdom*" (Matt 4:23, etc.); or even "the gospel of *God*" (Mark 1:14), which links directly to "the gospel of *Jesus Christ*" in Mark 1:1.[10] These varied expressions point both to the idea of a gospel as a message or proclamation and to a text that teaches authoritatively about the significance of the deeds and/or words of Jesus.

Early interpreters of these "gospels" quickly made a transition that added a uniquely Christian framework to the word *evangelion*, employing it specifically to denote a *book* dealing with the life and teaching of Jesus. Since books need to be read and interpreted, this raised the issue of who ought to have authority over the interpretation of these most important documents of the Christian faith.

The interpretation of the gospels involves another kind of evidence as well. The four gospels that entered the NT as *the* authoritative (canonical) sources of the life of Jesus were not the only gospels that were written. A recent book lists seventeen such works,[11] some preserved

---

10. The second-century epistle of Barnabas speaks of "the *authority* of the gospel" (8:3).

11. Ehrman, *Lost Scriptures*.

only in fragments, others known only because they are cited by other early Christian writers, and still others now recovered archaeologically in varying degrees of completion. Many of these extra-canonical gospels contain tidbits of biographical information about the life of Jesus absent from the NT accounts, precisely the kind of details that modern biographers include routinely to titillate readers studying the life of a famous person. And yet, for a variety of reasons, the young church declined to accept them into the elite list of gospels considered essential for Christian life, faith, and praxis.

The reasons for excluding some gospels were four in number. First, the extra-canonical gospels (and other books as well) were not considered to be ancient. In a world where "antiquity rather than novelty was respected,"[12] books that were more recent than the time of Jesus himself were viewed with suspicion. Second, some books were passed over because they were not believed to be apostolic, written either by one of the twelve or a close companion to someone in that group.[13] Third, some were omitted because they were not considered catholic, or "universal," which implied that they did not enjoy favor across a wide spectrum of individual Christian congregations. Fourth, it was assumed that books not written by an apostle advanced teachings not in line with the majority proto-orthodox view. These four criteria indicate that the first task of the interpreter of a gospel was to determine which gospel to interpret!

This process of adverse selection, that is, the omission of certain gospel accounts or even leaving out certain words or deeds of Jesus, is acknowledged in the pages of the NT itself. Near the end of the Gospel of John comes a simple statement: "Jesus also performed many other miracles in the presence of the disciples that are not written in this book" (20:30), calling to mind the oft-repeated explanation in the Hebrew Scriptures at the end of the description of the reign of a king: "Now the rest of the deeds of King _____ are written in the Book of the Chronicles of the Kings of Israel [or Judah]."[14] In other words, the gospels were not intended as complete histories or biographies of Jesus any more than the prophetic descriptions of Israelite and Judahite kings had been intended to offer complete histories of the kings of Israel and Judah. What came

---

12. Ehrman, *Lost Christianities*, 242.

13. Of course, the criterion of apostolicity is intriguing in light of the fact that the authors of all four gospels that did make it into the official NT canon are anonymous!

14. I have discussed this phenomenon and cited all occurrences of the phrase in "'History' and 'Writing.'"

into the canon of the NT has survived the process of selection, passed the test of theological character, and shown evidence of broad appeal by having been widely used in many different congregations. All of this underscores the crucial role of the *community* of faith in the selection of the literature that would be considered authoritative and normative.

The Gospels of the New Testament

Mark: 70–75 CE, written in Rome[15]

Mark was written by a native speaker of Greek who was not an eyewitness of the ministry of Jesus and was quite fuzzy about the details of Palestinian geography. His sources were oral reports from various individuals that may or may not have been edited into a coherent shape before Mark wrote his narrative. Mark was written to people who did not understand Aramaic, as indicated by his translation of Aramaic or Hebrew terms or phrases at several places in his narrative.[16] These translations would have been quite unnecessary for a Jewish audience.

All three synoptic gospels (Mark is cited below, parallels are attested in Matthew and Luke) use three "trap" questions about issues debated among the rabbis of his day, designed to show that the Jewish opponents of Jesus sought unsuccessfully to lure him into an untenable position. The three issues were:

1. taxes for Caesar (12:15–22), asked by Herodians and Pharisees;
2. resurrection (12:23–33), asked by Sadducees;
3. the great commandment (12:34–40), asked by a Pharisee.

Yet as the earliest of the four NT gospels, "it is noteworthy that Mark does not portray the Pharisees as having an active role in the final actions against Jesus. . . . The lethal opposition comes from the Temple authorities."[17] The significance of this fact will become apparent in chapters 4 and 6.

---

15. Many of the stances taken in this section are still hotly debated among NT scholars, and one could identify other cities as the provenance of each gospel, or the specific viewpoint of each with respect to the Pharisees, etc.

16. See 7:34; 10:46; 15:22; and especially 15:34, where Mark cites and then translates the Aramaic of Psalm 22 rather than the Hebrew original.

17. Brown, *An Introduction to the New Testament*, 146 n51.

Matthew: 80–90 CE, written in Antioch, Syria

The author of Matthew was also a native speaker of Greek who may have known either Hebrew or Aramaic, but whose audience apparently did not. He was not himself an eyewitness to the career of Jesus, but uses sources like Mark and "Q", a collection believed by NT scholars to contain mostly saying and parables of Jesus and used as a "source"[18] by the authors of both Matthew and Luke. He also attempted to use OT proof texts to define the person and function of Jesus, a feature to be analyzed in detail in chapter 4, and dated the birth of Jesus to the reign of Herod, who died in 4 BCE, another fact whose importance will be made apparent in chapter 4, as will his sharp attack on the Pharisees, whom he calls "blind guides" in 15:12–14, and whom he excoriates throughout chapter 23.

Luke: 85–95 CE, written in Achaia, Greece

This writer was a well-educated, Greek-speaking author, who knew the LXX, but had little or no knowledge of the MT. He was almost certainly not a Jew, and not an eyewitness. His sources include Mark and Q but apparently not Matthew. In contrast to Matthew, Luke dates the birth of Jesus to the decree of Caesar Augustus calling for a census that would be used as the basis for taxation. We know that there never was a census of the whole Empire under Augustus, although there were numerous local censuses. The census of Judea (not of Galilee) under Quirinius, the governor of Syria (mentioned by name in Luke 2:2), took place in 6–7 CE, probably at least ten years too late for the birth of Jesus.[19] Clearly, "although Luke likes to set his Christian drama in the context of well-known events from antiquity, sometimes he does so inaccurately."[20] At the least, it must be admitted that the year given by Luke for the birth of Jesus cannot be reconciled with the date chosen by Matthew.

"The vituperation that Matt 3:7 directs to the Pharisees and Sadducees, Luke 3:7 directs to the multitudes—a reflection of the Lucan

---

18. The German word for source is *Quelle*, from which the common designation "Q" derives. If Q ever existed as a separate document, it is now lost, and must be reconstructed hypothetically.

19. And twelve or thirteen years later than Matthew's date.

20. Brown, *An Introduction to the New Testament*, 233.

tendency to remove some of the local Palestinian color and generalize the message."[21]

John: 110 CE, written in Ephesus, west coast of Asia Minor (modern-day Turkey)

This author regards himself in the tradition of the disciple whom Jesus loved, but does not identify himself as John. "Plausibly there was a school of Johannine writing disciples."[22] He is thought by scholars not to have known of the Synoptic tradition. John is based more on non-biblical concepts than any other gospel, and hints at dualism or gnosticism among other Hellenistic or philosophical positions. He is also by far the most anti-Jewish of the four.

Acts

This is a book written as a sequel to Luke's gospel, documenting the activity of the followers of Jesus during the years immediately following his death and resurrection.

Epistles

None of the forty-six books in the Catholic OT canon is an epistle. But twenty-one of the twenty-seven NT books are. An epistle may be defined as an address in written form sent: to a specific community (nine Pauline epistles); to a particular individual (Timothy [2], Titus, Philemon); to a general (catholic) audience including all churches (James, Peter [2], John [3], Jude). The book of Hebrews, also called an epistle, was written by an author posing as a Jew, who knew no Hebrew (i.e., who quoted exclusively from the LXX).[23]

Several if not all of the NT epistles were dictated to a professional secretary. This is shown by statements such as, "I, Tertius, who write this

21. Ibid., 235.
22. Ibid., 334.
23. While Hebrews may be scored for having badly misunderstood/misstated the teachings of the Hebrew Scriptures in an attempt to demonstrate the superior interpretation of Judaism offered by his understanding of the Christian faith, subsequent chapters will indicate that its author was not alone in this regard.

letter, greet you in the Lord" (Rom 16:22), and by the description of 1 Peter 5:12 that Peter was writing "through Silvanus." However, some parts may have been written by the author, as in 1 Corinthians 16:21 ("This greeting is in my own hand") or Galatians 6:11 ("See with what large letters I write to you with my own hand").

Two special issues must be addressed about each epistle, especially those penned by Paul. The first is the fact that Paul does not quote any of the gospels, for the simple reason that his letters are all earlier than any of them.[24] But it is surprising that none of the gospels ever quote Paul either! The second issue is the manner in which these letters were transformed by early Christianity from addresses on topics relevant for a specific locale to their place in the general NT canon intended for all of Christendom.

Apocalyptic Literature

A final literary type contained in the NT canon is the Apocalypse of John, commonly known as Revelation (of John). Although other shorter passages treat the future apocalyptically, Revelation is the only NT book written entirely in the literary genre familiar from the book of Daniel and Second Zechariah (chapters 8–14) in the Hebrew Bible.

An Overview of the Period

In order to understand the literature of the Christian New Testament, it is essential to grasp something of the situation in which first-century Jews found themselves. At the time of the birth of Jesus, the Roman Empire had been the occupying power in Judea for almost seven decades. One of the most fateful decisions made by Rome involved the choice of an enigmatic man named Herod to serve as "King of the Jews." From the Roman perspective, Herod was a logical and perfect choice to serve as the leader of the Jews. He was the product of conversion to Judaism, and he was a local authority.

But to the Jews, Herod was an interloper, a fraud, and not truly a Jew![25] He was in fact an Idumean, the kingdom that had been known in

---

24. Paul's death is generally dated to the mid 60s in Rome.

25. On the differences between the Roman and the Jewish view of Herod, see Goldin, "The Period of the Talmud," 125–33.

earlier biblical times as Edom. And Edomites were certainly no favorite of the Jews (cf. Malachi 1:2 and the short book of Obadiah)! No matter how hard he might have tried, to the Jews in first-century Judea, Herod could never have been considered legitimate. And try hard he did. He inaugurated numerous building projects that were architectural marvels of the era, including a refurbishing and expansion of the Temple in Jerusalem, and the construction of an entire port city on the Mediterranean coast in honor of the Roman Emperor Caesar. Of course, the money for such projects came from heavy taxes levied against the Jews, and higher taxes did nothing to gain favor for Herod from those who paid them.

We have spoken earlier of the various branches of Judaism attested in this era, including the Pharisees, the Essenes, the Zealots, and the Sadducees. We also noted briefly that it was this last group that made league with Rome, promising to keep order and stability among the Jews in exchange for being granted control over Temple taxes. The key word here is "stability," for this was truly the highest priority of Rome throughout all of the provinces in its Empire. Scholars speak of *Pax Romana*, or peace Roman style, by which is meant the Roman obsession with order imposed by whatever force was deemed necessary.

The favorite tool employed to achieve Roman peace and stability was crucifixion, a particularly cruel method that illustrates and underscores the Roman obsession with stability and order. And it is clear the method was effective. First-century evidence from Josephus indicates that a person selected to be crucified was often simply anyone with a popular following, regardless of whether that following was political or theological, as the NT believes the case to have been with Jesus.

Taxation, regimentation, and exploitation under Rome had produced a social cauldron that was ready to boil over in first-century Palestine. Jews had responded in different, though not mutually exclusive, ways. First, some Jews viewed the problem as the punishment of God on a sinful society, but wondered how such a situation could be permitted to continue without hope of an end. Second, a second group of Jews ascribed the widespread suffering of everyday people to the work of demons or evil spirits, believed to be fallen angels who took delight in sowing greed, discord, and misfortune among the people of Israel. Third, some fantasized about a violent retribution, looking forward to a time when God would cleanse the holy land, and chastise the wealthy, the wicked, and the idolatrous as a prelude to the establishment of his own rule over the humble and righteous. Part of their fantasy world involved searching for signs on the political horizon that would portend the interruption of God into history once again.

Where does Jesus fit into this mix? First, his baptism at the hands of John, written after the fact, that is, with knowledge of all that would happen throughout the career of Jesus after this baptism, indicated his willingness to identify with the masses of people who longed for a spiritual renewal.

Second, according to John 3:22, Jesus began to baptize people on his own, and this identification with John surely had political overtones as well. John had been beheaded by Herod on charges of sedition stemming from his opposition to the divorce of Herod's unnamed Nabatean wife so that Herod could marry his brother's wife, Herodias[26] (see Mark 6:18). Such an action was a violation of the Levitical laws of incest, leading John to opine: "It is against the law for you to have her" (Matt 14:4). It is thus not difficult to understand why Herod felt compelled to kill such a popular opponent, and this Romanesque action was something the newly appointed Roman prefect, Pontius Pilate, both understood and applauded. For Jesus to affiliate with such a prophet as John was for him to make an open political and social statement of his own. It is of great significance that according to Mark, the public career of Jesus was inaugurated with this public baptism by John (1:9).

Third, Jesus developed a reputation as a healer and exorcist. Here was a point of contact with common people who were disenfranchised in every way. But the emphasis on social and physical healing would not be enough. What must be noted is the connection between *physical* health and *spiritual* renewal in the accounts of his activities.

Fourth, even the closest followers of Jesus longed for the moment when he would transpose his ministry of the spirit into a new arena. How, they wondered, could he "move beyond healing and wonder-working and suggest some practical ways by which the people's suffering under the reign of Herod Antipas might be reversed and then permanently overcome."[27]

This perception that the career of Jesus was linked to political issues led, perhaps inexorably, to his crucifixion. While he may have believed that his message was spiritual and dealt with the "kingdom of the heavens," both his own followers and the high government officials of Rome heard political overtones as soon as they heard the first word of

---

26. Herodias was the daughter of the Hasmonean prince, Aristobulus.
27. Horsley and Silberman, *Message and Kingdom*, 52–53.

his famous phrase, "*kingdom* on earth." For at least some of his followers, this was welcome, and it must be noticed that among his twelve closest associates there were those who appear to have been close to the thinking of the Zealots.

In this vein, it is notable for Luke to record that at his arrest, "when those who were around him saw what was going to happen, they said, 'Lord, shall we strike with the sword?' And a certain one of them [drew his sword, and] struck the slave of the high priest, and cut off his ear."[28] The zealotry strain among some of the close disciples of Jesus is evident also in the fact that among his original twelve were not only Peter who struck with the sword at the arrest, but also Simon the Cananaean (a name associated with the Hebrew root *qane'*, "to be zealous") who is specifically called by the synonymous Greek word *zelotes*. Included in the small group also were the brothers James and John, who were called in Mark 3:17 "the sons of thunder" (Boanerges).[29]

The political reality was that Rome crucified people like Jesus. As early as his baptism and affiliation with John, he had no doubt come to the attention of Herod Antipas, the younger son of Herod. The later entry of Jesus into Jerusalem on a donkey may have been a parody of Antipas, whose penchant for travel to popular gatherings on a giant white steed amidst a large entourage was well known.[30] Such an action virtually assured his death. In fact, Professor Ellis Rivkin of Hebrew Union College, following the suggestion of Josephus, has shown that it was Roman imperial policy to crucify anyone who became popular enough to attract a large crowd, regardless of the issues on which they spoke, just on the outside chance that such a charismatic person might someday decide to speak a seditious word that would induce his followers to cause trouble for Rome.[31]

In this context, we should note an interesting NT tradition. Following his resurrection of Lazarus, "many Jews . . . believed in him. But some

28. See also Matt 26:51 and Mark 14:47. John 18:10 identifies this person as Simon Peter!

29. It has sometimes been suggested that the name Judas Iscariot may have meant something like *'ish sicarii* ("a *sicarii* [a short dagger used in public assassinations] man"), whose actions suggested his belief that Jesus could withstand the military force of the Roman army. Linguistically, this is folk etymology only, but it may have sounded suggestive to the average person listening to an oral recounting of Jesus and Judas.

30. Detailed by Horsley and Silberman, *The Message and the Kingdom*. See especially page 80.

31. Rivkin, *What Crucified Jesus?* See especially page 91.

of them went to the Pharisees and told them the things Jesus did. Then the chief priests and Pharisees convoked a council to ask, 'What shall we do? For this man performs numerous miracles. If we let him alone, everyone will believe in him and *the Romans will come and take away our position and our nation*'" (John 11:45–48, emphasis added).

This kind of NT report, with its unlikely coupling of chief priests[32] and Pharisees, has led to the popular perception that the Pharisees were major opponents of Jesus throughout his career. But five NT notations show that caution must be exercised before drawing such a conclusion. First, it was the Pharisees who warned Jesus of the plot by Antipas to kill him (Luke 13:31). Second, a Pharisee named Nicodemus became an early follower (John 3:1–10).[33] Third, Joseph of Arimathea, "a prominent member of the Sanhedrin," took a great risk by appealing to Pilate for permission to give the body of Jesus a decent burial (Mark 15:43). Indeed, one of the purposes of crucifixion was to leave a decomposing body impaled without burial, serving as a grim reminder of the cruel fate awaiting any other perceived troublemaker. For Joseph to confront Pilate with the request to obviate this portion of the punishment Rome had decided Jesus took great courage. Fourth, it was a Pharisee member of the Sanhedrin named Gamaliel who defended the apostles of Jesus after his death (Acts 5:34ff). Fifth, Acts 15:5 mentions "some of those from the sect of the Pharisees who had believed."

While it is surely unfair to label all Pharisees as opponents of Jesus, the Sadducees were another matter entirely. Their political deal with the Romans depended on their ability to help keep order. And the New Testament is well aware of this dependence, as we saw in the passage just cited, showing their fear that, "the Romans will come and take away both our status and our nation" (John 11:48). It is thus probable and appropriate to conclude that the pro-Roman Sadducees were supportive of the crucifixion of Jesus.

---

32. The plural here is nonsensical, as there was only one high priest at any given time. It is also necessary to remember that the high priest was a Roman political appointee who often lacked the qualifications for the high priesthood demanded under Jewish law.

33. Whether or not modern scholarship accepts Nicodemus and Joseph as historical persons, it is clear that they were so portrayed in the NT.

The Founder of the Religion: Paul

Comparison between Jesus and Paul reveals a contrast between the two men in personality, education, political orientation, and style. Jesus was a simple teacher from the countryside who apparently had no formal education.[34] He spoke the common language of his people, Aramaic,[35] and only left the country of his birth for two short trips into nearby Tyre and Sidon (Mark 7:24). Paul was a well-educated, cosmopolitan citizen of Rome who spoke at least Greek and Hebrew, and wrote literate Greek. He traveled to numerous countries, visiting both European and Asian metropolitan centers of population. Familiar with rabbinic methods of interpretation, as we shall see below, Paul was also a mystic and a brilliant organizer.

Easily the most compelling aspect of Paul was his obsessive-compulsive personality. As a practicing Jew, he initially sought authority to bind and imprison those other Jews who were interpreting the faith in the new way. When he became a Christian, he attempted to destroy the very foundations of the Judaism to which he had been born and in which he had been educated. He was convinced that the second coming of Jesus would occur in his own lifetime, and used this belief as an incentive to evangelize every person with whom he came into contact. His method of garnering new converts is described in 1 Corinthians 9:20–22:

> To the Jews I became {or acted} as a Jew that I might win Jews; to those who are under *nomos* ["law"], {I became} as under *nomos* [although I myself am not under *nomos*], that I might win those who are under *nomos*. To those who are lawess [*anomos*], {I became} lawess [although I am not without divine law (*anomos theou*) but am under the *nomos* of Christ], that I might win those who are without law. To the weak I became weak, that I might win the weak. I have become all things to all people, in order that I may by all means save some.[36]

The Pauline dispute with Peter and James in Jerusalem illustrates the depth of his zeal. Acts 15 records what appears to be a doctored account

---

34. Use of the title "Rabbi" to refer to Jesus is an anachronism. While some modern scholars believe that Jesus was educated as a rabbi, John 8:19 chronicles an interesting exchange with some Pharisees who ask him the identity of his "father," probably seeking to identify his rabbinic "teacher."

35. He apparently could read the Hebrew text of Isaiah as well (Luke 4:16–17).

36. Words in brackets are in the Greek text, but interrupt the reading flow of the narrative. Words in {} are added for clarity.

of the first major dispute within the new faith, centering on a single question.[37] Did non-Jews need to convert first to Judaism before becoming Christian? While the leaders of the church in Jerusalem attempted to retain strong ties to their Jewish faith, Paul was certain that such ties would hamper his efforts to attract non-Jews into Christianity. Although he appeared at first to accept the minimal conditions laid down by James,[38] upon leaving Jerusalem he began to impose immediately upon the new faith his personal views of Judaism. We will examine specific examples of Paul's arguments in chapter 6.

According to Paul, Judaism had misunderstood its own history. Abraham had not become a righteous person because of his obedience to Torah, for he had lived 430 years before the giving of the Torah on Mt. Sinai (Gal 3:17).[39] In other words, Abraham had been deemed righteous by God because of his faith alone. Thus, Paul reasoned, anyone else, and clearly he meant non-Jews, could become righteous apart from observance of the Torah as Abraham himself had done. The Law, as Paul interpreted it, was not the five-fold torah known to the rabbis, including the oral torah to be ultimately codified in the Talmud, but the narrowly construed Greek idea of *nomos*, that is, rules and regulations, right and wrong. Thus Paul was free to set aside such a narrow and binding view of righteousness before God, and to declare righteous any person who accepted belief in the Jesus whom he preached.

At times, the Jesus whom Paul preached is barely recognizable as the person described in the gospels. Paul did not speak of one born of a virgin, but described Jesus as having been "born of the seed of David according to the flesh" (Rom 1:3), or as one whom God had sent "born of a woman, born under Torah" (Gal 4:4).[40]

Of particular interest in this regard is the fact that Matthew and Luke had used the virgin birth as an argument for the divinity of Jesus. Matthew's argument (1:20) is that "what has been conceived in [Mary]

37. Paul's own account in Galatians 2 is perhaps more credible.

38. Note that Paul delivered to the congregation in Antioch a letter containing the provisions of the agreement (Acts 15:30).

39. Cf. the rabbinic dictum, "There is no 'early' or 'late' in the Torah" (Steinsaltz, *The Talmud*, 149).

40. Paul's view is not unknown in two of the gospels. While both Matthew and Luke describe a virgin birth, the earliest written gospel (Mark) does not mention such an event, and the latest gospel (John 1:45) specifically describes Jesus as "the son of Joseph, whose father and mother we know." We will return to the subject of the virgin birth in chapter 4.

is from the holy spirit." Likewise, when Mary questions the angel about how she could become pregnant without a male partner, the Lukan (1:35) answer is, "The holy spirit will come upon you, and the power of the most high will overshadow you. And for that reason, the holy thing begotten shall be called the son of God." But Paul's explanation is that the divine nature of Jesus derives not from his virgin birth but from his resurrection. "He was declared in an act of power to be the son of God as a result of the resurrection from the dead" (Rom 1:4).

Again, the Pauline conception of the resurrection is instructive. The gospels would later give mixed signals. On the one hand, the resurrected Jesus could be depicted as a normal, physical person who could walk, engage in conversation and debate, and whose fully human, physical body required food (Luke 24:13–30). John 20:11–15 describe a person who was mistaken by Mary to be a gardener, while Matthew (28:9) depicts Jesus meeting with disciples who have no trouble recognizing him. John 20:24–29 also reports that one doubting disciple (Thomas) actually touched the hands and the side of the resurrected Jesus. On the other hand, Mark (16:12) reports that Jesus had appeared to the disciples "in a different form!" And John 20:19 describes Jesus materializing through locked doors, even though he was recognized once inside with his students.

In his most extensive treatment on the subject, Paul clearly argues for the mystical nature of the resurrection. The key passage here is 1 Corinthians 15:42–54: "This is the resurrection of the dead. It is sown a perishable, it is raised an imperishable. It is sown in dishonor, it is raised in glory. It is sown in weakness, it is raised in power. It is sown a natural body, it is raised a *spiritual body* [sic!]. If there is a natural body, there is also a spiritual one. . . . Look, I am telling you a *mystery*."

On the other hand, 1 Thessalonians 4:13–17 refers to a physical resurrection of the same body in which one has lived earthly life:

> We do not want you to be uninformed, brothers, about those who are asleep, that you may not grieve, as do the rest who have no hope. For if we believe that Jesus died and rose again, even so God will bring with him those who have fallen asleep in Jesus. For this we say to you by the word of the Lord, that we who are alive, who remain until the coming of the Lord, shall not precede those who have fallen asleep. For the Lord himself will descend from heaven with a shout, with the voice of an archangel, and with the trumpet of God; and the dead in Christ will rise first. Then we who are alive, who remain, will be caught up

together with them in the clouds to meet the Lord in the air, and thus we will always be with the Lord.

In chapter 4, we will examine more fully the ways in which these and other theological differences were treated by Paul and the writers of the canonical Gospels.

3

Early Jewish Principles of Interpretation

"'Is not My word like a hammer that breaks the rock in pieces?' [Jer 23:29]—as the hammer causes numerous sparks to flash forth, so is a scriptural verse capable of many interpretations" (*San* 34a).

Šiv'îm panîm la-tôrah—"The Torah has seventy faces" (*Bamidbar Rabbah* 13:15-16).

IN CHAPTER 1, WE surveyed the development of several bodies of literature that grew to become the most sacred and influential writings of Judaism (the Bible and the Talmudim), the *responsa*, three great works of Maimonides, and the still authoritative *Shulḥan Arukh* by Joseph Karo in the fifteenth century CE. We learned that while the Bible held its place of ultimate authority for all Jews, the early rabbis and their successors in the post-biblical era embraced the idea that biblical teachings needed to be reformulated and modernized (transvalued) in ways that would allow the core principles of the Bible to inform the periods of history in which they lived, long after the Bible had become a closed canon.

When we examine the reasons for their acceptance of the need for transvaluation in their own era, several preliminary points deserve mention, the first of which is located within the Bible itself.[1] Deuteronomy 17:8–11 reads as follows:

> Whenever any [legal] matter is too difficult for you, concerning justice, between blood and blood, between judgment and

---

1. See more on Nehemiah 8 later.

judgment, between stroke [of punishment] and stroke, in disputed matters within your gates, you are to arise and go to the place that YHWH your deity chooses. You are to come to the Levitical priests and to the judge who is in office at that time. You are to inquire [*darašta*], and they are to tell you the word of judgment. You are to act according to this word that is told to you in the place that YHWH chooses. You are to take care to observe what they instruct you. You are to act according to the instruction they give you. You are not to turn right or left from the word they give you.

In this passage, not only did the rabbis find clear evidence of the idea that interpretation is an integral ingredient in the process of seeking the divine will, but they also deduced "the legislative authority of the Sanhedrin and its successors, the Sages."[2]

Post-biblical Preludes to Rabbinic Interpretation

Philo of Alexandria[3]

We notice next that the rabbis had examples of non-literal, modernizing interpretation from the first-century CE authority, Philo of Alexandria. Philo, a member of one of the wealthiest families in Alexandria, Egypt, was educated in Greek institutions where his studies included logic, rhetoric, and Hellenistic literature, and was familiar with current developments in the analysis of the Greek classical literature. For centuries, these classics had been viewed in ways comparable to the reverence with which Jews viewed the Bible. But partially because of intellectual developments in philosophy, notably neo-Platonism, and in the natural sciences, and partly because "the duplicity and sexual rapacity of the gods in the *Iliad* present an obvious embarrassment,"[4] many Greek thinkers in Philo's day attacked the long-held Greek view that the Homeric stories of the gods reflected the moral values to which humans should aspire. Pious Greeks searched for a way to preserve the traditional values of Hellenistic society, and in their search turned to a method of literary interpretation

---

2. Tigay, *The JPS Torah Commentary*, 165.
3. See Goodenough, *An Introduction to Philo Judaeus*.
4. O'Keefe and Reno, *Sanctified Vision*, 103.

called "allegory."[5] A new school of thought arose to redeem the gods, who were often portrayed as capricious or immoral, and to protect them from negative attacks by skeptical philosophers. This was done by assigning meanings to the actions of the gods other than the plain sense of the stories themselves. Interpreters began to assign metaphorical, often philologically indefensible, meanings to the names of various deities, and to offer mystical interpretations of the ancient myths (stories about the gods) and legends (stories about human heroes).

Because of his Greek education, Philo, who remained an observant Jew all of his life, was able to exist in two different worlds. Not only did he observe Greek thinkers turning away from traditional interpretations of the Greek classics, but he also witnessed a sharp division of opinion among Jewish interpreters about their own classical works, in particular the Bible. Influenced by the emphasis paid to Hellenistic learning in the educational institutions of the Roman Empire, a large number of Jews turned their backs on Moses in preference for a Greek worldview, while others became increasingly isolated from Alexandrian society in a desperate attempt to remain loyal to traditional Judaism, which they continued to interpret narrowly. To reconcile the two different worldviews, Philo authored two major works in which he attempted to recast some of the stories of the Pentateuch using language he thought would speak to the educated Greek mind, defend Judaism against negative attacks from the same philosophers who had come to doubt the validity of their own classics, and "prove to his fellow Jews that Moses had already comprehended all the learning of the Greeks."[6]

In his movement to metaphorical interpretation, Philo pruned the narratives of the Bible of their stark literal meaning. Abraham became a natural philosopher rather than the biological ancestor of a particular group of people. And, Philo argued, the rituals of Judaism that estranged Jews from other people and cultures actually expressed universal ideals and values very much like Greek ideas of truth, honesty, virtue, and morality. For example, the struggle between Cain and Abel was not merely a story about murder and filial jealousy, but a picture of the struggle between material and spiritual essence. Biblical citations of God speaking

---

5. Greek *allegorein* refers to the process of describing one thing with reference to the meaning of another thing. For a complete documentation of the allegorical method of interpretation employed by Neoplatonists in reading Homer, see Robert Lamberton, *Homer the Theologian*.

6. Mowry, "Allegory," 82.

to Moses or the great prophets, sounding very much like ethnic boasts made by the Jews about themselves, were instead examples of the longing felt by all human beings to rise above the material world and find unity with the *logos* (pure reason), that is, the very mind of the gods.

Josephus[7]

A second example of exegetical latitude available to the rabbis came from the writings of a Jewish historian named Josephus, a later contemporary of Philo. Two of his works titled *Vita* ("life" or "biography") and *History of the Jewish War against Rome* contain spirited defenses of his actions as a Galilean general during the first part of the Roman attack on Judea that culminated in the conquest of Jerusalem and the destruction of the second Temple in 70 CE. However, the work that pertains directly to our survey of the principles of biblical interpretation among early post-biblical Jews is found in his twenty-volume series on *Jewish Antiquities*, the first ten volumes of which are devoted to a recounting of the biblical narratives themselves.[8] The principles of interpretation Josephus brought to his handling of the biblical text are instructive in numerous ways.

1. Josephus was working with the LXX rather than the Hebrew text from which the rabbis worked throughout this period and beyond.[9] This practice, which he shared with Philo, was not condemned by the rabbis, who knew well that the LXX included numerous textual changes from the Hebrew text, and realized that the LXX provided more than mere translations that could be explained via the movement from one language to another, several examples of which they cite.[10] The point is that both Josephus at the end of the first century and then the rabbis in their published works of the third and sixth centuries CE, knew and used this alternate textual version of the Bible. That they were not bothered by such variants indicates not only their openness but also their view that the *ideas* of Scripture

---

7. Feldman, *Josephus's Interpretation of the Bible*; and Mason, *Flavius Josephus*.
8. Mason, *Josephus and the New Testament*, 99.
9. Although the text of the Hebrew Bible had not yet been standardized, citations from the Talmud are an important source for understanding the movement in that direction.
10. *Meg.* 9a includes their discussion and listing of variants between the Greek and Hebrew texts. We note once again that it had been rabbis who produced the LXX.

were more important than full agreement of all details that a mechanical doctrine of inerrancy or literal accuracy would demand.

2. Josephus added to his account details that are lacking in both the Hebrew Bible of the rabbis and the Greek text of the LXX. For example, he gave the name of the man responsible for the construction of the Tower of Babel (Nimrod) and the name of the Egyptian princess who found and adopted Moses (Thermuthis); emphasized the cardinal (Greek) virtues of heroes like Abraham, Moses, Samson, Saul, David, and Solomon; shaped the story of the biblical Joseph to sound much like his own personal life; and saw no link between circumcision and the Abrahamic covenant with God made explicitly in Genesis 17, offering instead the rationale that circumcision helped to prevent Jews from assimilating into pagan cultures.

3. In addition, Josephus often offered explanations of biblical law that were similar to rulings codified in rabbinic writings only centuries later, indicating his familiarity with the oral debates taking place as early as the end of the first century CE. Yet, while Josephus was in agreement with many rulings that the *Tanna'im* were to codify later, he disagrees with numerous others.[11]

Pseudepigrapha[12]

The time period under consideration also witnessed the publication of a wide variety of documents known collectively as Pseudepigrapha ("falsely written"), that is, documents written by authors living in the period between ca. 200 BCE and 200 CE, but ascribed to a famous person who had lived in ancient times. The custom of such false ascription is difficult for modern thinkers to grasp. But there appear to be multiple reasons for such a practice. First, the Bible itself attests pseudepigraphic writings. Numerous psalms ascribed to David, Solomon, or Moses could not have been written by these worthies.[13] Virtually one-half of the book of Isaiah derives from the Persian or post-Persian era, long after the death of the eighth-century prophet whose name is assigned to the entire book.

11. Feldman, "Josephus," *ABD* 3:992–94 for examples.
12. The standard collection of this genre is edited by Charlesworth, *The Old Testament Pseudepigrapha*.
13. See my book, *God's Scribes*, 156–71 for a discussion of this phenomenon in Psalms.

And the ascription of the five books of the Torah to Moses is an obvious example of false ascription of authorship in the modern sense of the term. Should it be argued that these results of modern scholarly analysis were unknown two thousand years ago, it must be admitted that the ascription of the entire Mishnah to Moses, cited in chapter 1, cannot be explained away as an example of later writers who simply did not know the true authors of material.

This observation leads to a second point about authorship in ancient times. "Wisdom was the result of God's guidance and was often made possible through the devotion of a gifted teacher or rabbi."[14] The ancients were thus open about the fact that what they believed and taught had come to them from outside themselves, be it from God, a great teacher, or even via a dream or vision. When one adds the element of solidarity with the past that guided the authors in question, it becomes clear that the ruling principle was not deceit of readers but a sense of connection with the whole of Jewish tradition and praxis.

However the issues of authorship are determined by modern scholarship, for the purposes of our study, the salient feature of pseudepigraphic writing is its freedom in dealing with standard biblical accounts. In addition to texts that supply lengthy narrative additions to supplement biblical stories,[15] the Pseudepigrapha attest a very elaborate expansion of the concept of angels, a keen interest in apocalypticism, and a great emphasis on belief in bodily resurrection, all subjects that receive minimal attention in the Bible. Yet all three are much more important in rabbinic thought than they are in biblical thought.[16] Here we are not speaking strictly about methodological methods of biblical interpretation, but underscoring the freedom exercised by the authors of pseudepigraphic works to move beyond the scope of biblical narrative as they attempted to address questions pertinent to their own era. In the exercise of this freedom, both the boundaries and the literal understanding of biblical narratives were altered.

---

14. Charlesworth, "Pseudepigrapha, OT," *ABD* 5:539.

15. For example, the extensive supplement to the biblical account of the era of the Flood in 1 Enoch.

16. In addition, although pseudepigraphic literature mentions "messiah" only rarely, it includes references that became important in Christian doctrine.

The *Targumim*[17]

The word *Targum* (pl. *targumim*) refers to Aramaic translations of the Hebrew Scriptures. *Targumim* are extant for all biblical books except Ezra-Nehemiah (originally a single work) and Daniel, both of which were composed partially in Aramaic. There are three main versions of the *Targumim* for the Torah (Pentateuch): *Onqelos*, *Pseudo-Jonathan*, and *Codex Neofiti*. The chief version of the Prophets is known as *Targum Jonathan*. A variety of fragmentary versions are available for several books, and many books among the Writings have separate Aramaic translations of their own.[18]

According to the rabbis, the origin of the custom of offering explanatory comments about the Hebrew original of the Bible, a practice that was continued and extended by the Aramaic *targumim*, may be traced back to Nehemiah 8:1-8, which describes the reading of the Torah by Ezra to the Judahite returnees to Jerusalem in the fifth century BCE. During the reading, several scholars and Levites were dispersed among the crowd for the purpose of explaining the Torah to the people. Verse 8 notes that not only Ezra, but "*they* read from the book, the divine Torah, explaining [it] to give the meaning so that [the people] understood the Bible." The reference to "reading" is taken by the rabbis to mean the reading of the Hebrew Scripture, but the additional "explaining" they identify as "the *Targum*,"[19] by which they meant that an oral Aramaic translation was offered concurrently with the Hebrew text.[20]

The book of Nehemiah also alludes to the fact that Aramaic translations of the Hebrew Scriptures became necessary because fewer people were able to understand Hebrew once Aramaic had replaced it as the native language of more and more Jews, especially those living in Palestine.[21] At least by the era of the *Tanna'im*, it became customary to translate simultaneously into Aramaic the passages of the Hebrew Torah that were being read aloud in worship, one person reading in Hebrew and a sec-

---

17. An excellent treatment of the *targumim* is that of Kolatch, *Masters of the Word*, 1:157-225. Note his documentation of the fact that Maimonides knew the tendency of Targum Onkelos to alter statements describing God in anthropomorphic terms on pages 186-87.

18. See Alexander, "Targum, Targumim," *ABD* 6:320-31 on the extant copies.

19. *Meg.* 74d.

20. See *Meg.* 3a.

21. In Nehemiah 13:23-24, Nehemiah laments the fact that many children produced from intermarriages between Jewish men and Ashdodite, Ammonite, and Moabite women "did not know how to speak Judean" (i.e., Hebrew).

ond person offering an oral rendition into the more familiar vernacular Aramaic.[22] In this way, two goals were met. On the one hand, the special status of the Torah in the original Hebrew was retained,[23] while on the other hand, the *meaning* of the sacred texts was made understandable to the non-scholarly worshippers.

Of greatest interest for our theme is the fact that the *Targumim* were viewed by the rabbis as a vital step in the mastery of "oral torah."[24] While the Hebrew text required a person who was capable of *reading* from the sacred scroll, the Aramaic translation itself was offered orally based upon what the translator *heard*.[25] Because of the greater flexibility provided by the strictly aural context in which they occurred, not only were the *Targumim* important links in the *oral* component of biblical interpretation, they shared features of numerous interpretative principles with Midrashim. A translation could offer only a single line of interpretation, while a Midrash could include give and take, pro and con, much in the manner of rabbinic debates themselves. In choosing from among a variety of possibilities for rendering specific Hebrew words into Aramaic, the *Targumim* served as commentaries on the biblical text; they were not attempts at literal or word-for-word equivalency. By the time of the 'Amoraim, Targum Onkelos had become the accepted translation, as indicated by the judgment of Rabbi Yehudah (referring to *Onkelos*): "One who translates a verse on his own is a liar, and one who adds[26] is a blasphemer" (*Kiddushin* 49a). Clearly *Onkelos* is closer to what we might call a translation, while two *targumic* versions that originated in Israel (*Targum Yonatan* and *Targum Yerushalmi*) incorporate additional *haggadic* and Midrashic materials that move well beyond translation into the realm of interpretation. It should be remembered that even *Targum Onkelos* existed only in oral form for centuries before it was edited into the fixed, written form to which Rabbi Yehudah was referring.

---

22. This is clear from the rulings governing the public reading of the Torah, given in detail in *Meg.* 4:4, 10.

23. The translator (*meturgeman*) was not allowed to look into the Torah text itself, to avoid the impression that the translation itself was written in the sacred text.

24. Note the statement in *Sifrei Shoftim* 161: "Scripture leads to [the study of] *Targum*, and *Targum* leads to [the study of] Mishnah."

25 According to Rashi, commenting on *Meg.* 23b, the tradition was to read only one verse at a time in Hebrew so that the *meturgeman* might not err.

26. To the Hebrew text, which all *Targumim* do consistently!

A classic example of *Targumic* commentary that extends well beyond a simple translation of the text, only one among many that could be cited, occurs in Exodus 7:1. The Hebrew text has YHWH telling Moses: "Look, I have made you a deity [Elohim] to the Pharaoh, and your brother Aaron will be your prophet." There was no problem in viewing Moses filling "the role of God in negotiations with Pharaoh, who claimed divinity for himself."[27] But the idea that Moses, *the* prophet par excellence,[28] needed someone else to function as his prophet had an uncomfortable ring to it. *Targum Neofiti* solves the problem nicely, describing Aaron as the *meturgeman* ("translator") for his brother whenever Moses needed to speak to the Pharaoh.[29]

Historical Development

Alongside their awareness of the ways in which the Bible had been defended with recourse to secular modes of interpretation, the rabbis understood that more than 1500 years and scores of human authors and editors had been involved in the formation of their canon of Scripture and Talmud. In an era that witnessed a world no longer germane to the time-bound narratives of the Hebrew Bible—that is, that lacked a king, a nation, political independence, or a Temple—Jewish rabbis embarked on the task of reformulating the core values of the Bible in a fashion that would speak to the new realities of their world.[30] As we have seen, they offered these reformulations in their Mishnah and Gemara (Talmud), followed by the codes and rabbinic *responsa* of subsequent eras.

---

27. Sarna, *JPS Exodus*, 36.

28. See Numbers 12; Deuteronomy 13:2–6 and 18:18.

29. Logically, of course, this explanation makes little sense. The book of Exodus clearly depicts Moses, reared in the palace of the Pharaoh, as someone who would have been as fluent in the Egyptian language as Aaron.

30. In chapter 5 we will return to specific examples of how this rabbinic reformulation, or transvaluation, worked.

The Hermeneutics of the Rabbis[31]
ha-midôt še-ha-tôrah nidrešet bahin[32]

With these preliminary considerations in mind, we may now examine the ways in which the rabbis began the task of biblical interpretation that preserved the Bible for Judaism; defended Moses against assaults from Greek philosophy, Christianity, Islam, and internal opponents like the Karaites; and transformed a static body of written literature into a dynamic system of belief, morals, faith, and praxis. It is self-evident that the work of the rabbis demanded rules of fair play to regulate their discussions and debates, that is, principles of interpretation to which they felt bound, and which were designed to establish appropriate boundaries within which their examination and reformulation of the Bible could occur. While the true task of the rabbis was to reformulate for their own era the values of Scripture to which they were committed, they deemed it obvious that not every opinion was equally learned or valid. So we must ask how a debate winner was determined, or how a particular opinion came to be held by the majority, and recommended to the community as appropriate *halakhah*. The entrance of the rabbis into the field of hermeneutics addressed precisely these issues.[33]

Hermeneutics is the discipline of explaining or interpreting a literary text. The word itself refers to that branch of analysis concerned to establish *rules* and *principles* of proper interpretation. Hermeneutics is related closely to exegesis (to explain, interpret), and the two words are often used interchangeably. However, while hermeneutics establishes general *rules* for the interpretation of literature, exegesis refers specifically to the *application* of those rules.

The starting point for our analysis of the hermeneutics of the rabbis lies in the distinction made by the rabbis between two basic methods

---

31. For a brief discussion of these thirteen hermeneutical principles, see Kolatch, *Masters of the Word*, 1:90–95.

32. "The principles by which the Torah is interpreted," the Hebrew phrase by which the rabbis referred to the rules they felt committed to follow.

33. The bibliography on the subject is enormous. Among the more accessible and reliable sources are (with full publication information offered in the bibliography): Jacobs, "Hermeneutics"; Mielziner, *Introduction to the Talmud*, 117–87; Neusner, *Invitation to Midrash*, 45, 48, 49, 51, 54–55; Neusner, *The Judaism Behind the Texts*, 124–27, 131–33, 153–57; Porten, "Midrash," *ADB* 4:818–22; Steinsaltz, *The Talmud*, 147–54; Strack, *Introduction to the Talmud and Midrash*, 93–98 and notes on 284–97; Trepp, *Judaism*, 260–75.

of biblical interpretation, the plain (most obvious) sense (*peshaṭ*) and a more complicated sense that requires examination in greater detail (*drash*). The *peshaṭ* explains a biblical passage in the most natural or obvious fashion according to its grammatical construction and its contextual intention, and the rabbis believed that this plain sense was to be preferred.[34] The *drash* required a more intensive searching, often leading to an artificial deduction, and could be employed generally in a case where the plain sense was difficult to ascertain. But the rabbis could also move beyond the *peshaṭ* in cases where a literal understanding clashed with their own cultural sensitivities. That they understood the implication of such instances is clear in the following astonishing statement: *halakhah ʿôpheret miqra'*, meaning "*halakhah* uproots Scripture" (*Sot.* 16a).

The Talmud[35] includes the following passage that illustrates the difference between *peshaṭ* and *drash* in dramatic fashion. In a long discussion about people deemed qualified to serve as witnesses in a legal procedure, the Mishnah makes the following judgment: "A friend or an enemy [is ineligible]. By 'friend' is meant one's best man; by 'enemy,' anyone who because of hard feelings has not spoken to [the principal involved in the legal dispute] for three days." Then the rabbis (i.e., a majority of the *Tanna'im*) added one additional qualification: "Israelites [Jews] are not *ipso facto* to be suspected on such grounds."[36]

The *'Amoraim* who contributed the gemara to this Mishnah made some interesting additions. First they supplied a specific biblical reference on which it appeared that the *Tanna'im* had based their ruling, Deuteronomy 24:16: "Fathers shall not be put to death for sons, nor sons put to death for father. Each person shall be put to death for his own sin." Then they asked about the *peshaṭ* of the biblical verse, supplying a rhetorical answer to their own question: "What does this teach? Is it [not] that fathers shall not be executed for sins committed by their children and vice versa?" Third, they noted that a different biblical verse (Lev 26:29) had made the same point even more explicitly. And this suggested a fourth point to them. Since the *peshaṭ* on which the Mishnaic ruling rested was clear from Leviticus 26:29, a deeper meaning should be sought for Deuteronomy 24:16: "'Fathers shall not be put to death on account of

---

34. Hence the rabbinic dictum: "A verse does not depart from its *peshaṭ*" (Shab 63a; Yeb. 13b; and *passim*).

35. San. 27b.

36. I.e., Jews are presumed not to give testimony of bias or prejudice against another Jew.

children' has to mean 'fathers shall not be put to death *on the testimony* of their sons.' Likewise, 'sons shall not be put to death on account of fathers,' has to mean, 'nor sons *on the testimony* of their fathers.'" This is quite a radical movement from *peshat* (the family of a criminal ought not to be punished for his crime) to *drash* (the testimony of relatives cannot be accepted in a criminal procedure).

It was specifically for passages like these that rules of fair play were needed in the search for answers to crucial questions: When could one move beyond the plain sense? What limits should be set to govern the imposition of a *drash* on a biblical passage? How could two apparently contradictory passages be treated? What about cases where both a *peshat* and a *drash* appear applicable? No matter how complicated an issue might be, "arbitrary explanations of the Biblical text" were not acceptable. In each case, the rabbis were required to "follow fixed principles of interpretation."[37]

As early as the first century CE, the great Rabbi Hillel set forth a series of seven principles to be followed in the interpretation of Scripture. But a critical moment in rabbinic methodology was reached in the second century, when the famous Rabbi Akiva propounded the theory that the language of the Torah was different from human language. Because it was divine language, Akiva argued, not a word, not a syllable, and not even a single letter should be deemed superfluous.[38] Two points are important. First, because of his view that the biblical text was divine language, Akiva exhibited little appreciation for the *peshat*. Second, since he believed the language of Scripture to be divine rather than human, he argued that the Bible must be read and interpreted differently from the ways in which humanly authored texts are approached.

Although Akiva did gain a following among some of his rabbinical colleagues, his view of biblical language did not win the day. Rather, it fell to his most outspoken critic, Rabbi Ishmael ben Elisha', to coin the famous dictum that became the watchword of rabbinic biblical interpretation: "The Torah spoke in ordinary human language." Assuming the truth of Rabbi Ishmael's dictum meant that the language of the Bible could be

---

37. Steinsaltz, *The Talmud*, 147.

38. For example Akiva interprets Leviticus 21:9 to mean that the daughter of a priest who commits harlotry before her marriage should be burned to death, drawing his conclusion from the presence of the letter *vav* at the beginning of the verse. Amusingly, Rabbi Ishmael retorts, "Just because you interpret the extra letter *vav*, we should take her out and burn her?" Their argument is recounted in *Sanhedrin* 51b.

subjected to human analysis.³⁹ Apparent contradictions, inconsistencies, obscure references, all could be brought into the realm of human intelligence and examined using rules of grammar, syntax, logic, philosophical coherency, and plain common sense. As noted earlier, this certainly did not imply that every rabbi could champion his own favorite interpretations, no matter how farfetched. It meant that the *community* of rabbinical scholars, working together, would accept responsibility for shaping biblical teachings into meaningful instruction for the lives of ordinary Jews. Rabbi Ishmael then outlined a series of thirteen rules of exegesis that became standard among rabbis involved in biblical interpretation:

1. Rabbi Ishmael's first rule is known in Hebrew as *Qal va-ḥomer*, literally "light and heavy," "easy to hard," or "lenient to stringent." Students of Greek philosophy can recognize a similar rule that was used by Hellenistic rhetoricians, known as an inference *a fortiori*. A *Qal va-ḥomer* syllogism, like its Greek counterpart, consists of a major premise, a minor premise, and a conclusion, the process more generally known as deductive reasoning. Taking two statements that relate to each as major to minor, the rabbis argued that whatever is true about the simple or plain biblical statement is all the more true about the more complicated one, and vice versa. In practical terms, they were trying to understand a complicated biblical statement in terms of one that was plain and simple, or easy to understand (*Qal*). In addition, when dealing with a *legal* issue, they argued that *Qal* describes not only the easier meaning to understand but specifically the more lenient treatment, the *ḥomer* implying the more stringent one. Since an argument *Qal va-ḥomer* is one of the most frequent devices used by the rabbis, examples abound in Talmudic and other rabbinic discussions of *halakhah* and the biblical passages on which they are grounded.⁴⁰ The following examples are a representative sampling.⁴¹

Example: Shabbat is considered more important than an ordinary religious holiday by the rabbis. Therefore, any activity permitted on

---

39. For the view that this dictum applies much more narrowly than I am assuming here, see Steinsaltz, *The Talmud*, 151.

40. For example, a detailed fourth-century CE work, *Mekhilta de-R. Ishmael*, includes a long section devoted to the laws listed in the book of Exodus 20:19—23:33. Many are explained by reference to the principle of Qal va-Homer.

41. Some of the examples to follow are cited by Mielziner, *Introduction to the Talmud*. For more detailed definitions of these thirteen and numerous other hermeneutical principles, but without concrete examples, see Steinsaltz, *The Talmud*, 147–54.

Shabbat is also permissible on a mere holiday. Conversely, anything prohibited on a holiday is all the more to be prohibited on Shabbat.

Example: The biblical law "eye for an eye" was taken by the rabbis to mean not that the offender's physical person should be harmed to punish him for having harmed another, but that the extent of the harm done to the injured person should be calculated and expressed in terms of a monetary equivalent paid by the offender. They discovered biblical justification for this interpretation in Exodus 21:29, which stipulates that when an ox with a history of goring is not confined by its owner and subsequently has gored to death a human, the ox must be stoned, and the negligent owner must also be put to death. But the following verse in Exodus reads: "If a ransom is demanded, [the ox owner] shall give as redemption whatever is demanded [in monetary payment]." Thus, if the Torah expressly allows monetary compensation for a person deemed guilty of a capital crime and deserving of the death penalty according to a *peshaṭ* reading of the text, monetary compensation should be all the more acceptable in cases that do not require capital punishment to begin with. In other words, a ruling applied to a minor problem "must never surpass in severity the original law in [the major example] from which the inference was made."[42]

Example: Exodus 22:7–9 deals with a situation in which one man agrees to hold money (or unspecified "goods") for a neighbor, and the money turns up missing. In such a case, it is impossible to know whether the money has been hidden away by the trustee, stolen by a third party, or merely lost. The biblical context states quite explicitly that a trustee must make restitution to an owner whenever property or money under his care for another is stolen. The ruling of the rabbis extends this principle to cover instances of lost property as well: "It follows *Qal va-ḥomer*: if he must pay for theft, which is near to accident, then surely he is liable for loss, which is more akin to negligence."[43]

2. The second hermeneutical rule of Rabbi Ishmael is called *gezerah shavah*, "a similar decision," that is, a question pertaining to analogous situations. Analogy was also well known among Greek philosophers as the principle by which two things that are similar may be compared

---

42. Mielziner, *Introduction to the Talmud*, 134.
43. *Baba Metzia* 94b.

and contrasted. Whenever "A" is clearly understood, and is recognized as similar (or analogous) to "B," which is less easily grasped, "B" should be defined with reference to "A." It should be noted in the following examples, that the principle of *gezerah shavah* is employed to compare and contrast two or more biblical statements which each contain the same word or Hebrew root. Conceptual comparisons were made using rule number three introduced below.

Example: Exodus 21:2 sets forth regulations governing the treatment of "a Hebrew slave." But the phrase itself, "Hebrew slave," is ambiguous. It may mean an Israelite who has been sold as a slave (i.e., a slave who is a Hebrew), or it may refer to a non-Israelite owned by an Israelite (i.e., a slave belonging to a Hebrew). This ambiguity is solved by reference to Deuteronomy 15:12, where the same regulation appears to be repeated. But in Deuteronomy, the word "brother" (member of the group) is added as an explanatory gloss before the phrase "a Hebrew male or female slave," clearly a reference to an Israelite who is a slave. Thus Exodus 21:2, which is ambiguous, must be interpreted in light of Deuteronomy 15:12, which is explicit and clear. And this must be done by an appeal to the rule of *gezerah shavah*, which functions to supply an omission or ambiguity in one verse by analogy to the more explicit provisions in another verse.

Example: Leviticus 16:29 occurs in the context of a long passage giving to Moses numerous details about the yearly observance of Yom Kippur. One of the requirements for individual Jews on Yom Kippur is described in the biblical verse as follows: "you must afflict [or humble] yourselves."[44] However, no specific form of expressing humility or self-denial is included in the biblical text. So the rabbis turned to other biblical texts. An important reference elsewhere in the Pentateuch links the word "afflict" with "hunger" (Deut 8:2–3). The book of Isaiah (58:3) offers a clear link between affliction/humbling oneself and fasting, while Psalm 35:13 portrays an innocent man protesting his troubles to God even though he had, among other things, "humbled myself with fasting." By appeal to the rule of analogy, *gezerah shavah*, the rabbis[45] determined that the generic expression in Leviticus 16:29 also referred to fasting, and

---

44. Or, as *JPS* translates the phrase: "you shall practice self-denial." The word *ləʿanôt* can describe affliction, humbling experiences, or even the trauma of rape (2 Sam 13:12).

45. Cf. the Midrashic commentary to Leviticus 16, known as *Sifra*.

that fasting should become a requirement for acceptable observance of Yom Kippur.[46]

3. Rabbi Ishmael's third rule deals with the generalization of a specific biblical law. Its Hebrew name is *Binyan 'Av* ("formation of a leading rule"). As a principle, *Binyan 'Av* was used to extend a simple biblical formula to allow coverage of situations not mentioned specifically but obviously similar. This principle is comparable to the rule of *gezerah shavah* just discussed. But whereas the *gezerah shavah* dealt with biblical instances of specific *verbal* identity, the *Binyan 'Av* searched for broader *conceptual* similarities.

Example: Deuteronomy 24:6 has the clear and simple rule: "No one may take a hand mill or an upper millstone as pledge [i.e., collateral for a loan], because he would be taking a life as a pledge." This appears to be a very specific law dealing with two items described in precise detail, a hand mill and an upper millstone. Yet the reason given for the law in Deuteronomy is quite broad: loss of either item would deprive a family of the means of preparing their food. The *Tanna'im* deduced from this specific biblical reason a general principle for lending. "Everything used to prepare food is forbidden as collateral."[47] They give as biblical justification the final phrase in Deuteronomy 24:6: "because it is [someone's] life," (i.e., means of staying alive).[48]

Example: Exodus 21:26–27 state that if a slave owner knocks out either the eye or the tooth of a slave, that slave has to be set free, and this biblical law becomes a straightforward ruling in the Mishnah. But the discussion of this Mishnaic ruling in the Gemara extends these two specific biblical examples to provide that the mutilation of *any* member of the body of a slave by a master triggers the immediate manumission of that slave. Their line of reasoning is significant.

---

46. The *Tanna'im* (*Yoma* 8:1) added other restrictions as well: drinking (even of water), washing or bathing, use of perfume or bodily ointments, wearing of leather footwear, sexual intercourse. Obviously they were concerned to plumb the full meaning of the verbal root "to afflict."

47. *Baba Metzia* 9:13.

48. Modern Jewish scholars have extended this principle to exclude things like the tools of a carpenter or mechanic, the car of a salesperson, or even the office equipment of a businessman, all of which should be deemed ineligible to serve as collateral for a loan because they all control a person's means of making a living and staying alive.

A Tanna' taught: "He [a non-Jewish slave] goes out [free] as a consequence of [losing] his eye, tooth, or protruding limbs which do not grow back. Now, as for [the loss of] his tooth or eye, it is well: these are written.[49] But how do we know [the loss of] the protruding limbs? By analogy with tooth and eye. Just as these are patent blemishes, and do not grow back, so [is a slave to be freed for the loss of] all [limbs which are] patent blemishes that do not grow back."[50]

Example: Deuteronomy 19 is a chapter devoted to the concept of "cities of refuge,"[51] cities to which anyone who had committed unintentional homicide could flee to avoid revenge at the hands of the deceased person's relatives seeking revenge in a moment of anguish over the recent death of their loved one. As an illustration of the kind of person who would be eligible to flee to one of these cities, Deuteronomy 19:4–6 spells out in some detail the kinds of incident the law has in mind. Verse 4 assumes a case involving two men who had no history of enmity between them, and further assumes that the death is unintentional. Verse 5 offers a very specific example of such a case: "If someone enters the forest with his friend to cut wood, and his hand thrusts forward the axe to cut down the tree, but the iron [axe head] slips off the handle, strikes his friend, and kills him, he may flee to one of these cities [of refuge] and remain alive." Verse 6 notes that the law intends to protect the slayer from a relative who is seeking revenge "in the heat of his anger."

The rabbis realized this rule needed to be extended to cover a wide range of accidents that resulted in a death. So they added the following examples of what would be ruled "accidental homicide," making the slayer in such cases eligible for protection from family revenge: two men working on a roof when the roller used to flatten the mixture of clay and straw slipped out of one man's hand and killed the other; one man letting a heavy jar down from the roof by rope when the rope breaks, allowing the heavy jar to fall on and kill his working partner; one man descending by ladder and falling accidently upon another man, killing him; a piece of chopped wood flying through the air and striking a second man.[52] And then, realizing that they could not mention every possible accidental

---

49. Here the Amoraim cite the biblical passage in question, Deuteronomy 24:6.

50. *Kiddushin* 24a.

51. The provision for these six cities is found in Numbers 35:10–28, which lists several examples of homicide that do *not* qualify the slayer for refuge.

52. *Makkot* 2:1.

situation, the rabbis added an even more general provision stipulating that the location where an accident had occurred should be a place where the deceased person was working or otherwise to be found habitually, and concluded that in each qualifying case, the deceased man must have entered willingly into the activity that resulted in his accidental death, and the slayer must have acted without malice or prior hatred for his fellow.[53] These last two qualifiers are, of course, precisely the two mentioned in the biblical text under examination!

4–6. To grasp the function of the next three rules given by Rabbi Ishmael, it is necessary to understand the two words "general" (*kelal*) and "particular" (*peraṭ*) as the rabbis employed them. When a general law is followed by a particular application (#4), the law is presumed to cover only the particular(s) that Scripture enumerates. On the other hand, when a particular term is followed by a general description (#5), the rabbis assumed that the law refers to anything included in the general and that the particulars were merely illustrative examples of that general principle. Finally, when a general rule is given, followed by one or more particular examples, and then another general principle is enumerated (#6), the assumption was that only things closely resembling the particular(s) given in the middle are affected. In short, the rabbis accepted the proposition that wherever Scripture spoke in general terms it intended to include everything similar or related to those terms. But whenever Scripture spoke in specific terms using lists of particular things, the burden fell upon interpreters to determine when the particulars should be limited to the things listed specifically by the Bible and when they should be extended to cover other things not listed specifically. In other words, a determination had to be made about whether a case before the rabbis properly fell in the same generic category covered in the Bible. The trick was to know which was which, that is, when a ruling should be limited and when and how the meaning of a specific text needed to be extended.

4. *Example*: Deuteronomy 22:11 reads: "You will not wear a mixed fabric [*šaʻaṭnez*], wool and linen together." Since the general term, "mixed fabric," is followed immediately by a single particular, "wool and linen together," the prohibition of wearing a garment of mixed fabrics is restricted to the specific mixture of wool and linen.

---

53. *Makkot* 2:2.

Example: Leviticus 1:2 explains the kinds of animals acceptable for use as an offering. "When one of you brings an offering to YHWH, you must bring that offering from animals, from a herd [of cattle] or from a flock [of sheep or goats]." The word "animals" is a very general term that includes an uncountable number of species. But cattle, sheep, and goats are quite specific. They are all animals, of course, but not all animals are cattle, sheep, or goats! So the Talmudic tractate dealing with sacrifices concludes that sacrifices are to be selected from herds and flocks, "but not wild animals,"[54] using not the generic term for "animals" (*behemah*) found in Leviticus, but the broader term used in the Genesis creation stories (*ḥayyah*).

5. *Example*: According to Exodus 22:9, "if a man gives his neighbor a donkey, an ox, a sheep, or any animal to guard, and it dies or is wounded or driven away while no one is looking," the two parties must appear in court and take an oath to determine the guilt or innocence of both the guarding neighbor and the property owner. Since the specific examples of donkey, ox, and sheep are followed by the phrase "or any animal" (*behemah* here, the same word found in Lev 1:2), the particulars are deemed to be a non-exhaustive list exemplifying a general rule that covers *any* kind of animal delivered for safekeeping.

6. *Example*: Exodus 22:6 opens a short section on responsibility for theft in cases where one man has entrusted something of value to another for safe keeping, concluding that "if the thief is captured, he must pay double." But what if the thief is not caught? In that case, the trustee must appear in court to determine whether he himself may be the thief (22:7). Once it has been shown that the trustee did not steal the property, both parties must appear together in court and take an oath to determine the guilt or innocence of both the guarding neighbor and the property owner. If there is a conviction of the owner, the trustee, or a thief, the penalty is stipulated using a general-particular-general structure. "For any matter of trespass [general], for ox, for donkey, for clothing [particulars], for anything lost [general] that has been identified by the owner, the guilty party 'shall pay double to his neighbor'" (22:8). All of this is included in the biblical verses.

---

54. *Zevahim* 84a.

But Exodus 22:8 reappears in the middle of a rigorous Talmudic debate about numerous instances of liability,[55] with emphasis on how to determine the liable party, when double payment should be made, and when the restitution should be four- or five-fold. The *Tanna'im* gave a simple ruling with no biblical citation: "the determination of double payment applies both to a thing possessing the breath of life and to a thing that does not possess the breath of life." The *'Amoraim* naturally asked, "From where is this derived?" Then they proceeded to cite Exodus 22:8 and tied it to the formula we are examining. "'For every matter of trespass' is a generalization; 'whether it be for ox, for donkey, for sheep, for clothing' is a particular; 'or for any manner of lost thing' generalizes again" (literally, "returns and generalizes"). This indicated to the *'Amoraim* that they faced

> A generalization preceding a particular which is in its turn followed by another generalization, and in such cases, we include only that which is similar to the particular. Just as the particular here mentions an object that is movable and has an intrinsic value, so any object that is movable and has an intrinsic value should be included. Real estate is thus excluded, not being movable; slaves are similarly excluded as they are on the same footing [in the eyes of the law] with real estate; bills[56] are similarly excluded, because although they are movable, they have no intrinsic value; sacred property[57] is also excluded because the text speaks of "his neighbor."[58]

The following five rules of Rabbi Ishmael cover technical modifications of the three preceding rules dealing with "general" and "particular."

7. The seventh rule examines passages that contain a general statement lacking a particular explanation or a particular example without a clear general principle. In such instances, the general and the particular are to be examined as if they formed only a single and inseparable expression.

---

55. E.g., if sparks from a hammer started a fire, or if flax being carried by a camel blew into a retail shop and caught it on fire.

56. I.e., a note signed as evidence of a debt. Such a note has a face value that must still be collected, but the value of the note itself is not intrinsic; the note is merely an extrinsic representation of what will become an intrinsic value only upon payment.

57. Owned by the community rather than by any individual.

58. *Baba Kamma* 62b.

Example: Leviticus 17:13 requires that when a hunter catches an animal or a bird that is kosher for eating, "he must pour out its blood and cover it with dust." Here "cover" (*kissah*) is a general term, while "dust" (*'aphar*) is a particular substance. Thus the rabbis recognized a problem of definition in the Hebrew word "cover," which has a variety of meanings. Taken alone, for example, it could mean simply to hide the animal blood from one's sight. And so, the particular substance with which the rabbis considered it proper to "cover" blood had to be limited to "dust," and nothing else (like a closed container). Why? Because "this is a general that requires a particular,"[59] and the Hebrew phrase, "covered with dust," functions as a single idea.

8. Rule number eight deals with a more intricate form of interpretation. If a biblical passage specifically names a particular example that is clearly already included in a general provision, the example must be illustrative only, and not inclusive. So the general provision must apply.

Example: Deuteronomy 22:1–3 deal with the duty of a person to restore a lost animal to its rightful owner, mentioning explicitly first an ox and a sheep, either of which must be kept safe until the owner comes seeking them (22:1–2). Almost as an afterthought, or an expansion of the principle just stated, verse 3 adds two more particular examples: "Oh, and you must do the same thing for a donkey. And you must do the same thing for a garment," before adding a final statement that is very general: "you must do the same with anything a neighbor has lost and you have found." The rabbis took the particular mention of a donkey as an obvious extension of the general class of "animal." But then they wondered about the addition of the word "garment," which falls outside the animal classification of the other three particulars. "Why is 'garment' mentioned separately? . . . To teach that as a particular, a garment has special characteristics that allow a rightful owner to claim it: the specific size that fits its owner, a unique pattern or color scheme, even a name tag. So any item that has such markings must be included."[60] This concluding generality, of course, teaches that there are *no* exceptions to the rule.

9–11. Rules nine, ten, and eleven involve additional ways to deal with general-particular problems. When should a combined general-particular

---

59. Cf. *Hullin* 88b.
60. *Baba Metzia* 2:5.

statement be decided on the side of leniency and when in favor of stringency? Are there cases where a biblical rule should be either lenient or strict depending upon changing circumstances? If a particular seems to be included in a general but the Bible describes it as something "new," does the generalization control, or the particularization?

12. Rabbi Ishmael's rule number twelve involves context, a principle of literary interpretation more familiar to modern critics than some of the preceding eight. The rule that "a thing is taught by its context" (*davar ha-lamed me-inyanô ve-davar ha-lamed misôfô*) is complicated by the fact that context may refer to the immediate surroundings of the text, or may be extended to a far broader appeal including the whole of biblical narrative.

Example: Both Exodus 20:15 and Deuteronomy 5:19 include a familiar member of the Ten Commandments: "do not steal". At first glance, this would seem to be a general and extremely broad prohibition whose *peshat* appears to be so unambiguous that disagreement about its meaning would seem unlikely. But two different sets of anonymous rabbis disagreed sharply about the verse, illustrating in the process both aspects of rule twelve about Scriptural context.[61] When the *immediate* context of the verse is considered, it becomes clear that the offenses preceding the prohibition against stealing (murder and adultery) deal with capital crimes. This is the context that convinces Rabbi A.

> Rabbi A taught: "'You shall not steal' [Exod 20:15] refers to the stealing of human beings."[62]

> Rabbi B disagrees: "You say, 'Scripture refers to the stealing of human beings,' but perhaps it is not so. Maybe it refers to the theft of money."

> Rabbi A retorts: "I will tell you: Go forth and learn from the thirteen principles whereby the Torah is interpreted [one of which is that] a law is interpreted by its context. Of what does the text speak? Of capital punishment [i.e., for murder or adultery], hence this too refers to [a crime involving] capital punishment."

But the rule about context allows either an immediate or a wider biblical context to be considered. So the following argument about the same prohibition occurs between two more rabbis.

---

61. Both discussions cited below are from *Sanhedrin* 86a.
62. I.e., kidnapping, which is also a capital crime.

Rabbi C taught: "'You shall not steal' refers to theft of property."

Rabbi D disagreed: "You say thus, but perhaps it is not so. Maybe Scripture refers to the theft of human beings" (a capital offense).

Rabbi C: "I will tell you: Go forth and learn from the thirteen principles whereby the Torah is interpreted [one of which is that] a law is interpreted by its context. Of what does the text[63] speak? Of money matters. So this too refers to the theft of money."[64]

These two disputes illustrate the fact that agreement could not always be achieved. Even depending upon context was not a panacea, for individual judgment could differ between honorable opponents. All sides to the arguments above believed they were following the rules faithfully. But they differed as a result of the specific context each chose by which to interpret "do not steal." It is also significant that there is no condemnation of any of the individuals involved, and no final decision binding all Jews to only one of the two possible interpretations.

13. The final rule of Rabbi Ishmael deals with two different biblical verses that contradict each other when read as *peshaṭ* (*šenei khetuvim ha-makhḥishim zeh et zeh 'ad sheyavo ha-katuv ha-shelishi ve-yakhri'a beineihem*: two verses contradict one another until a third verse reconciles them). In instances of contradictory Scriptural statements, the two competing verses must be reconciled by reference to a third verse (or multiple additional verses) wherever possible.

Example: Two passages in the Torah appear to contradict each other with respect to the appropriate way of preparing the Passover meal. Exodus 12:8–9 prescribes that the only proper way to prepare the Passover sacrifice is to roast it by fire, and specifically states that it is not to be boiled (*bišsel*) in water. But Deuteronomy 16:7 flatly disagrees: "You may boil [*bišsel*] it." On the surface, therefore, Deuteronomy appears to allow what Exodus prohibits. Second Chronicles 35:13 resolves the contradiction by adding an explanatory phrase to the verb "boil": "They cooked [*bišsel*] the Passover offering *over the fire* according to custom."[65] The ad-

63. Here Rabbi C cites Leviticus 19:11–13 which refer to stealing money, robbery, or withholding wages from a worker. These verses are all located well outside the immediate context of the Ten Commandments.

64. Which is not a capital offense.

65. Or "as prescribed" (with JPS). A *mishpaṭ* refers to a custom that has acquired the force of law over time.

dition of this extra phrase modifies the verb *bišsel*, which normally refers to "boiling" food in water,[66] and turns its meaning into "roasting."

Example: The story in Genesis 22 has long puzzled, horrified, and fascinated readers of the Bible. How could a decent God ask a man to sacrifice his own son just to prove his obedience? The answer is that the *peshaṭ* of this passage is contradicted by teachings found elsewhere in the Bible. In one treatment, the rabbis recount 22:2 with their own explanatory comments ascribed to Abraham (italicized below) phrase by phrase:

Then [God] said, "Take your son,"

But I have two sons!

"Your only one."

Each is the only one of his mother!

"Whom you love."

I love them both!

"Isaac!"

This treatment assumed that Abraham was troubled by the incident, despite the biblical picture of him as fully and instantly obedient to the demand of God. It also addressed the issue of why God took so long to tell Abraham the full truth in the Genesis account under consideration. Why did he not simply say, "Sacrifice Isaac," and be done with it? Was God reluctant? Did he work into his demand slowly to prevent Abraham from going into shock?

The rabbis then turn to another interesting Midrash that illustrates how the troubling and contradictory biblical statements in Genesis 22 must be reconciled: teachings found elsewhere in Scripture show that Abraham had not understood God correctly. The Midrashic explanation begins just after Abraham had been alerted to the ram provided for sacrifice in place of Isaac.

[Then] Abraham wondered. "O God, You too indulge in lying. Yesterday You said that 'your descendants will be named after

---

66. Note that Exodus 12:9 includes the phrase "in water."

Isaac' [Gen 21:12]. But then You retracted and commanded, 'Now take your son' [Gen 22:2]. And now you are ordering me, 'Don't lay your hand upon the boy' [Gen 22:12].

So the Holy One, blessed be He, said to him: "O Abraham, I will not profane My covenant [Psalm 89:35], and I will establish My covenant with Isaac [Gen 17:21]. Although I ordered you, "Now take your son up," I will not change what has gone out of My lips [Psalm 89:35]. Did I say, "Slaughter him?" No! I said "Take him up." You took him up. So, now take him down.[67]

Two things stand out in the story. First, the author of the Midrash gives careful attention to the vocabulary of the text, and plays upon the dual meanings of one key word. The Hebrew verb *'alah* is often used in biblical narratives with its basic meaning, "to go up." In the context of sacrifices made to God, the noun *'olah* (formed from *'alah*) describes a sacrifice that is completely burned until the entire animal being sacrificed *goes up* in smoke.[68] However, the verb *'alah* also has a "causative" sense when spelled with a prefixed letter *Heh*, and that is the form of the verb found in Genesis 22:2. It is this verbal form that is translated "offer him [Isaac] up as an *'olah*." But the rabbis knew that the verb *ha-'aleh* could mean either "offer up [as a sacrifice]" or simply "bring [someone/Isaac] up," that is, to the top of a mountain. They also knew the specific Hebrew word, "to sacrifice" (šaḥat), which is unambiguous. In God's answer to Abraham, the *Midrash* plays upon these two words and their meanings. God did not ever intend for Abraham to "sacrifice" (shaḥat) Isaac, merely to "bring him up" (ha-'alehhu) to the top of the mountain where further instructions would be given.

Now this rabbinic explanation may not be satisfactory to the twenty-first-century mind, and we will notice in chapter 6 that it did not satisfy the authors of the NT. But before we dismiss it, we must remember that Isaac was not killed. In fact, this story was probably composed during a period of time when kings from surrounding countries, and even some people in Israel (2 Kings 23:10), killed their own sons in times of national stress, hoping to convince their deity that they were sincere and pious, and hoping also to gain divine support for their political policies. In that context, the story takes on a different hue. The most sincere man of all, the most obedient to God, the most faithful, *thought* that he should

---

67. Translated from *Midrash Rabba: Genesis, va-yera'*, LVI, 8.

68. Such a sacrifice is described in English by the well-known phrase, "whole burnt offering."

sacrifice his son to prove his piety, but *he was mistaken*! Despite what Abraham may have thought he had heard, in the end, the story shows clearly that God never intended the death of Isaac.[69]

Second, the *Midrash* serves as a perfect example of the knowledge base of the entire Bible from which the rabbis worked. They presumed that even the greatest man of faith ever to live had his own moments of private doubt, for surely Abraham must have seen the contradictions between the promises of future blessing through Isaac and the command to take his life before those promises could be kept. So the rabbis used their vast knowledge of the Bible—in an era before concordances or computer programs with search engines made such things far simpler—to pull citations from elsewhere in the book of Genesis and in the book of Psalms in order to solve an apparent contradiction. That they have God cite to Abraham verses from books that had not yet been written when Abraham lived was not an issue with them. They needed a way to resolve the biblical picture of God acting in apparently arbitrary and contradictory ways. And, playing within the rules, they found it.

The examples just cited should not be taken as evidence that one or more of the thirteen principles of Rabbi Ishmael were always used in every examination of a biblical passage. Followers of Rabbi Akiva continued to follow some rules that underscored their belief that the language of Scripture was other-wordly. Thus two of their rules came to be known by the names of "inclusion" (*ribbui*) and "exclusion" (*mi'ut*), both covering some variation in the rule of general and particular. Their rule of inclusion was tied to Hebrew particles like *gam* ("also"), *'af* ("even," "also"), or *'et* ("with").[70] Exclusion was signaled by the particles *'akh* ("although," "if only"), *raq* ("only"), or *min* ("from," "out of"). Followers of Akiva also continued to insist that special Hebrew constructions using an Infinitive Absolute (which repeated a finite verbal form for emphasis or emphasized the linear aspect of action) had special significance that was other-wordly. It was against the use of such interpretations that Rabbi Ishmael noted sharply that "the Torah speaks in the language of human beings," cited above.

Two additional, widely accepted principles of Scriptural interpretation deserve mention. *'Ein mukdam u-me'uḥar ba-Torah* ("there is neither

---

69. The importance of their careful distinction will become more apparent in chapters 4 and 6 as we examine the ways in which the New Testament explains this incident.

70. The particle *'et* can also be used to indicate a definite direct object.

early nor late in the Torah") expresses the idea that the Torah often does not proceed in strict chronological sequence (*Pes.* 6b). *'Ein mikra' yotze' mi-ydei peshuto*, "a Scriptural verse never loses its plain meaning [*pešaṭ*]," even in cases where some additional interpretation is deemed appropriate (*Shab.* 63a; *Yev.* 24a).

Still, even the use of a number of principles that fall outside the thirteen standard ones we have surveyed does not dim the realization that the thirteen are illustrative of the fact that rules were firmly established to set boundaries within which scriptural argumentation could occur.

Post-Rabbinic Jewish Hermeneutics

The Talmudic system of transvaluation created by the rabbis flourished in the face of the Saducean position that only the Pentateuch, taken literally, should be accorded authoritative status in Jewish life. A similar view of biblical authority arose in the eighth and ninth centuries CE, when the rabbis faced a vigorous challenge from the Karaites.[71] There was a major difference between the Scriptural views of the Sadducees and the Karaites: the Sadducees had rejected the Prophets and the Writings of the Bible, both of which the Karaites accepted as canonical. But both groups denied the authority of oral torah, the rabbinical disputation that had produced the written Talmud. The rise and development of the eighth-century Jewish schism known as Karaism provides the material for a case study in the methods of dealing with fundamental disagreements within the broader Jewish community. At least in part because their founder, Anan ben David, was slighted in favor of his younger brother for a post of rabbinic leadership; ben David and his followers decided to reject the results of rabbinic scholarship and took the position that the Bible alone was authoritative.[72] Post-biblical rabbinical interpretations or reformulations had no weight of authority whatsoever for this new group, and their numbers were swelled by two other factors. First, the study of the Talmud was a difficult and arduous occupation that required a lifetime, and typically did not result in a consensus on many important issues, as we have illustrated. Second, many Jews believed that a simplification of

---

71. Literally, "readers," i.e., of the Bible (*miqra'*).

72. This was not a new idea in Judaism. Apparently the members of the Qumran community (ca. 250 BCE–73 CE) had also denied the validity of "oral torah" (see, Schniedewind, "Qumran Hebrew," 235–52). This was in an era when such discussions were common (cf. both Sadducees and Christians in addition to the Qumranites).

their authority structure would make Judaism less foreign to the ruling Muslim-majority world in which they lived. As the Muslim claimed to look only to the Qur'an for guidance, the Karaite looked to the Hebrew Bible as his only guideline.

However, as indicated by the extended discussion in chapter 1, nothing could be more basic to Rabbinic Judaism than the value and sanctity of oral torah. The rabbinic commitment to teaching and learning of Bible and Talmud became and remained an integral component of Jewish life and worship, and served as the backbone for a fully developed system of education that could not simply be ignored in favor of a Bible-only mentality.[73] In short, for a group of Jews to deny *in toto* the authority of this literature was an assault that could not go unchallenged, because it struck at the very heart of Judaism.[74] Rabbinic Judaism responded to the Bible-only stance of the Karaites with intellectual and literary weapons. The brilliant Saadia Gaon[75] offered his own translation of the Scriptures into Arabic, thus making accessible to far larger numbers of people the literature about which the great debate was raging. Saadia also penned an authoritative work on the *hapax legomena* of the Bible,[76] using literary examples to illustrate that even the meanings of key biblical vocabulary could not be understood without the help of the Mishnah.

Alongside these two specific issues addressed by Saadia, a third battle front developed. The Karaites:

> Took up the scientific study of Hebrew, developing Hebrew philology to an advanced stage and liberalizing the entrance requirements into Karaism in much the same way Paul liberalized entry into Christianity. The Rabbis countered by trumping the Karaite ace. They studied Hebrew even more assiduously, developed even better Hebrew grammars, made the Bible even more accessible to the people, interpreted laws even less stringently.[77]

---

73. See Kolatch, *Masters of the Word*, 1:79–81.

74. Catholic theology also affirms the value of post-biblical tradition, as we will note in chapter 4.

75. For a full discussion of his life and influence, see Malter, *Saadia Gaon*.

76. His famous *Pitron Shivim Millim* ("Interpretation of Synonymous Words").

77. Dimont, *Jews, God and History*, 204. Dimont's view is very similar to that expressed by Roth, *A History of the Jews*, 153–55. Bamberger gives a rather more negative assessment of all Karaite achievements in his section on "Karaism," in *The Story of Judaism*, 143–45. For a different view of the impetus for the interest in Hebrew grammar study, see William Chomsky, *Hebrew*, especially 117–20.

In other words, Rabbinic Judaism, led by Saadia Gaon, met the Karaite challenge with the argument that the Bible itself could not be understood without the Talmud because the explanations of the rabbis pointed to the true teachings of Scripture more faithfully than a literal reading of them could do. In particular, Saadia pointed to numerous rare biblical words that appeared only once or twice in Scripture, and argued that these words demanded definitions supplied only in the dialect of Hebrew used by the rabbis in the Mishnah, by which time many of them had become more common. Perhaps of greatest importance, this desire of the Karaites to return to the Bible alone prompted the rabbis to expand the scope of their intellectual activity to include dialogue with Greek philosophy (particularly Aristotle), translation of the Bible into vernacular Arabic, and forays into Hebrew grammar and lexicography based upon similar models being published in Arabic and Greek.

Our survey of the rabbinic principles of interpretation as well as their clash with the Bible-only mentality of the Sadducees and the later Karaites highlights perhaps the single most important aspect of rabbinic thought. The rabbis believed everything they taught was truly based upon the Bible, which remained *the* source of all truth and *halakhah* for them. As we noted also in chapter 1, the names they gave to their literature testify to this same idea. Their "Mishnah" was an updated and applied repetition of biblical principles, their "Gemara" was merely the explanation and justification of that repetition. The *'Amoraim* assumed that the teachings of the *Tanna'im* were correct, but, as illustrated above, still took the trouble to ask repeatedly, "How do we know this?" [from biblical authority] about what their predecessors had taught. More than any other factor, this commitment to the Bible compelled them to take the necessary steps to bring their own views into harmony with Scripture. As one modern rabbinic authority has phrased it, "this system of artificial interpretation was mainly calculated to offer the means of ingrafting the tradition on the stem of Scripture, or harmonizing the *oral* with the *written* law."[78]

In practical terms, the rules set in place to govern debate about Scripture helped to determine which opinions prevailed with the majority and which would not. Whenever an individual rabbi offered an opinion, his colleagues would be quick to ask for his biblical foundation. When citing biblical texts, an individual rabbi would be required to show

---

78. Mielziner, *Talmud*, 186.

whether and how the original words could be related to his current interpretation of them. Here he would attempt to persuade others that an analogous situation existed, that a simple view of one matter elucidated the more complicated issue at hand, or that either the immediate or the general context of Scripture pointed in the direction of his position. Equally importantly, his colleagues were also free to challenge him. But when they did, they were not allowed merely to offer an alternative opinion. Their challenge had to show that he had misapplied one or more of the rules of interpretation common to the whole community of scholars. In short, opponents of a particular position were also required to stick by the rules in making their challenges! Post-Talmudic scholars of Judaism responded to this rabbinic example in various ways.

Rashi[79]

The greatest "son" of the Talmudic rabbis was the erudite expositor, Rabbi Solomon ben Isaac (Rashi, 1040–1105). Rashi was a child of Christian Europe who nonetheless held fast to a strict observance of Jewish life, faith, and culture. Born in France and trained in France and Germany, his concern was to make the Bible and the Talmud accessible to the Jewish people as a whole. For him, the élite within Judaism were not determined by the accident of birth or family bloodlines, but by scholarship and erudition, and he was determined to make accessible the foundational texts necessary for rigorous scholarship. To that end, Rashi wrote running commentaries on the Bible and the Talmud offering insights into word meanings, grammar and syntax; he also included in his vast writings an eclectic selection of rabbinic teachings, folklore, and Midrashic stories.

But Rashi and his followers[80] did not treat biblical and rabbinic literature by creating summary statements or compendiums of laws. Their trademark became the use of *responsa*, or answers offered to specific questions that continued to arise in daily life. Whereas the masters of the Talmud had declined to anoint specific opinions as *the* answer to this or

---

79. From here to the end of this chapter, our discussion is not specifically about early Jewish biblical interpretation. But it must be remembered that in all of the interpretations offered by Rashi and Maimonides, and later by the two antagonists that became "Reform" and "Orthodox" Judaism, every interpreter perceived himself to be following in the footsteps of the founding fathers of Judaism, precisely the "rabbis" whose methods of interpretation we have been outlining.

80. See the authoritative text by Kolatch, *Masters of the Word*, 2:1–84.

that problem, the purpose of the *responsa* was to offer Jews authoritative conclusions to problems on which they could act with confidence that they were fulfilling Jewish law properly. Yet Rashi was aware of the dangers that could attend the publication of opinions by individuals working alone. So he organized the rabbinic community of his day into a scholarly body that worked together to seek consensus on the questions brought to them.

Maimonides

This focus upon the *minutiae* of Scripture took a new turn in the work of the great philosophical scholar Moses ben Maimon (Maimonides, 1135–1204), whose works were introduced briefly in chapter 1. The rabbis were Jews speaking to Jews, and they had been concerned to demonstrate within the Jewish community how their rulings reflected faithfully the teachings of the Bible. Rashi had written in Hebrew as a Jew speaking to Jews whose lives were more and more intersecting with Christian France. But Maimonides played to a larger audience, writing in both Hebrew and Arabic as a Jew whose audience included both Jewish and non-Jewish readers. As a lifelong student of Greek philosophy who lived in a world dominated by Muslim law and religion, Maimonides came to believe that the truths of Greek thought and the teachings of the Bible were consistent with each other. To demonstrate his conviction, he turned to rationalism as the method by which biblical teachings could be defended in the court of Greek philosophical thought and could commend Judaism to the worlds of Islam and Christianity.

One example of his dialogue with the non-Jewish world will suffice. During the Middle Ages in which Maimonides lived, it was widely believed by Christian and Greek thinkers that the existence of God could be demonstrated by reason. Many scholars, including Maimonides and his Christian contemporary, Saint Thomas Aquinas, devoted themselves to offering rational "proofs" of God's existence linked almost genetically to Aristotle's Unmoved Mover or Plato's Prime Cause. By contrast, the existence of God was something the rabbis had taken for granted, and none of their energy had been expended on its proof. The innovation offered by Maimonides was his philosophical rationale for the laws of the Torah, all of which were grounded in the existence of God, which he believed he also had demonstrated through reason.

In his commentary on the Mishnah for non-scholars, Maimonides went even farther in his attempt to fuse together the traditions of the rabbis[81] with the ethics of Aristotle. His philosophical training shines through most clearly in his attempt to distill the basic beliefs of Judaism into the form of a creedal statement quite similar to the early creeds of Christianity and the shorter creedal statement of Islam, the *Shahadah*.[82] In fact, the Jewish critics of Maimonides attacked him precisely on the basis of the similarity between his creed and those of the two other faith systems. Yet a careful reading of his thirteen articles of faith shows that Maimonides was not merely copying other traditions by compiling a list of essential Jewish beliefs. As the following chart demonstrates, virtually each statement sets Jewish belief in sharp contrast to either the Christian or the Islamic world.

"I believe with full faith"	Contrast with Christianity or Islam
[1] . . . that the Creator, may His name be blessed, creates and guides all creatures, and that He alone made, makes, or will make everything.	This excludes both 'Allah and Jesus Christ, the *Logos* of John 1, from any participation in the act of creation. God acted alone.
[2] . . . that the Creator, may His name be blessed, is unique [יחיד] (*yaḥid*), and there is no uniqueness like His in any form, and that He alone is our God, who was, is, and will always be.	Thus there can be no other person to share deity with God.

---

81. Which the rabbis asserted were "Mosaic" in origin.
82. See my *Encyclopedia of Religion*, 86–89.

early jewish principles of interpretation   87

"I believe with full faith"	Contrast with Christianity or Islam
[3] . . . that the Creator, may His name be blessed, has no physical body, is not affected by physical phenomena, and that there is no comparison whatsoever to Him.	This precludes an incarnation.
[4] . . . that the Creator, may His name be blessed, is the First and the Last.	A direct challenge to the statement made about Christ in the book of Revelation 1:8, 11; 21:6; 22:13.
[5] . . . that the Creator, may His name be blessed, to Him alone is it appropriate to pray, and it is not appropriate to pray to any except Him.	Contrasts with the Christian custom of praying or acting "in the name of Jesus," and with the Muslim prayer offered "in the name of Allah."
[6] . . . that all the words of the prophets are true.	In opposition to the Christian idea that some parts of the Jewish Bible were *passé* and could be set aside, or the Muslim idea that many biblical passages had been corrupted by Jews and no longer were accurate or true.
[7] . . . that the prophecy of Moses was true, and that he was the father of the prophets, both those who preceded him and those who follow him.	Neither Jesus nor Muhammad has offered a prophetic teaching that surpasses Moses.
[8] . . . that the entire Torah now in our possession is the one given to Moses our Rabbi.	In both its written and oral forms, i.e., both the Bible and the Talmud.

"I believe with full faith"	Contrast with Christianity or Islam
[9] ... that this Torah will not be changed, nor will there be another Torah from the Creator, may His name be blessed.	The unchangeable character of the Bible disallows a New Testament or a Qur'an.
[10] ... that the Creator, may His name be blessed, knows every act of humans, and all of their thoughts, as it is written, 'He forms their hearts all together, He comprehends all of their acts' [Psalm 33:15].	One statement upon which all three Abrahamic faiths could agree.
[11] ... that the Creator, may His name be blessed, rewards good to the keepers of His commandments, and punishes the transgressors of His commandments.	God alone is the great Judge of all the world, but his evaluations will be made against the standards of divine commandments in the Bible and the Talmud.
[12] ... in the coming of the messiah. And even though he may delay, nevertheless I will anticipate every day that he will come.	i.e., he has not yet come!
[13] ... that there will be a resuscitation of the dead whenever the desire rises up from the Creator.	While both Christianity and Islam also teach a doctrine of resurrection, the Pauline idea of immortality (1 Cor 15:53) differs from 13.

Methodologically, this initial publication of Maimonides stands in contrast not only to the Talmudic disputations of the rabbis, but also to the writings of Rashi, neither of which had attempted the systemization of biblical interpretation into a creedal statement. This contrast continued with the publication of a second major work by Maimonides titled *Mishneh Torah*, a compendium of rabbinic oral Torah arranged systematically, explained rationally, and designed to enable rabbi and lay person alike "to find authoritative answers quickly."[83]

The work of Maimonides destined to find lasting fame was his *Teacher/Guide for the Confused*,[84] in which his debt to philosophy comes to the fore. One of his students wrote to Maimonides asserting that the logic of Aristotle required Jews to choose between reason and faith, that is, to choose Aristotle and abandon their traditional beliefs, or to hold those beliefs while turning their backs on their own intellectual abilities. In response, Maimonides attempted to demonstrate that logic alone fell short of explaining Judaism. God, for example, the ultimate foundation of all Jewish thought, cannot be described by human language, for a finite medium (human language) cannot adequately explain infinity. Maimonides believed that philosophy could state only what God is *not*, but could never express what God *is*. Thus when the Bible uses an anthropomorphic term to speak of the "hand," the "arm," or the "face" of God, such description is an accommodation to the limitations of the human mind and the boundaries of finite human language. God has no such physical features,[85] just as he does not exhibit human emotions like "anger" or even "love." Since anything finite cannot have existed before time, Maimonides concluded that God alone was eternal and therefore infinite. Accordingly, the actions of God are often beyond the human ability to understand and explain them.

Miracles must likewise be regarded as metaphors or exemplars of the sovereignty of God over nature, but must not be taken as literal fact. Sacrifices do not feed or please God, for God cannot be hungry and pleasure is a human sensation. Rather, sacrifices were a medium used to express Israelite worship at a time in world history when all people assumed the anthropological character of many gods. Now that it could be done intellectually, Maimonides believed it necessary to move beyond the idea of sacrifices designed to satisfy the needs of God and replace those sacrificial rituals with forms of devotion that impact real life and

---

83. Trepp, *Judaism*, 64.
84. Mentioned briefly in chapter 1.
85. Here Maimonides was following the precedent of *Targum Onkelos*, which frequently altered biblical terminology seeming to imply that God had physical features. See Kolatch, *Masters of the Word*, 1:185.

the needs of real people. The Talmudic masters had recognized the reality of history that had made Temple sacrifices impossible, but had continued to debate questions involving appropriate Temple worship and sacrifices in the belief that these things would be restored to Judaism in the future. Maimonides accepted the loss of Temple and sacrifices as permanent, yet ultimately unimportant in light of newer and better knowledge of the world. According to Maimonides, the *exoteric* meaning of the Bible is its literal sense, which he deemed sufficient for ordinary Jews. The *esoteric* meaning(s) of the Bible is/are its philosophical sense, which Maimonides sought to uncover for educated (philosophically trained) Jews. Allegorical interpretation was his way of getting at the philosophical meanings of Scripture. But allegorical interpretation was legitimate only when the underlying philosophical idea had been demonstrated by "proof," that is, reason. The following summary of Maimonides is directly on point.

> All our knowledge can and should be a way toward God. The knowledge of nature leads on the way to perception of God. Since truth streams to man only out of God, it therefore becomes the bond between God and man. Study gives humans the happiness of direct connection with God, the love of God and his nearness (but never mystical union with God). Those who study recognize God as the moral being and take God as guide. They build their lives on Mitzvot ("commandments"); theory becomes ethical practice. The ultimate blessing of communion with God is found in life eternal. But not only elitists, dedicating their lives to study and contemplation, but even average Jews who see God in anthropomorphic terms have a share in life to come. Maimonides is a Talmudist, a rabbi. But in his philosophical work he places Talmud study beneath philosophical study.[86]

Addenda

Toward Reason and Enlightenment

It would be misleading to imply that all rabbinic disputes continued in the gracious spirit of the Hillel-Shammai differences of the Talmudic era. In fact, it would be impossible even to review all of the conflicts among Jews that have occurred since the death of Bar Kosiba in 135 CE. The hermeneutical principles of the rabbis continued to be honored until the

86. Trepp, *Judaism*, 295–96.

late seventeenth or the early eighteenth century. At that time, an interesting switch occurred. Jews, who had been denied citizenship throughout Europe, had lived in self-contained ghetto isolation for centuries. There the rabbi was the supreme authority on all matters, not only religious, but also legal, medical, social, and sexual. When Jews were allowed to attend public universities, young students heard for the first time the teachings of non-Jews on the Bible, on medicine and science, on history, and on law. The predictable reaction was a rush away from a Judaism that seemed so out of date and arcane when compared to modernity. The local rabbi likewise suffered by comparison to the sophisticated university professor.

Reform Judaism was a response to the loss of young people to this new stimulus, attempting to harmonize the power of tradition and the lure of modernity. And the tool of Reform was the reformulation of the principles of Judaism into the language of the new, enlightened world, as Reform rabbis attempted to do for their era what their predecessors had done in theirs. The ghetto rabbis who stood to lose both status and authority reacted angrily, as might be expected. Their conflicts with Reform were reminiscent of the clash between the Pharisees and the Sadducees or the rabbis of the Talmud and the Karaites.

There were three different circumstances in which such conflict rose to the surface, attesting numerous methods that qualify as extreme, including invective, (threats of) excommunication or the withholding of rabbinic approval for life cycle events, and especially harsh and uncompromising *ad hominem* attacks in denunciation of Jews who differed from the majority. The first of these circumstances involved the Karaites and Saadia Gaon, discussed above.

The second involved the *Ḥasidim*. And while the history of their rise and influence does not need to be repeated here,[87] one aspect of the Hasidic movement that deserves mention is the sharp controversy which the new movement engendered with the ruling rabbinate of the times. Rabbi Elijah ben Solomon, the famous "Vilna Gaon" of Lithuania, became a central figure in this controversy.[88] As we saw above, the Karaites had wished to forego the study of Talmud in an attempt to return directly to biblical authority, but had nonetheless devoted themselves assiduously to rigorous study. By contrast, the chief doctrine of the *Ḥasidim* emphasized the idea that personal piety was superior to *all* forms of scholar-

---

87. A good survey may be found in Bamberger, *Judaism*, 243–49.
88. Shulman, *The Vilna Gaon*.

ship and study. The resultant groups of adoring followers that grew up around the early leaders of the *Ḥasidim*, the Baal Shem Tov and many of his successors, were deeply troubling to the serious and staid rabbis of the day. Clearly the opponents of the *Ḥasidim* feared that the development of blind personal attachment to a particular Rebbe was very close to a form of personality cult.[89]

A watershed date appears to be 1771, the year of a terrible plague that swept through Vilna, when several hundred children died.[90] Once they determined to their own satisfaction that the plague had been caused by the spread of *Ḥasidism*, Vilna Jewish authorities, headed by the Gaon himself, proclaimed a rabbinic ban of excommunication against the *Ḥasidim*. A counter ban was quickly issued by the *Ḥasidim*, books were burned by both sides, and a bitter fight ensued. Wording from a 1781 ban against the *Ḥasidim* includes the following: "They must leave our communities with their wives and children . . . and they should not be given a night's lodging; their *sheḥiṭah* [ritual slaughter of kosher meat] is forbidden; it is forbidden to do business with them and to intermarry with them, or to assist at their burial."[91]

Now it cannot be doubted that such a decree produced severe hardship upon many a Jew identified with the *Ḥasidim*. For persons to be unable to make a living, to be barred from participation in the closed

---

89. See Dan, "Hasidism," *EJ*. It has been argued that one of the reasons for the fierce opposition to the Hasidim was the suspicion that it had, "Shabbatean tendencies." Rifat Sonsino's article, "Shabbetay Zevi," 71–83, includes a helpful survey of the issues of Shabbetay's conversion to Islam, the residual effects of his career on his followers, and a good basic bibliography.

90. Shulman, *Vilna Gaon*, 128.

91. Dan, "Ḥasidism," *EJ*. As many modern *poskim* have pointed out, there is no hint anywhere that one is forbidden to marry the daughter of a member of one of these groups, or that a rabbinic wife was doing anything wrong by staying with her husband, even if he were a member of one of these groups. I believe the case of King Jannaeus' wife may present an instructive earlier parallel here, assuming that King Jannaeus and Johanan the High Priest are one and the same person, as both the numismatic evidence and the descriptions of them in the Talmud would suggest. Thus it would seem that the members of these groups were still considered Jews of good legal standing even after the destruction of the Second Temple. Was marriage permitted between Sadducees and Pharisees, or between Sadducee and rabbinic families at the time of the Mishnah? Considering the literary silence about any such prohibition, the onus would seem to be on anyone who would claim that there was any restriction of this nature at the time. I have summarized my own view of the evidence here, but wish to acknowledge my dependence on an exchange of private correspondence with Dr. Liz Fried of New York University.

societal structure into which they had been born, to be prevented from celebrating the major life cycle events stretching from birth to bar mitzvah to marriage to proper burial—these were serious punishments for the average Jew to endure. And there seems to have been little of the milk of human kindness to soften any of the rhetoric spewed forth by both sides. Indeed, a further example of the depth to which the animosity of the rabbis against the Ḥasidim reached is exemplified by an incident when the Vilna Gaon left his own town secretly, rather than meet with two Ḥasidic representatives for a discussion that might have eased the tensions. "By refusing to see the two representatives of the *chassidic* [sic!] movement, the Gaon crystallized the controversy that would be synthesized only many decades later."[92] And it is important to note that the chief objections raised against the new movement often had little to do with ideology. Rather, "the *Mitnaggedim* [opponents] attacked the Ḥasidim because of the way they behaved."[93]

Yet another aspect of the controversy was the practice by each side of denouncing the other to the secular authorities, "leading to arrests of various Ḥasidic leaders and mutual calumnies of a grave nature."[94] This meanness of spirit vented against the Ḥasidim did not abate until a more dangerous "foe" arose, a foe against which both sides would make common cause in opposition: the advent of Reform Judaism and the age of the *Haskalah*.[95]

Haskalah, Reform, Orthodoxy

It is not possible here to offer a complete review of the history of the Jewish *Haskalah* ("Enlightenment") and its relationship to the European age of Enlightenment or to chronicle in detail the rise of the movement known as Reform Judaism. New ideas played roles of special importance in the new age of modernity, the Enlightenment that spread throughout Europe in the seventeenth and eighteenth centuries. A particularly significant idea was the emphasis placed upon individualism, one

---

92. Shulman, *Vilna Gaon*, 129.

93. Including charges of excessive drunkenness. Dan, "Ḥasidism," *EJ*.

94. Ibid. We may recall here the custom followed by the *Tanna'im* who had kept classroom discussions private for fear that local secular authorities might become involved in Jewish life.

95. Shmuel Sermoneta-Gertel called to my attention the excellent chapter on the battle between *ḥasidim* and *maskilim* by Mahler, "Heḥasidut ve-Hahaskalah," 64–88.

concomitant of which was the movement of religion from the public into the private sphere. That is, theological beliefs came to be viewed as matters of individual, personal conscience rather than as matters of concern for the public at large or for society as a whole.

A second influential idea arising out of the enlightenment was scientific empiricism, which ushered in new methods of determining truth, seeking verification in the world of experience via a new, skeptical approach that threatened to undermine the basis of all religious faith. In particular, new methods of seeking supporting proof from external data about the meaning of written texts catapulted biblical interpretation into a new sphere of scholarly engagement. While the *'Amoraim* had sought data to support each Mishnah they interpreted, they had done so with careful appeal to the Bible, the basic sacred text of Judaism. Scientific inquiry now demanded information from sources well outside the Bible, including the results of modern physical science and its new understanding of the material universe. Such ideas had the effect of transforming social reality as well. Distinct subgroups lost their significance as rights and responsibilities came to be viewed as devolving upon individual members of society via their allegiance to the state, not their religion. What ensued was a sense of discontinuity with the past, and the authority of religious communities began to be relegated to a voluntary, complementary role *vis-a-vis* society as a whole.

The emerging capitalism of England and Western Europe clearly contributed to the creation of a new social culture. So too did the revolution in philosophical thought, as did also both the American (1776) and the French Revolution.[96] For our study, the influence of Napoleon Bonaparte was critical, especially his attitude of intellectual and cultural imperialism demanding that Jews respond to the political implications of the new trends in philosophical thought.

One response to the sense of discontinuity with the past was exemplified by the great Dutch scholar Baruch Spinoza (1632–1677), whose challenge to the past was expressed most forcefully in his response to the ways in which western European scholars began to read and interpret the Bible. Though he was born into an observant Jewish home, Spinoza, influenced by independent Christian scholars with whom he studied in Amsterdam, abandoned Jewish rituals, openly broke the laws of *Kashrut*, and turned his back on the observance of great Jewish festivals. These

---

96. The French "Declaration of the Rights of Man" (1789) was an especially transformative occasion.

actions prompted his excommunication from the Jewish community. But many of his ideas took root among free-thinking Jews, and he continued to flourish as an independent scholar.[97]

Moses Mendelssohn (1729–1786)[98] fashioned a response to enlightenment that differed from the positions taken by Spinoza. He too was born into a traditional Jewish home, but, unlike Spinoza, he followed Jewish ritual and religious observances throughout his life. At the same time, Mendelssohn, trained in philosophy at Berlin University, was thoroughly modern, conversant with the prevailing intellectual theories of his age, and so much at home with modernity that he was elected to the Prussian Royal Academy of Sciences.[99] Thus he was "a human being in the street, but a Jew at home."[100]

The importance of Mendelssohn to the development of Judaism in the modern world had many facets. As was indicated by the extended description in chapter 1, the rabbinic commitment to teaching and learning of Bible, Mishnah, and Gemara became and remained an integral component of Jewish. He was acknowledged as well versed in rabbinic texts, even by his opponents (see below). But he embraced modern critical scholarship of the Bible enthusiastically, and saw in it the means of continuing in his era the task accomplished by the rabbis in theirs: reformulating core values found in the Bible and translating them into the modern idiom. To this end, he translated the Bible into modern German, publishing along with it his own explanatory comments between 1780 and 1783. The title of these comments, *biur* ("clarification") hints at the dual *foci* of Mendelssohn's method. In the Talmud, a *biur* is a specific kind of explanatory comment intended to clarify and justify the reasons why an interpreter was moving beyond the surface of a particular text. The choice of the title by Mendelssohn not only shows his familiarity with Talmudic thought, but also his willingness to use modern scientific

---

97. He refused a chair of philosophy offered by Heidelberg University, persisting in earning his living as a lens grinder, fiercely retaining complete academic freedom. His most enduring work was his *Theological-Political Treatise*, published anonymously in 1670, in which he argued the Bible was a work of political science rather than of religion.

98. Two books by David Sorkin offer valuable information about Mendelssohn and the Reform movement: *Moses Mendelssohn* and *The Transformation of German Jewry*.

99. King Frederick II refused to sign his confirmation appointment.

100. On this slogan, which Mendelsoohn epitomized, see Breslauer, *Understanding Judaism*, 121.

exegesis even when he was compelled by the new modern method to move beyond what the Talmudic masters had said.[101]

The Chasam Sofer[102] of Frankfurt, Dresnitz, Mattersdorf and Pressburg (Hungary) *seriatim*, deserves attention in the context of our discussion both because of the role he played in opposing Reform and for the methods he employed in that opposition.

The first incident in his life that apparently awakened him to the danger at hand occurred during a trip to Vienna, probably in 1786, when Sofer was still a young man/student. Walking into the parlor of his host, Rabbi Sofer observed the man's daughter-in-law having her hair cut by a male barber. Despite his youth and the fact that he was a guest in the home, he immediately rebuked her for immodesty. Later that same evening, his host explained to the young rabbi that the infatuation many Jews had with modernity would soon pass and should simply be ignored in the meantime. But Rabbi Sofer came to interpret the immodest act of the young woman and the other examples of loose behavior he had observed in Vienna as somehow to be coupled with the activities of Moses Mendelssohn, the leader of Reform Judaism.

Once he had become a leading scholar in his own right, Rabbi Sofer began to view Mendelssohn and his followers as more and more audacious and dangerous on many fronts. He became convinced that Mendelssohn's translation of the Bible into German was not for the purpose

---

101. Despite his translation of the Bible into German and his own exegesis published also in German, Mendelssohn was committed to the Hebrew language, in which he was fully at home, as his involvement with numerous Hebrew periodicals attests.

102. A convenient survey of his life and times is presented by Shulman, *The Chasam Sofer*. Even though Shulman is not a rigorous historian, I have chosen to cite him extensively because he is a modern orthodox biographer who is openly sympathetic to every goal of Rabbi Sofer, and his treatment captures the deep spirit of animosity born by the rabbi and his followers for everything modern or "Reform." An independent assessment of Rabbi Sofer's importance is given by Moshe Shraga Samet (*EJ*): "He finally brought to an end the debate which was being hotly waged as to whether the *Shulhan Arukh* was still to be regarded as the final authoritative code. The principle of complete submission to the *Shulhan Arukh* became one of the fundamental doctrines of Orthodoxy. In addition he ruled that from then onward no distinction existed from the point of view of their religious importance between an insignificant custom and an explicit biblical prohibition. Sofer's attitude made him the undisputed leader of the rabbis of Europe who organized themselves between 1817 and 1821 to frustrate the first efforts of the Reform movement in Berlin, Hamburg, and Vienna. From this struggle which, as a result of his direction, ended in partial success, Sofer emerged as the recognized leader of Orthodoxy, a status which he maintained until the end of his life." Samet's article includes primary bibliographic sources for the published works of Sofer.

of helping people learn Bible nearly so much as it was to teach literary German to Jews who knew only Yiddish. And this would enable them to read all kinds of secular literature that was tainted with the poison of the *Haskalah*.[103] Further, though he knew that Mendelssohn was well schooled in traditional Jewish texts, he noted that the commentaries of Mendelssohn avoided Midrashic explanations and stuck close by the "plain" meaning of biblical texts. This was an insult to his own traditional conviction that Midrashic and Talmudic knowledge enabled a scholar to unlock the "deeper" levels of meaning in Scripture, including those that might appear irrational to the untrained eye.

More than two decades after his first direct contact with the poison that was Reform, Rabbi Sofer became involved in an issue with far-reaching consequences, an issue that offered him the opportunity to vent his twenty-five-year frustration and anger at the new movement. Following in the wake of changes set in motion by the conquests of Napoleon, many Jews began to be drafted into the German (and other) armies early in the nineteenth century. Jewish soldiers in the region of Westphalia who had difficulty finding kosher food to eat for Passover, appealed to the rabbinical council of Westphalia, seeking permission to be allowed to eat legumes (*qitniyot*). The ban on legumes was not based on Scripture or Talmud, was fairly recent (probably dating only from the fourteenth century at the earliest), and was a ban that had been temporarily lifted on numerous occasions previously. When the Westphalian rabbinical council ruled in favor of allowing *qitniyot* for the soldiers, their decision was apparently standard and based on broad precedent. However, there was a difference. The rabbinical council was headed by a Reform leader named Israel Jacobson. In his argument, Jacobson developed lines of reasoning based not on *halachah* but rather on his non-*halachic*, Reform point of view. In doing so, Jacobson turned a *halachic* ruling into an ideological weapon against the Torah.[104]

Rabbi Sofer did not object to the conclusion that had been reached, for he admitted that the decision did have, "a background of *halachic* opinion on which to rely."[105] Nevertheless, he determined that the decision would have to be overturned because it had been handed down by people whom Rabbi Sofer distrusted personally. Their contempt for his

---

103. Shulman, *Vilna Gaon*, 70.
104. Shulman, *Chasam Sofer*, 162.
105. Ibid., 163.

way of life meant that they simply had no right to offer *halakhic* rulings of any sort, for nothing they could say would ever have validity, even when they were correct. In other words, since it was clear that the overall purposes of these enemies of Torah were wrong, "the advocates of Reform did not have the right to play with the traditions of Jewish communities," because they did not evince proper, "appreciation for the worth of that which they sought to change."[106]

Two other issues deserve brief mention. First, in the early nineteenth century, as the Reform movement gained in strength and in numbers, virtually every Jewish community in Europe seeking a rabbi found itself faced with the dilemma of choosing either an Orthodox student or a student from within the Reform movement. One part of the Orthodox response to this challenge was to devolve upon their rabbinate greater authority than it had ever wielded before. And to support this stance, Rabbi Sofer issued a formal ruling that "a rabbi had the right to bequeath his position to his son (as he himself eventually did)."[107] Such a system of succession was designed to guarantee a depth of *halakhic* continuity never before seen, for a new rabbi was not really new at all, but a son who had already served a *de facto* co-regency with his father-teacher before assuming the reigns of leadership alone. There proved to be little chance of innovation from the rulings of such men. "The Reform movement manipulated and exploited all changes and all innovations as tools . . . to drive a wedge into the Orthodox camp. Rabbi Sofer responded with equal firmness. All change and all innovation was henceforth suspect and forbidden."[108] To further clarify his unstinting opposition to Reform in any guise, Sofer coined, "many pungent and pointed epigrams . . . which became the slogans of the Orthodox. [T]he best known is his application of the Talmudic dictum 'ḥadash 'asur min ha-Torah'[109] to mean that any innovation, even though from the point of view of *halakhah* it be unimportant, is strictly forbidden simply because it is an innovation."[110]

Second, Rabbi Sofer, who was "firmly opposed to the learning of general studies,"[111] faced an attack from Reform leaders who wanted to

---

106. Ibid., 165.

107. Ibid., 199, and see further his discussion of the issue in the chapter titled "Strengthening Orthodoxy," 197–206.

108. Ibid., 200.

109. "A new thing [i.e., *halakhic* ruling] is forbidden from the Torah."

110. Samet, "Moses Sofer," *EJ*.

111. Shulman, *Chasam Sofer*, 200.

close down his Yeshiva because of the narrowness of its curriculum. At a time when the political status of Jews in Europe was a topic of great debate both in legislative halls and in newspapers, a dichotomy formed in the minds of many Jews. On one side were those who believed that the gaining of greater civil rights for Jews justified a movement on their part to reform and modernize many aspects of their religious and social practices. On the other side, many Jews seemed to feel that a permanent status as second-class citizens was a small price to pay for the opportunity to remain loyal to Torah as they understood and practiced it. The curriculum of Jewish educational institutions went directly to the heart of this debate. Rabbi Sofer himself "viewed the very aspiration for equality as a sign of dissatisfaction with the traditional way of life of the community and a desire for partial assimilation with gentile culture."[112] In the end, the opponents of Rabbi Sofer could not force the closing of his Yeshiva, nor could he simply wave his rabbi's wand and make them disappear.

Approaching the end of his life, and seeing absolutely no possibility of rapprochement with his opponents, the rabbi wrote the following: "When these Reformers first appeared and began to change customs and to begin all sorts of things that had never been done before, I argued with them. But now, after all these years, I see that there is no point in trying to communicate with them. They are lost to the Torah."[113] In this frame of mind, Rabbi Sofer wrote, "If we had the power, in my opinion, we should thoroughly expel such people from our community."[114] But nowhere is there found a more poignant expression of Rabbi Sofer's soul than in the final will and testament which he addressed to his son. Two of his statements stand out:

"Do not touch the books of Moses Mendelssohn."[115]

"Do not say that the times have changed. We have an old Father, blessed be He. He does not change and He will not change."[116]

---

112. Samet, "Moses Sofer," *EJ*.
113. Shulman, *Chasam Sofer*, 205.
114. Ibid., 206.
115. Ibid., 253.
116. Ibid., 154.

The Modern Agenda

The challenge of the Karaites had been met by rigorous scholarship and open, if confrontational, debate about the issues involved. The views of the Ḥasidim had evoked sharp and bitter responses, including official bans issued by traditional rabbis that brought hardship to those who were sympathetic with the views of the Ḥasidim. Orthodox animosity against Reform became so bitter that innocent Jewish soldiers were denied the right to eat otherwise acceptable food, not because the Reform Rabbis had rendered a *halakhically* incorrect opinion, but simply because they were Reform rabbis and served on a rabbinical council whose rulings could not be accepted!

In the clash between Reform and Orthodoxy, the spirit of the Talmudic masters was stood on its head. Debate that had once served to sharpen opinions on both sides became the cause for suspicion and shrill cries for excommunication. The innovators of Talmudic fame, who had preserved Judaism by their innovative interpretations, were now claimed as the exclusive property of those who decried the very spirit of innovation. Teachings of the men who had reformed Judaism in antiquity in the spirit of modernity and with an attitude of interpersonal civility were now frozen in time and viewed by Orthodox Jews with greater veneration than the rabbis had granted even to the Bible. Hillel and his peers had accepted the need to reconstruct biblical teachings in an effort to keep alive the *principles* for which they stood. Orthodox extremists took some (but certainly not all!) of the *conclusions* drawn from those principles and declared them to be binding for their own day, essentially making their own favorite Talmudic passages into a new Bible to be interpreted literally and harshly. Among Orthodox extremists, there was little or no appreciation of the fact that the very thing that had kept what they believed to be "true" Judaism alive had been its ability, and willingness, to innovate, to remain dynamic rather than static.[117] In their hands, Judaism became "dry bones in urgent need of the breath of life."[118]

A balanced view of the controversy demands an admission that the Reform Movement ran away from these "dry bones" as hard as Orthodoxy ran toward them, but the important point for this chapter is the sad picture of Jewish interpreters working in complete isolation from the

---

117. A comparable evaluation of Orthodox methodology has been articulated clearly by Maslin, "The Fury of Orthodoxy," 19–24.

118. Ibid., 24.

principles of hermeneutics forged by the classical rabbis and accepted by them as rules of guidance for debate and discussion.

In the coming chapters we will see that in establishing the early forms of their own faith, Christianity followed hermeneutical principles very similar to those articulated by the rabbis. And we will learn sadly that extremism was not limited to Judaism. Both of these Abrahamic faith systems proved capable of abandoning the liberal hermeneutical principles with which they were inaugurated in favor of monolithic views that produced intolerance and meanness. To do so, the extremists within each system also had to abandon the spirit of the very founders and builders of their faith whom they now sought to canonize and appropriate for their own purposes.

4

Hermeneutics of the New Testament, the Early Church, and Beyond

In chapter 3, we surveyed several examples of the rabbinic awareness that the Bible needed to be updated and reformulated ("transvalued") to meet the needs of a society living in a post-biblical world, and offered an overview of the literature that they produced to express their reformulations. Now we must examine the way in which early Christianity responded to that same awareness. At the outset it is important to remember that the first Christians were Jews who shared the post-biblical world of the rabbis and who were called upon to respond to the same set of *stimuli* faced by the rabbis: the destruction of the Temple at which they prayed and worshipped; life without a Jewish king, an independent nation, an army, or its own economy; and above all the immutable fact of Roman domination. The literary responses produced by the early Christians to these *stimuli* are no less astonishing than those of the rabbis.

We must also bear in mind that the early Christians were busy producing their New Testament literature during the same general period of time that the rabbis were carrying on the debates that would ultimately produce the Mishnah early in the third century CE. But this does not mean that we may set a rabbinic text alongside a NT text uncritically. At the outset, we should note that numerous scholars, led by Jacob Neusner, have argued that the Mishnah must be examined historically using the critical tools applied to the Hebrew Bible and the New Testament. In particular, Neusner's concern has been to demonstrate that rabbinic materials, including the Mishnah, the two Talmudim, and several early medieval Midrashic compilations, do not provide historically reliable data, especially when they are ripped uncritically from the context of the later periods during which they were actually composed.[1]

While it is true that the *written* forms of rabbinic opinion are later than the earliest written documents of the New Testament, the position of Neusner has often been taken too far. He is correct that scholars may not compare rabbinic literature with the NT in an uncritical search for parallels. But the process of setting the Mishnah into written form is more accurately perceived as an exercise in the *preservation* of rabbinic discussions held much earlier rather than the *creatio ex nihilo* of ideas and positions never discussed until the time of their literary creation. Thus while some *mishnayot* may in fact have been expanded in a period later than the NT, many others were not. And even those that were expanded can often be linked back to the germ of an idea born much earlier than the publication of the Mishnah. In addition, while the Mishnah was continuing to develop orally until the time of its publication in ca. 220 CE, and thus many of the words attributed to early sages actually come to us in the phrasing of their successors, what ultimately became the text of the NT was in a state of growth for some six decades (ca. 50–110 CE) from oral traditions to pre-canonical gospels ("Q"?) to canonical literature. This means, of course, that all of the sayings of Jesus in the NT also come to us from his followers well after his death.

Further, just as the Mishnah originated in oral form (*tôrah še-be-'al peh*), so also did much of the New Testament begin as oral communication from Jesus that was only later interpreted in the preaching of luminaries like Paul and Peter before it was set in writing by Paul, the gospel writers, and others. Only following the death of Jesus did the impulse arise on several fronts to select, assemble, and set in writing his teachings and other incidents of his life.[2] In addition, while it is certain that the contributors to the written Mishnah were selective in their choice of

---

1. It would be impossible even to list here the hundreds of books that have flowed from Neusner's pen. His earliest work was the three-volume set titled, *The Rabbinic Traditions about the Pharisees Before 70*. It was beginning with subsequent publications that Neusner's views became more skeptical about the historical value of the Mishnah. For a convenient summary and beginning bibliography, see Saldarini, "Pharisees," *ABD* 5:289–303. It should also be noted that other scholars have sought to balance the special pleading of Neusner.

2. Luke 1:1 asserts that "many have undertaken to compile an account of the things on which there is deep conviction among us."

which rabbis to quote and which opinions to include, the same impulse applies equally to the NT, as the Gospel of John openly attests.[3] In both cases, the compilers of the Mishnah and the NT made choices about which theological positions should be included as essential to the faith systems each side represented, choices that inevitably led to the exclusion of other ideas. However, one major difference must also be noted. Unlike the rabbis, early Christian authors never made explicit their principles for interpreting Scripture. In the examples offered below, it is necessary to infer the methodological rules by which each Christian interpreter appeared to be governed in specific cases.

It is also important to remember that the rabbis and the early Christians were attempting to interpret the same biblical text. While the rabbis viewed their work as a "repetition" of their tripartite Bible (*Torah, Nevi'im, Ketuvim*), Christianity soon came to view its most widely revered writings as a "New" testament that updated and reformulated the "Old" testament or covenant. Given the similarity of the context in which the interpretations of the rabbis and the NT authors took place, we should not be surprised to find hermeneutical principles and exegetical methodology common to both bodies of literature. The burden of our entire study is not to choose any particular argument over another, Jewish or Christian, but to demonstrate the *methods* that were employed in reaching them. Thus while specific rabbinic or NT theological conclusions may reflect eras later than the authority quoted as their source (whether Hillel, Jesus or any other individual!), the methods by which those opinions were derived cannot be demonstrated to have changed appreciably during the three hundred year period with which we are concerned (ca. 100 BCE–200 CE).

The Rabbinic Methodology of Jesus in Matthew[4]

We begin our examination of the NT use of the OT with the Gospel of Matthew. It has become commonplace to speak of the "Jewishness" of Jesus, often without a serious attempt to describe exactly what is meant by the description. Since the Gospel of Matthew quotes from the Old Testament more than any other NT book, and since Jesus is the central

---

3. According to John 20:30, "Jesus also performed many other miraculous signs in the presence of his disciples, which are not written in this book."

4. See a different approach by Sigal, *The Halakhah of Jesus of Nazareth*.

figure in it, we may examine the ways in which some of the teachings of Jesus are presented by Matthew to learn whether and in what ways Jesus was perceived as having taught and interpreted the Bible as a Jew.

In the Gospel of Matthew, the most concentrated group of Jesus teachings from the OT are introduced by the formula, "You have heard that it was said,"[5] attested six times in Matthew 5, the opening chapter of the Sermon On the Mount. This is the Greek equivalent of a common introductory formula in Talmudic debates, where the Hebrew/Aramaic phrases *še-neʾemar* ("as it is said") or *di-khtîv* ("as it is written") are specific formulae used to introduce a quotation from Scripture[6] on which an individual rabbi wished to comment. Each time Matthew uses the formula, an OT law is cited, followed by his understanding of the opinion of Jesus about each one. All six may be crucial to an understanding of the method of Jesus in dealing with Scripture, but are more important as a window into the mind of Matthew who chose and transmitted the examples, arranged them together in one place, and appended his understanding of their true meaning. In other words, what the gospel presents is the way in which Matthew perceived Jesus to have understood the Jewish Scriptures.

Example 1 (5:21–22): "You have heard that it was said to the ancients, 'do not commit murder,' and 'whoever commits murder shall be liable for judgment.'" Here we are given a citation of one of the Ten Commandments, "Do not commit murder" (Exodus 20:13) followed by a conflation of one phrase in Deuteronomy 17:8 ("bring disputed cases to court") and all of Leviticus 24:17 ("If a man takes the life of a person, he must be put to death").

Interpretation: "But I [Jesus] say to you that anyone who is angry with his brother[7] shall be liable for judgment."

As noted, the introductory formula used in Matthew by Jesus is quite rabbinic, as is his freedom to offer a personal opinion about the

---

5. Once a shortened formula is used ("it has been said"), and twice a more complete formula is attested ("you have heard that it was said to the ancients").

6 This formula is used by the *ʾAmoraim* who are attempting to justify a specific ruling by the *Tannaʾim*. See for example the way in which the discussion about times for reciting the *Shemaʿ* in *Berakhot* 2a are explained, or *Berakhot* 8a, where the synagogue prayer known as *the* prayer (*Tefillah*) is discussed. The comparable phrase *ka-katûv ba-tôrah* ("as it is written in the Torah") is attested in Neh 10:35, 37; and 2 Chron 25:4.

7. "For no reason" (*eike*) is added by some manuscripts.

meaning of the passage being cited. Jesus would surely have been aware that the Hebrew Bible itself lists jealousy (e.g., 2 Samuel 20:10), anger (e.g., Genesis 4:5–6), and hatred (e.g., Deuteronomy 19:11) as motives that could lead to the final act of murder. To these passages we may add the clear statement of Leviticus 19:17: "You must not hate your brother in your heart." In fact, the tenth commandment, "Do not covet" (Exodus 20:17), seems designed to blanket all of the others with the idea that inner motivation must be controlled so as not to lead to the actual commission of unlawful acts. As *Sefer ha-Ḥinnukh* phrases it, "At the root of this precept lies the reason that an evil thought causes a person multiple misfortunes."[8] We should also note here the rabbinic concept that "baseless hatred" of one Jew for another was a contributing cause to the destruction of the Second Temple in 70 CE.[9]

Clearly, neither the idea nor the interpretation offered by Jesus is new. Rather, Matthew is seeking to underscore the *identity* of the rabbi offering the idea as well as his *authority* to do so. We will see the importance of this distinction a bit later.

Example 2 (5:27–30): "You have heard that it was said, 'you shall not commit adultery.'" This is a direct quotation from Exodus 20:14.

Interpretation: "But I say to you, 'everyone who looks at a woman lustfully has already committed adultery with her in his heart.'" This teaching does indeed seem to be a radical reformulation by Jesus. As was also the case with example one, it recognizes the relationship between emotions and deeds, and its contrast with a supposed standard opinion of other rabbis is carefully drawn in the definition of a lustful look itself as the commission of "sin." Rabbinic law did not consider an evil thought to be a sin, and would not punish a person unless such a thought produced an unlawful action. But although they would not administer punishment in such cases, the rabbis were not totally silent on the specific point being made by Jesus, according to Matthew, who appears to define the taking of a lustful look as an act, but does not offer an opinion about whether such an act should be punished, and if so, in what way.

In the Mishnaic tractate *Kiddushin*, devoted to marriage and male-female relationships, there are extended discussions about conduct that is

---

8. Mitzvah 38 in *Sefer ha-Ḥinnuch*.
9. See the extended discussion of this principle in *Yoma* 9b.

proper or improper. For example, the rabbis strongly advised men against allowing themselves to be alone with a woman other than a mother, sister, wife, or daughter. One particularly interesting report found in the Gemara[10] has the following *haggadah* that was intended to serve as a precept by example: "Rab and Rab Judah were walking on a road, and a woman was walking in front of them. Said Rab to Rab Judah, 'Lift your feet before Gehenna,'" that is, walk faster to get in front of the woman so as not to continue looking at her. This is an example of the rabbinic admonition to "build a fence around the Torah" (*Pirkei 'Avot* 1:1), to avoid not only action prohibited by law but also actions that brought one close to the boundary of unlawful action. In short, both the rabbis and Jesus were concerned about the link between inappropriate observation of women and the possibility that such observation might lead to an unlawful act that could not be recalled. While the rabbis clearly believed that to avoid such looking was a safeguard against the commission of a forbidden sexual act, Matthew's Jesus labeled the lustful look itself a "sin."

It would be fascinating to be able to read the debate that surely would have ensued between Jesus and other rabbis about this distinction. What, it might have been asked, should be the penalty for the lustful look? Since the look of lust itself is defined by Jesus as adultery, should the man who looks with lust be executed as any other adulterer? And since the biblical penalty for adultery was death for both the male and the female,[11] someone might well have asked whether the female object of the improper glance should also be stoned? However the debate might have gone, it is clear that Jesus has employed hermeneutical rules 4 and 5 of Rabbi Ishmael, arguing from a general principle (adultery is absolutely forbidden) to the conclusion that a particular circumstance leading to that general (lustful looking) should also be proscribed. Thus while the rabbis may have debated with Jesus about his formulation, they would easily have recognized the method employed to derive it.

Example 3 (5:31-32): "It was said, 'whoever puts away his wife, let him give her a certificate of dismissal.'"

Interpretation: "But I say to you, 'everyone who divorces his wife except for unchastity makes her commit adultery, and whoever marries a

---

10. *Kiddushin* 81a.

11 Note Leviticus 20:10-14, which repeats five times the provision that *both* the man and the woman involved in illicit sexual relations are to be executed.

divorced woman commits adultery.'" In this example, Matthew does not portray Jesus as having quoted the entire verse cited from Deuteronomy 24:1, and what is omitted makes the interpretation of Jesus seem far more innovative than it actually was. Here is the entire verse: "If a man takes a woman and marries her, and she does not find favor with him because he finds something obnoxious about her, he may write a bill of divorce for her and send her away." Now the phrase "something obnoxious" is the difficult Hebrew wording ʿervat davar, literally "a matter of nakedness," which the LXX renders by aseksemon pragma, "a dishonorable deed," itself as ambiguous as the Hebrew it translates. Matters of nakedness or deeds of dishonor could include adultery, of course, but would not be limited to that single example. The Greek of Matthew 5:32 does not follow the LXX here, but employs the phrase, "except for the cause of *porneia*." Again, the word *porneia* is itself almost as ambiguous as the Hebrew phrase ʿervat davar in Deuteronomy. Although it can refer to fornication or any other kind of unlawful sexual intercourse, its primary meaning is "prostitution" as opposed to adultery.[12]

The Mishnaic discussion of divorce[13] ends by citing three competing opinions about the meaning of this Hebrew phrase, ʿervat davar, omitted by Matthew. The conservative school of Shammai ruled that "A man may not divorce his wife unless he has found unchastity in her," specifically citing Deuteronomy 24:1. The liberal school of Hillel ruled that divorce was permissible "even if she spoiled a dish for him," but cites the *same* biblical phrase as its authority![14] Rabbi Akiva offered yet a third ruling, seemingly more liberal than that of Hillel, authorizing divorce even if a man found another woman who was prettier. This opinion was linked by Akiva to yet another biblical phrase included in Deuteronomy 24:1 but also omitted by Matthew: "she has not found favor in his sight." It is clear that while the ruling of Jesus was radically different from those of Hillel and Akiva, the conservative Shammai, who lived some fifty years earlier than Jesus, had interpreted the Hebrew text of Deuteronomy itself in a manner very close to what Matthew argues that Jesus appeared to teach. And, as we have noticed often before in their discussion of other issues, there was no movement among the rabbis to decide once and for

12. See Arndt & Gingrich, *Greek-English Lexicon*, 693.

13. See *Gittin*. The citations of Shammai, Hillel, and Akiva are in *Gittin* 9:10.

14. Shammai and Hillel lived slightly earlier than Jesus, and it is likely that he would have been aware of their schools of thought and teachings.

all among the three opinions of Shammai, Hillel, and Akiva, all of whom were well known and respected in their group. That Jesus agrees with Shammai on the matter of divorce is interesting, as is the fact that both Shammai and he were offering not a more liberal but a more restrictive and conservative interpretation.

There is yet another Hebrew phrase in Deuteronomy 24:1 that demands attention, "a writ of divorce" (*sefer kərîtût*), cited from the LXX in the Greek text of Matthew, yet receiving no comment or explanation from Jesus. The rabbinic word for this phrase is a *geṭ*, and we have already alluded to the complete tractate devoted to it (*Giṭṭîn*). But to understand the rabbinic views of divorce, we must turn to a related tractate devoted entirely to the matter of marital agreements: *Ketubbot*. A *ketubbah* was a marriage contract that a man was required to give to his bride at the time of the betrothal, in many ways similar to a modern pre-nuptial agreement. It sets forth in writing the obligations to a wife that the groom agrees to fulfill, including his legal obligation to her if he should decide to divorce her. Adultery by the wife could invalidate the entire marital contract, and trigger a release of the husband from his obligation to continue to support her. This is the context in which Hillel and Akiva offered such apparently liberal opinions about the rights of a man to divorce his wife. If his reason were only that he did not like her cooking (Hillel) or that he had found someone more attractive (Akiva), he would be required to complete all of his financial obligations to her set forth in the *ketubbah*. Because the *ketubbah* would have been negotiated before the wedding, and thus before anger or disillusionment with the relationship had begun, and because the bride would have been represented by a person who was committed to protecting her (a father or a brother), her security would virtually always be safeguarded. Lacking a reason to invalidate the *ketubbah* (like adultery or a comparable act of lewdness or prostitution), the dissatisfied husband could gain his divorce, but would have no legal way to avoid his continuing financial responsibilities.

Before concluding this example, we must note that Matthew added a second proviso to the teaching of Jesus, again siding with Shammai, by stating that a woman who was divorced for a reason other than adultery was being forced to commit adultery, the penalty for which was execution. Similarly, a man who married a divorced woman also committed adultery. We are not made privy to the rationale for this ruling. But we note that the opinion also directly contradicts the presumption in Deuteronomy 24:1 that marriage to a legally divorced woman is allowed under certain conditions, and further illustrates the freedom Matthew perceived Jesus to exercise by setting aside a clear biblical teaching in favor of his own opinion. As noted above, quite unlike the liberal rulings of the rabbinic majority providing greater latitude for divorce, the rulings of Shammai and Matthew's Jesus are ultra conservative and far more restrictive than that of other rabbis or of the Hebrew text itself. Whether the conservative rulings of Shammai and Jesus offered more protection for a woman than the automatic triggering of a *ketubbah* payment envisioned by Hillel and Akiva[15] would be a matter of personal opinion. In either case, both the concern of Jesus to quote and interpret Scripture and the freedom to depart from it are rabbinic to the core.

Example 4 (5:33–37): "You have heard that it was said to the ancients, 'Do not make false vows; fulfill your vows to the Lord.'" Here we do not find a specific biblical verse being cited but a *pastiche* of two verses. Leviticus 19:12 reads, "You must not swear falsely by My name and profane the reputation of your deity," while Deuteronomy 21:22 (English 23) adds: "When you make a vow to YHWH your God, do not delay its completion."

Interpretation: "But I say to you, 'Don't take an oath of any kind[16] ... but let your "Yes" be "Yes" and your "No" be "No." Anything beyond these is from the evil one.'" By contrast to this opinion of Matthew's Jesus, both the Hebrew Bible and the Talmud presume the necessity of oath-taking in an orderly society, and both include statements of limitation designed to regulate the procedure of taking and fulfilling oaths appropriately. The Mishnaic tractate *Shevu'ot* is dedicated to these regulations, setting forth restrictions on oaths taken rashly, oaths made by witnesses during a trial procedure, oaths that were inherently improper or illegal, and oaths using one of the names of God. So Jesus would appear here to be plowing new ground by denying the validity of oath-taking under any circumstance. But once again, this opinion was not unique among Jews.

Whereas the Pharisees and Sadducees had become deeply involved in the political machinations of the Hasmoneans and the Romans, another group of Jews, the Essenes, chose a different tactic. Framing themselves into a tightly structured society, members of this sect were required to

---

15. Certifying that the man obtaining a divorce on flimsy grounds is liable for the payment of the *ketubbah* without challenge.

16. Or "Don't take an oath at all."

pass through a one-year period of probation and a two-year non-permanent probationary status before entering into full membership. As noted earlier, the Essenes agreed with the Pharisees on most issues of *halakhah*, and cited as authoritative a much larger body of literature than that acknowledged by the Sadducees. But they also viewed the Hasmoneans as illegitimate holders of the office of high priest, and on this point, their dissent was so strong that they refused to frequent the Temple, going so far as to initiate their own system of animal sacrifices outside the Temple. Two segments of the group are attested. Several thousand of them gathered together at the NW shore of the Dead Sea near Qumran. But many others continued to live scattered among the general populace.

A prominent feature of the Qumran community was a common fund into which all personal resources were pooled. Food and clothing were purchased from this common fund, to ensure that all food was kosher, and that all clothing was made of only one kind of material as prescribed by Leviticus 19:19. Among those who did not live in the Qumran community, group rules called for a level of hospitality so strict that no Essene could exclude any other Essene from his house for any reason. When the scattered Essenes traveled, they brought only weapons as protection against brigands, knowing that in every city there was an appointed person responsible for providing visiting Essenes with food, lodging, clothing, and any other necessities.

Because the Qumran order prohibited marriage, the membership grew only by adopting abandoned children, and by the addition of people who became disillusioned with the political or social situation in which they found themselves and fled to their desert retreat. Yet the other order did marry, permitting sexual intercourse only for the purpose of producing children. Both orders prohibited slavery, which Philo says they considered an "injustice that outraged the law of equality."[17] Yet they maintained strict levels of rank among themselves.

Both orders placed emphasis on sexual purity, because they all anticipated a great apocalyptic battle between the sons of darkness and the sons of light. To be ready to participate in this holy battle, it was necessary to abstain from sex so as to be ritually holy at all times. Biblical Israelites had stayed away from women for two days and had washed their garments in preparation for receiving the Ten Commandments (Exod 19:10–15). Uriah had refused intercourse with his wife while his battalion

---

17. All citations of Philo in this section are from *Every Good Man is Free*, 12–13.

remained at war (2 Sam 11:11). In rabbinic Judaism, the high priest was given short rations on the eve of Yom Kippur, and kept awake all night long to prevent even an inadvertent seminal discharge that would render him cultically impure and thus unfit for his Yom Kippur duties.[18] In the spirit of such restrictions, because they could not know the precise moment of the great final war, at least one order of the Essenes refrained from sex at all times so as to be ready at every moment.

The Essene view of oath-taking is of special significance for our study of the opinion of Jesus offered by Matthew. On the one hand, when they were ready for final admission into the sect, the Essenes were required to swear oaths taken so seriously that they were obligated to die rather than break one of them.[19] In fact, a member who was excommunicated for a breach of conduct often died of starvation rather than break the oath he had taken to eat only foods deemed kosher by the group standards. On the other hand, they advocated abstinence from oaths, teaching that a person's entire life should exhibit a standard of trustworthiness. In the words of Philo, "any word of theirs has more force than an oath; swearing they avoid, regarding it as worse than perjury, for they say that one who is not believed without an appeal to God stands condemned already."[20] Josephus also reports that they viewed "swearing on ordinary occasions as worse than perjury."[21] It is this second, fully Jewish, aspect of oath-taking that Matthew's Jesus adopts along with the Essenes into his own system of *halakhah*.

Example 5 (5:38–42): Here Matthew presents the opinion of Jesus on the matter of *lex talionis*, widely known as "an eye for an eye." Because of the importance of this concept in the Bible and in rabbinic theology, we will examine it in detail in chapter 5 as a parade example of the rabbinic freedom to transvalue a plain biblical teaching. In chapter 6, we will compare the opinion of Jesus with those of the rabbis.

Example 6 (5:43–48): "You have heard that it was said, 'You shall love your neighbor and hate your enemy'" Here we encounter not merely

18. Mishnah *Yoma* 1:1–8 contains several other provisions beginning seven days before Yom Kippur to ensure that the high priest did not become cultically impure and thus unable to offer prayers of repentance for himself, his family, and the entire congregation.

19. Josephus describes these in some detail, *Wars of the Jews*, 2, 8:7.

20. Philo, *Every Good Man is Free*, 13.

21. Josephus, *Wars of the Jews*, 8:6, cited by Pope, "Oaths," *IDB* 3:577.

hermeneutics of the new testament, the early church, and beyond 113

a patching together of two partial verses from the Bible, but the representation as biblical of a commandment nowhere to be found, forging a straw man that was the exact opposite of the teaching of the Hebrew Scriptures. The "love your neighbor" phrase was well known to Jesus from Leviticus 19:18, as his citation of it elsewhere attests.[22] But the phrase "hate your enemy" is unknown in the Bible, as indeed is its bipolar opposite, "love your enemy."

Interpretation: "But I say to you, 'love your enemies.'" To introduce this unusual commandment, Jesus calls upon hermeneutical rule 2, the rule of analogy (*gezerah shavah*). An airtight general rule found in the chapter of Leviticus to which Jesus refers has two sides: "do not hate your brother" (19:17), and "love your brother" (19:18). Nothing is said about an "enemy." Rabbinically, Jesus could have extended this general principle governing the treatment of a covenantal equal (a "brother") by reference to a third verse in the same pericope that ties the first two together. "There shall be a single standard for you. It shall be for the resident alien as well as for the native" (Leviticus 24:22). Thus any treatment that is commanded with respect to a "brother" (i.e., a member of the community, an Israelite) must also apply to everyone else as well.

This brief survey of six interpretations of the OT by Jesus as Matthew portrayed him yields several results. First, we have seen that many of these opinions were known to other Jewish thinkers of the era. Second, we have noted that Matthew depicts Jesus as typically leaning in the direction of conservative rulings, standing on its head the idea that the Pharisees were the arch fundamentalists and Jesus was more liberal in loosening the demands of law upon his followers. Third, we have seen that the *method* of approaching Scripture was well within the boundaries observed by other Jewish authorities. If the significance of his conclusions as presented by Matthew is not to be sought in terms of the radical and innovative, we might ask how Matthew believed Jesus viewed his own teachings. A passage later in the Gospel of Matthew holds the key, a teaching grounded in a word ("yoke") common to many classes of Jewish interpreters.

In biblical literature, the word "yoke" (*'ol*) is used in two distinct ways. Literally, it refers to the yoke used on cattle or oxen.[23] Figuratively,

22. See Matthew 22:39.
23. E.g., in Num 19:2 or 1 Sam 6:7.

it is used to refer to transgression,[24] or to involuntary servitude.[25] Thus in certain early poems and in prophetic literature, we find references to the breaking of such a yoke with divine assistance.[26] Of signal importance is the use of *'ol* in Jeremiah 27, where the prophet perceives the inevitability of the conquest by Nebuchadnezzar of Babylon, and reports that God himself had commanded him (Jeremiah) to make "bonds and yokes"[27] to place upon his own neck. The symbolism involved is clarified immediately in the prophetic oracle that follows. Any nation that refused to submit willingly to Nebuchadnezzar by placing its neck voluntarily under his "yoke," would be punished and destroyed by God, and only those who submitted to the plan of God to use Nebuchadnezzar would be spared (27:11). This is clear in the advice from Jeremiah to the Judahite King Zedekiah: "Place your neck into the yoke (*'ol*) of the King of Babylon. Serve him and his people, so that you may live" (27:12).

Here we see for the first time the idea of a difficult "yoke" that may be accepted or rejected, with drastic consequences attendant upon either choice! And it is this picture on which the *Tanna'im* drew in their discussions. In rabbinic thought, recitation of the *shema'* was connected to the act of accepting the "yoke of the kingdom of the heavens,"[28] and was perceived to presume the acceptance of God as one's King. In terms of language only, there is an apparent Mishnaic distinction drawn between "acceptance of the yoke of the kingdom of the heavens" and "acceptance of the yoke of the commandments." In fact, however, as a well-known Mishnaic passage makes clear, via the recitation of the *shema'*, the pious Jew both voluntarily takes upon himself the yoke of the kingdom of the heavens, and concordantly also accepts upon himself the obligation of keeping all the commandments of *halakhah*.[29] As we noted in chapter 1, the importance of such an acceptance is illustrated by the fact that Rabban Gamaliel himself was known to have recited the *shema'* even on

---

24. Made clear in Lam 1:14.
25. As the example of Rehoboam in 1 Kgs 12 illustrates repeatedly.
26. See for example Gen 27:40; Jer 2:20; 5:5; 30:8; Ezek 34:27; Isa 9:3.
27. *Môserôt û-môṭôt* in 27:2.
28. *Ber.* 13b.
29. *Ber.* 2:2. We should also compare the expression *'ol torah* ("the yoke of torah") in *'Avot* 3:6, which is juxtaposed to *'ol malkhut* ("the yoke of the kingdom") and *'ol derekh 'eretz* ("the yoke of appropriate behavior"). Of course, acceptance of "the yoke of the commandments" is one of three things (along with circumcision and *miqvah*, the ritual bath, expected of a convert to Judaism.

the first night of his wedding, reminding his students that he would not avoid "the yoke of the kingdom of the heavens even for a moment."[30] Two things appear clear. First, we note the voluntary nature of the choice between whether to accept the yoke of *halakhic* Judaism or not, and second, we find the assumption made by the rabbis that acceptance of the yoke implies a *halakhically* correct life.

This background prepares us to investigate a well-known passage in Matthew that portrays Jesus speaking about his own idea of *halakhah*, or his perception of a Jewishly appropriate life of obedience to God. Matthew 11:29 attests a figure of speech chosen by Jesus that would have been quite familiar to his audience: "Take my yoke upon you and learn from me." What else could Jesus have meant than a call for students to study and follow his personal interpretations of *halakhah*?

What seems to have been overlooked by commentators on this passage is that Jesus cites Jeremiah 6:16 here, assuring his audience that through observance of his *halakhic* interpretations, "you will find rest for your souls." The passage in Jeremiah specifically refers to the necessity of searching out the classical ways of faith to learn where "the good way" may be found, and how to "walk in it."[31] Both his choice of the word "yoke" and his citation of Jeremiah imply that Jesus perceived his own *halakhic* teachings to represent the "good" and acceptable way in which Jews should exercise their Judaism in order to obtain a life of peace and rest. Here Matthew portrays Jesus as doing what many a good first-century rabbinic teacher would have done, namely commending his own *halakhic* interpretations in preference to those of other Jewish authorities. And the chief rationale for the choice of the *halakhah* of Jesus was that his yoke was bearable or gentle (*chrestos*[32]) on the neck and light (*elaphron*), while that of other teachers was less so.

The idea that the *halakhic* opinions of Jesus were to be preferred to those of any other teacher because they offered an option of torah observance that was bearable also lurks in a rhetorical question recorded in Acts 15:10. Addressing the question of whether to require non-Jews to become Jewish first before they could become Christian, Peter, sounding

---

30. *Ber.* 2.2, 4.

31. "This is what YHWH has said: 'Stand near the pathways and see. Inquire about the ancient paths, "Where is the good road?" Walk in it and you will find rest for your lives.'"

32. Given the phonological similarities between the two, *chrestos* may be a play on *christos*, the "christ, messiah."

in this instance very much like Paul, asks: "Why do you test God by placing upon the neck of the disciples a *yoke* that neither our ancestors nor we have been able to bear?"

This understanding of *halakhah* as a way of life, "the good way" of which Jeremiah and Jesus spoke, is attested elsewhere in the NT. It may be found in the search by Saul for "anyone belonging to this *way*" (Acts 9:2), as well as in the description of Apollos as a man who "had been instructed in the *way* of the Lord" (Acts 18:25), or Felix as one who possessed "a more exact knowledge about the *way*" (Acts 24:22). The statement in Hebrews 10:20, speaking of "a new and living *way*," is also appropriate in this context, and it is also plausible to connect here the statement of Jesus in John 14:6: "I am the *way*."

Before leaving our analysis of the six interpretations of OT law offered by Jesus in Matthew 5:21–48, we must note the manner in which these six are framed in the overall gospel narrative. The prelude to the six (5:17–19) cites Jesus affirming that he intended to abolish nothing of the law, but to fulfill it completely, a statement fully concordant with the commendation of his own personal *halakhah*. And this he proposed to do by offering a way of life that would enable his hearers to exceed the righteousness of the "scribes and Pharisees" (5:20). The postlude in chapters 6 and 7 does not mention the Pharisees again, but classifies those who refuse to accept the *halakhah* of Jesus as "hypocrites" (6:2, 5, 16; 7:5); gentiles who were overly concerned with meaningless repetition in prayer (6:7) and with material things (6:32); or "false prophets" (7:15). In sum, those who accept and follow the rulings of Jesus are "wise" (7:24) and those who do not are "foolish" (7:26). Matthew then closed this literary section of his gospel with the observation that those who heard Jesus "were amazed at his teaching" (7:28).

Matthew took up this theme once again in chapter 23 of his Gospel: "The scribes and the Pharisees have seated themselves in the chair of Moses. So practice and observe all that they *tell* you, but do not practice the way they *act*, because they speak and do not practice" (23:2–3, emphasis added). This contrast between words and deeds is fully rabbinic in emphasis. But in the explanatory paragraphs that follow, the text of Matthew records a movement by Jesus to condemn other rabbinic authorities that becomes vitriolic. His six-fold refrain[33] is aimed at "hypocritical scribes and Pharisees" (vv. 13, 15, 23, 25, 27, 29) who are also "blind guides" (vv.

---

33. Repeated for what would be a seventh time in verse 14, lacking in the earliest manuscripts.

16, 24), "blind men" (vv. 17, 19), "fools" (v. 17), and finally "serpents, or a brood of vipers" (v. 33). The target of these epithets, the Pharisees whose methods Jesus followed and many of whose opinions he echoed, are thus the enemy not because of their exegetical *methods* or even their teachings, but because of the moral and ethical deficiencies in their personal lives.[34]

One final piece of evidence from the Gospel of Matthew is important. On numerous occasions Jesus is portrayed as willing to engage in dialogue with other rabbinic thinkers, receiving questions from Temple authorities (9:18; 21:23; 22:23), "scribes"[35] (8:19) and Pharisees (9:11; 12:2; 16:2; 19:3; 22:15) alike. Even though Matthew viewed at least some of their questions as attempts to trap Jesus (22:15), he portrays Jesus as always ready to engage in this common rabbinic practice of defending his positions against questions for the mutual enlightenment of all sides in the debate. But if Jesus did not mind debate, Matthew apparently resented it deeply. For him, Jesus was not only correct on every point, but so powerful in his presentations that his opponents soon realized they dare not ask him any more questions (see 22:46). One can hardly imagine a more *un*-Jewish circumstance.[36]

Parenthetically, a fascinating report in Luke 2:41–51 is related to the issue of Jesus and other Jewish authorities. Twelve-year-old Jesus and his parents[37] traveled to Jerusalem for the Passover celebration. Following the celebration, the parents traveled homeward for a full day before realizing that Jesus was not with them. When Mary and Joseph returned to Jerusalem, they located their son only after a three day search: "They found him sitting among the teachers in the Temple, listening to them, and asking them questions" (2:46). Clearly, then, according to Luke, asking questions (and presumably learning from the answers) was something Jesus had done since childhood! Such an embarrassing episode that reflected negatively upon Mary and Joseph is shaped by Luke in a creative manner. Although it was Jesus whom Luke portrayed as asking questions, we

34. As noted in chapter 1, personal conduct was one of the reasons for the preference of the rulings of Hillel over those of Shammai.

35. Pharisees who specialized in making copies of the Scriptures by hand. Since they were an important part of the sect of the Pharisees, the appropriate translation of the phrase identifying them should be "scribes of the Pharisees."

36. This information should inform the current debate among NT scholars about whether Matthew was or was not Jewish. Our analysis shows a distinct difference between the very rabbinic ways in which Jesus used Scripture to frame his theological positions and Matthew's interpretation of his debates with other Jewish authorities.

37. Surprisingly, Mary refers to Joseph as the "father" of Jesus!

are told that everyone present was amazed at *his* answers (sic!). In other words, both Matthew and Luke failed to recognize the true meaning of numerous instances of interaction between Jesus and Jewish scholars.

Before leaving the Matthean view of Jewish Jesus, one final episode is of interest. The Talmud[38] teaches that God originally gave to Moses a total of 613 precepts. According to the rabbis, subsequent sages and prophets attempted to reduce these 613 to a more manageable number. In Psalm 15, "David" reduced them to eleven, Isaiah to six (33:15–16), Micah (6:8) to three, Isaiah again to two (56:1), and finally Habakkuk to one (2:4). In this context, it is not surprising that a certain Pharisee should have asked Jesus to identify the greatest commandment in the Torah.[39] For his answer, Matthew has Jesus cite Deuteronomy 6:5, the verse immediately following the *shemaʻ*. "You will love the Lord your God with all your heart, with all your soul, and with all your mind." But although Matthew's Jesus cites the verse, he does not quote it exactly. The Hebrew text reads, "You will love YHWH your deity with all of your heart, with all of your life, and with all of your strength." Thus a cursory comparison of the two versions appears to indicate that Jesus has added a new concept not found in Deuteronomy, the love of God with the mind.

The usual Greek word for "mind" is *nous*, one of the three parts into which Plato divided the human person. It was perceived as higher than the other two (body, spirit), and in this tripartite division, "mind" (*nous*) is the seat of human thought. It may be used vigorously, or allowed to lie undisturbed.[40] However, the word used by Jesus in all three gospel accounts is not *nous*, but *dianoia*, a more intellectual term in standard Greek literature, best translated "reflection" or even "thought," that is, not the seat of thought, but the process of thought itself through mental reflection. One may possess a *nous* without using it, but *dianoia*, thinking, reflection, implies the active use of mental capacities. In other words, the addition of "with all your thoughts" is a perceptive way to summarize the Hebrew text that follows the *Shemaʻ* in the *veʼahavta* ("And you will love the Lord your God"). To hold the commandments of God in the heart, to teach them diligently to children, to converse about them sitting, walking, lying down, or arising, even to employ physical symbols to aid one in remembering them, all point to a lifestyle of reflection on life's

---

38. *Mak.* 23b–24a.

39. See Matthew 22:34–40; Mark 12:28–31; and Luke 10:25–27 also contain this account.

40. As every teacher knows well!

most important issues. With one deft phrase, Jesus aptly summarized Deuteronomy 6:5, neither adding to nor subtracting from it.

The Methodology of Paul

Given the Jewish/rabbinic methodology of Jesus seen in Matthew, we would expect to find comparable rabbinic methodology in the writings of Paul. He was personally quite proud of his Jewish education (Gal 1:14; Phil 3:4–5), and the story of his life recounted by Luke in the book of Acts (5:34; 22:3) claims that he had studied at the feet of the great rabbinic scholar Gamaliel,[41] himself a prominent member of the famous Hillel school whose liberal opinions were often cited by the rabbis. Surely a person trained in the Hillel school would be familiar with rabbinic methods of exegesis. However, our expectations meet with some difficulties as we begin to analyze Paul's own words.

The most unusual aspect of Paul's teaching was his attitude toward law.[42] The legal rulings of Jesus had been calculated to produce appropriate observance of Jewish law among his followers, and Bart Ehrman is directly on point to note that "even when [Jesus] appears to abrogate the Law of Moses . . . he does so in order to bring out what is, in his judgment, their true meaning and intent."[43] In sharp contrast to this attitude of Jesus as depicted in the gospels, Paul often seemed openly antagonistic to law as a controlling principle in life, and appeared to be more interested in showing that the law had become invalid than in trying to interpret it for his era. Such an attitude would have been anathema to the rabbis, of course.

The fact that Jesus held opinions against a majority of other rabbis, or even opinions shared by no other rabbi, would not have been unusual, and would not have caused him to be singled out for condemnation. But denial of the inspired Torah was one of only a few sins that the rabbis believed would deny a person a place in "the world to come."[44] This rab-

---

41. A fact Paul surprisingly omitted from his self-portrait in Philippians.

42. In the discussion that follows, I have used Torah to describe the Pentateuch, and *torah* to include both written Scripture and "Oral Torah," the rabbinic teachings that came to be published in the Talmudim.

43. Ehrman, *Lost Christianities*, 232.

44. See Mishnah *San.* 10:1. The other such offenses are denial of the resurrection, using the name of God inappropriately so as to profane it, teaching doctrine from books other than the Bible, and using "charms" while chanting Scripture to cure physical ailments.

binic exclusion of a Torah rejecter from the future world follows closely on the heels of an extended discussion demonstrating that even people who have committed horrible sins will enter into the world to come only if they have received adequate punishment in this life. In other words, for the rabbis, appropriate punishment for sin needed to be administered in this life so that the sinner could be "paid up" and ready to enter into the next life. But there could be no punishment stern enough for the person who denied the basic source book of their entire system of belief. On this issue, Paul stands alone in his disdain for law among those claiming to be trained as a rabbi or teacher of Jewish law.

We are left to ask why this should have been the case. Why did Paul stand apart from the rabbis for whom a lifetime engaged in seeking torah, written and oral, was the highest and the most satisfying goal to which anyone could aspire? They were quite aware of the impossibility of complete and accurate observance of every precept found in torah, yet remained committed to the effort.[45] Three points are significant here. First, the rabbis taught that a person who had sinned and then repented was more pleasing to God than a person who had never sinned.[46] Looking closely at their rationale, it is clear that they believed everyone had failed in some way to keep the whole of torah. A person who repented was one who had acknowledged his shortcomings and had taken steps to correct them, whereas any person who had not repented was one who had refused to admit his need of repentance and atonement before God in the first place. The second point is a corollary of the first, for the rabbis believed that repentance was a necessary component of torah observance precisely because they agreed with Paul that no one could achieve perfection in this life.[47] Even an imperfect knowledge of torah taught them not only their failings but also the necessity and power of repentance. And repentance, "returning" to God, was an oft repeated and explicit commandment in Scripture.[48] Third, they believed that true repentance could be verified only if a resulting change in life occurred whereby the

---

45. Note for example, the saying attributed to Rabbi Tarfon: "You are not obligated to complete the task, but you are not free to abandon it either" (*'Avot* 2:21).

46. *Ber.* 34b. And cf. also the discussion in Mishnah *Makkot* 3:14–16.

47. See the lengthy discussion in *Yoma* 86a–b; 87a.

48. The Hebrew word *šûv* means either to turn or to return. Thus, repentance (*təšûvah*, the noun formed from the root *šûv*) involved turning away from wrongdoing and towards God.

repentant person turned his back on the sin for which repentance had been made.

Paul allowed no such latitude. Viewing his personal inability to keep torah fully as evidence that no one could be fully torah observant, he overlooked the idea that repentance for failure to keep the law perfectly was an integral part of torah itself. Thus it was that Paul came to view law as "the dispensation of death" (2 Cor 3:7) or "the dispensation of condemnation" (3:9); described the Israelite covenant as "bondage" (Gal 4:1–7) or "slavery" (4:21–23); and ultimately labeled the law itself a "body of death" (Rom 7:24), "the law of sin" (7:25), or "the law of sin and death" (Rom 8:2). To be sure, in Romans 7:13—8:11, Paul speaks of two different laws: "the law of God," with which he agreed in his mind (Rom 7:22) and "a different law" in his body that fights against this law of God (Rom 7:23).[49] For Paul, the "inner person" or mind (*nous*) agrees with the law of God but is prevented from following it by "the law of sin" in the body. The law of God is thus a good thing for Paul, but another law prevails because of the flesh/body. While "the law of God" may not be co-terminous with the Torah of Moses, it can be inferred that the Torah of Moses reflects the "law of God," at least in part.[50]

Still, this is an astonishing disconnection between Paul and the Jesus seen in Matthew, a difference that may be attributed only partly to the different audiences each was addressing. But it must also be remembered that all of the writings of Paul precede Matthew by decades. Paul was attempting to jump-start a mission to non-Jews, while those who came later, like Matthew and the other gospel authors, were attempting to retain some link between Jesus and Judaism to provide a cover of legitimacy for the new faith. On the one hand, in arrogating to himself the freedom to move beyond the teachings of the Torah taken literally, Paul was utterly rabbinic![51] On the other hand, by abolishing the entire system, Paul did exactly the opposite of what Jesus had claimed to do.[52] Unlike Jesus, Paul

---

49. Here Paul has adapted Plato's body/soul dualism, probably from Stoic philosophers. In this perspective, the mind is the part of human nature that partakes of the divine nature, while the body is the seat of passions that keep the mind from being in tune with God.

50. I am indebted to my colleague Delbert Burkett for some of the points made in this paragraph.

51. Note that Hillel, the teacher of Paul's own teacher, had stated clearly that there are two torahs: oral and written (see *Shabbat* 31a).

52. Note Matthew 5:17: "Do not think that I have come to abolish the law and the prophets. I did not come to abolish, but to fulfill."

thereby removed the ancient foundation upon which he claimed to be building his personal theology. In citing proof texts from the Pentateuch to cinch his arguments, he was surely doing what his own teachers had taught him. But in rejecting the authority of that same Pentateuch insofar as it reflects the "law of God," Paul undercut his own arguments via sheer circularity. What must be noted is that while Paul rejected the *conclusions* of his teachers, he nevertheless continued to employ the *methods* they had taught him in the formulation of his own ideas. This may be demonstrated in three specific ways.

First, Paul was an expert in a method of argumentation known among the rabbis as *haraz*,[53] the ornamental stringing together of biblical verses, phrases, or even single words for the purpose of clinching an argument. Among numerous Pauline examples that could be cited, one of the most inventive is 2 Corinthians 6:14–18, where Paul makes a passionate argument against marriage between Christians and unbelievers. As proof of the validity of his argument, he follows his opening statement ("Do not be yoked together unequally with unbelievers") with allusions to or direct citations from the books of Deuteronomy, Leviticus, Ezekiel, Jeremiah, Isaiah, 2 Samuel, and Hosea. Similarly, in Romans 3:10–18, to recommend the condemnation of anyone who argued, "let us do evil that good may come" (Rom 3:9), Paul cites proof texts from Psalms 14, 53, 5, 140, 10, 59, and 16.

Second, Paul frequently employed questions much in the way that the later 'Amoraim would do in the Gemara.[54] We have noted their most frequent opening question whenever they considered a Mishnaic teaching: "How [or from what source] do we know this?" Such a question enabled them to offer answers to their own questions, founded upon biblical citations and logic. Paul's writings are filled with such questions. "What shall we say then" (Rom 4:1)? "Is the law sin" (Rom 7:7)? "Shall we continue to sin that grace may abound" (Rom 6:1)? These rabbinic-like questions cry out for Paul's answers, which he then offers. We do

---

53. The full Hebrew phrase is *haraz bedivrei torah*.

54. This may also be connected to a style of disputation familiar in the Greco-Roman world known as the "diatribe," a form of debate with an imaginary opponent. But neither Paul nor the rabbis seem to have had imaginary opponents in mind when framing their questions. A biblical precedent may be found in Micah 6:1–8, where the prophet formulated both sides of an argument before arriving at his conclusion. Neither the 'Amoraim nor Paul were employing a particular hermeneutical rule with such questions, but were wrestling in general with the contextual meaning of biblical principles.

not know how Paul might have fared in a debate against his peers, but it is safe to conclude that were Paul debating other rabbis, they would be asking questions of him and he of them, demanding "proof" according to their accepted rules.

Third, he matches his negative statements about the law with equally positive statements in other contexts, essentially contradicting himself on the significance of the Torah: "The entire Torah is fulfilled by one word, 'You will love your neighbor as yourself.'" Not only does this statement from Galatians 5:14 acknowledge what Paul elsewhere asserts is impossible (fulfilling the Torah), it echoes a famous ruling by Rabbi Hillel, the teacher of Gamaliel and thus the intellectual grandfather of Paul (see Acts 22:3).[55] Elsewhere, Paul makes seemingly unequivocal statements about the law. "The Torah is holy, and the commandment is holy, righteous, and good" (Rom 7:12). "The Torah is spiritual" (Rom 7:14). Perhaps it was this side of his feelings about the Torah that kept Paul interested in citing it as proof of his personal theological positions. In chapter 6, we will examine several specific instances of the ways in which Paul attempted to transvalue the Hebrew Scriptures in the process of forging the theological underpinnings of his new faith.

The Argument from Prophecy

As we saw above, the method of argumentation employed by Jesus in Matthew 5:28–48 was thoroughly rabbinic, and his positions on virtually every point are known elsewhere among Jews from Shammai to the Essenes, a fact of which we should assume he himself was aware. We also noted that only to someone like Matthew, apparently unfamiliar with rabbinic argumentation and the multi-faceted teachings they produced, could the way in which Jesus related to Scripture have seemed amazing. This impression is heightened by the way in which Matthew structures his narratives appealing to biblical prophecy.

Among the more than sixty citations of the Old Testament in the Gospel of Matthew, eleven are explained as OT predictions that are fulfilled in detail by the life of Jesus. Unlike the citations in Matthew 5 that purport to be from the mouth of Jesus, these explanations derive from

---

55. In *Shabbat* 31a, Hillel tells a potential convert, who demanded to be taught the Torah while he stood on one foot, that the entire Torah was, "What is hateful to you, do not do to your neighbor." He then adds, "Everything else is commentary. So, go study the commentary."

the mind of the gospel writer himself. The Matthean formula used to introduce such citations is: "This happened in order to fulfill what was spoken by the prophet."[56] In chapter 6 we will examine some of these fulfillments in connection with the discussion of the virgin birth concept and the suffering servant interpretation. Here we must ask what Matthew meant by his assertions that an OT prediction was being fulfilled in the life of Jesus.

Matthew's treatment of the flight to Egypt by Jesus and his parents offers a good example of his method. Immediately after his account of the miraculous birth of Jesus, Matthew begins in chapter 2 to narrate the story of King Herod determined to destroy the baby future king. Warned in a dream, Joseph took mother and child to Egypt (2:13), where they stayed until Joseph learned in a second dream that Herod had died, making it safe for the family to return home (2:19–20). Interesting here is Matthew's failure to cite a virtual literary parallel in the life of Moses. Exodus 4:19 records the words of YHWH to Moses who had fled to Midian after killing an Egyptian: "all the people who were seeking your life are dead." In the case of Joseph, Mary, and Jesus, the angel of the Lord says in the second dream that, "those who were seeking the life of the child are dead."

The flight of Joseph and his family to Egypt had occurred, Matthew explains, "in order that what was spoken by the Lord through the prophet might be fulfilled: 'I have called My son out of Egypt'" (2:15). Here Matthew offers not only a quotation of Hosea 11:1, but perhaps also a reference to Exodus 4:22, where collective Israel is named the "son" of God. Matthew's statement leaves the impression that no one had correctly understood the words of Hosea until they were fulfilled by the life of Jesus.[57] Such a view missed the point made by both Hosea and the book of Exodus, both of which use a grammatically singular word ("son") as a collective noun to refer to the entire group of Israelites who had exited Egypt.

But Matthew's story is not limited to the words of Hosea. It continues with a description of Herod's rage at the failure of the magi to give him the location of the baby as he had demanded of them, prompting the mad king to kill "all the male children who were in Bethlehem and in all its environs from two years old and under" (2:16). The grief that enveloped the region of Bethlehem caused an outcry that Matthew

---

56. Ten times using the Greek verb *plerein* (1:23; 2:15; 2:18; 2:23; 4:15; 8:17; 12:18; 13:35; 21:5; 27:9) and once its compound synonym *anaplerein* (13:14).

57. The same kind of interpretation is prevalent in the *pesharim* of Qumran.

believed "fulfilled" (2:17) words of Jeremiah (31:15) spoken more than six hundred years earlier. No modern critical exegete would relate the eighth-century words of Hosea or the seventh-century words of Jeremiah to this first-century CE incident for which there is no evidence in Roman history of the era. But for Matthew, the specter of a monarch slaughtering male babies recalled the story of the Exodus (Exodus 1:22), providing an instant parallel between baby Jesus and baby Moses, both of whom managed to escape a savage ruler with the help of clever parents. Thus the author who would argue later in his narrative that Jesus was greater than Jonah (12:41) or Solomon (12:42), announced at the beginning that he was the new Moses.

This relationship between Moses and Jesus is considered more than once in the Gospel of Matthew. In 8:4, after healing a leper, Jesus instructed the man to follow Mosaic (Pentateuchal) procedure leading to an official pronouncement of healing. This he did, according to Matthew, "as a testimony to them," an obvious reference to the priests whose certification of cleanliness would become a certification of the power of Jesus to heal.

In 19:7–8, Jesus claims Moses as his ally in the divorce question, stating that Moses (again, the Pentateuch here) had only permitted liberal divorces because of the hard-heartedness of his people, and repeating his own view, discussed above, that *porneia* alone provided adequate cause for a man to divorce his wife. This is an astonishing picture. Jesus admits openly that his own view of divorce is not that taught in the Pentateuch, yet boldly announces that his interpretation was what Moses *would* have taught if his audience had been able to accept it. This position is very close to the view expressed by the *Tanna'im* in *'Avot* 1:1 (discussed in chapter 1), that their Mishnaic reformulations of Scripture were actually the teachings of Moses![58]

In 22:24, Jesus answers a trick question from the Sadducees, who cited Moses in an attempt to confuse Jesus about marriage in the next life. The answer of Jesus accused the Sadducees of failure to understand "the Scriptures or the power of God" (22:29).

In 23:1, "the scribes and Pharisees," soon to be excoriated as described above, were said to occupy "the chair of Moses." This was Matthew's way of highlighting the superiority of Jesus to the current interpreters of Mosaic legislation.

---

58. Note again the statement, "*halakhah* uproots Scripture," in *Sot.* 16a.

But it is chapter 17 that underscores the importance of Moses for an accurate understanding of the greatness of Jesus according to Matthew. In this scene, Jesus takes Peter, James, and John to a high mountain, where he is transfigured before them with shining face and clothes as white as light (17:2), chatting with Moses and Elijah (17:3).[59] The appearance of Jesus with Moses the Lawgiver and Elijah the quintessential prophet elevates him to the highest rank in Judaism. No doubts about the authority of Jesus could remain when the voice of God was heard ordering the disciples to obey, "My beloved son with whom I am well pleased" (17:5).

The concept of prophecy fulfillment in Matthew is complicated and difficult to pin down to any single idea or definition.[60] For one thing, the Matthean idea that a specific historical event in his own day fulfilled utterances from prophets living hundreds of years earlier finds no parallel among the methods of interpretation practiced by the rabbis because nothing in rabbinic theology compared to the Christian idea that Jesus had inaugurated the final era of history during which Scripture was being confirmed and completed. The Greek verb *plerein* can connote ideas as disparate as meeting a requirement, completing, infusing an object (or saying) with meaning, or confirming the truth of someone or something.[61] When referring to a prophetic utterance as Matthew uses it, "fulfillment" appears to imply the earlier prediction of a predestined event. In this sense, it may be a reflection of the kinds of biblical commentaries written by the sectarians at Qumran called *pesharim*[62] (explanations, interpretations). These Essene students of Scripture believed that the truth of Scripture was largely hidden beneath an apparent plain-sense layer, and needed to be lifted out of its bed of mystery in order to speak to the specific historical context in which they lived. Matthew felt similarly, that events in the life of Jesus had been foreshadowed or predicted long ago, waiting to be revealed fully only in the life of Jesus.

Two additional aspects of the Matthean use of the OT must be clarified. First, the authorial decision to cite OT texts as being fulfilled by the life and work of Jesus must be distinguished from the intention to quote

---

59. Although Matthew fails to make the connection, we are reminded of the transfiguration of Moses (Exod 34:30–35) shortly after he had re-written the Ten Commandments.

60. On the Greek verb *plerein* and its cognates, see Delling, *TDNT*, 283–311. On the Hebrew *male*, "to fill, be filled", cf. Snijders, *TDOT*, 297–307.

61. See Gundry, "Fulfill," *ISBE* 2:366–69, for biblical examples of these definitions.

62. Horgan, *Pesharim*. See especially the *pesher* on Habakkuk 2:1.

accurately from the teachings of Jesus. Second, however, as one final example indicates, these citations point to an author who often appears unaware of the ways in which the Hebrew language expressed ideas. This may be seen most clearly with reference to Matthew's perception of Zechariah 9:9 (see Matt. 21:1–11). The Hebrew text reads as follows: "Behold, your [future] king will come to you, righteous and victorious (or endowed with salvation), mounted on a donkey, a colt, the foal of a female donkey." The reference is clearly to a single animal only, a donkey that was still a colt and naturally the offspring of a female. Zechariah thus underscores the significance of a king being able to ride a young colt that had not been saddle-broken. In the hands of Matthew, who did not recognize the poetic parallelism of the Hebrew text, the verse cited from Zechariah depicted two different animals, a donkey and her colt, *both* of which were to be brought to Jesus. Without recognizing the impossibility of what he was describing, Matthew then noted that, "The disciples went ... and brought the donkey and the colt, and laid on *them* their garments, and he (Jesus) sat on *them*" (21:6–7, emphasis added).

One aspect of prophecy in the Hebrew Bible does have to do with fulfillment. In the poetry of Second Isaiah, writing in Babylonia in the mid-sixth century BCE, the historical "evidence" that YHWH alone was divine, standing apart from idols or false gods, was his ability to predict the future and then make it happen.[63] The book of Daniel, from the mid second century BCE, records a similar phenomenon in the case of the haughty King Nebuchadnezzar, who heard a voice from heaven announcing, "Your kingdom has been removed from you" (4:31). The proof that YHWH alone is sovereign (4:28) follows: "Immediately ["at that moment"] the word concerning Nebuchadnezzar happened" (4:30). In other words, the only One who can predict the future accurately is the One who will create that future.

But there may be a simpler explanation for the way in which Matthew employed the term "fulfill." Long before Matthew, the prophet Samuel had chastised Saul with the following words: "To obey is better than a sacrifice" (1 Sam 15:22). The rabbis came to view this statement as an indication that faithfulness and obedience to God fulfilled everything that the Torah demanded, including seemingly insignificant as well as obviously important commandments. This is shown during the long discussion in *Makkot* 23a, b–24a, where one conclusion is that all of the 613

63. See *inter alia* 48:3: "I declared original things long ago. They issued from My mouth and I proclaimed them. I acted suddenly and they happened."

commandments in the Torah are reducible to one, "Seek Me and you will live" (Amos 5:4b). An alternative choice is also suggested from Habakkuk 2:4: "The righteous person will live by faithfulness." This is close to what Jesus apparently had in mind when he stated that he had come "not to abolish but to fulfill" both the Law and the Prophets (5:17), and his use of "fulfill" may have prompted Matthew's choice of the word in the context of other specific prophetic utterances that he believed foreshadowed or predicted various events in the life of Jesus.[64]

Typology

Closely related to the idea that an event in the life of Jesus "completed" or "fulfilled" a prophetic word from the past was the conception that earlier biblical narratives often prefigured a coming event. Said another way, an early event could be seen as a "type" of a later event so that when the second event occurred, a deeper meaning of the original narrative would come to light. The New Testament treatment of the Binding of Isaac in Genesis 22 is a classic example of typology. This simple and yet utterly complex story of Abraham preparing to sacrifice his son Isaac has spawned hundreds of interpretative attempts among Christians and Jews alike. Perhaps the first thing to be noticed is the different ways in which Jews and Christians refer to the incident. What Jews call the 'Aqedah ("the binding") of Isaac becomes the "sacrifice of Isaac" in Christianity, dating from early post-NT writings.[65]

As we saw in chapter 2, the Midrashic conviction of the rabbis was that God never intended for Isaac to die, but that the whole story was about whether Abraham would obey or not. For the modern Christian interpreter, "the picture of Isaac sensing the solemnity of the occasion and yet walking in perfect obedience, while carrying the wood upon which he is to be sacrificed, ranks among the most christological portraits found in the OT."[66] Yet it would be inaccurate to label one view Jewish and the other Christian. In fact, in some post-biblical Jewish literature, Isaac plays a much more prominent role than that given to him in Genesis.

---

64. The distinction made by John Dominic Crossan between "history remembered" and "prophecy historicized" in *Who Killed Jesus?*, 4 is useful but does not account for the full range of the word "fulfill" as used in Matthew.

65. For references, see Hicks, "Isaac," *IDB* 2:731 and Robert Martin-Achard, "Isaac," *ABD* 3:470.

66. Hicks, "Isaac," 729.

Josephus, anxious to show Isaac as the worthy son of Abraham, portrays a grown man throwing himself on the altar built by Abraham, indicating his willingness to help his father respond in obedience to God.[67] Philo apparently viewed the incident as equivalent to a sacrifice because it showed the *intention* of Abraham.[68]

Scholars are divided over whether the story of Abraham and Isaac acquired actual redemptive significance prior to the time of the NT,[69] but nowhere in the original Genesis account or in any later rabbinic interpretation of it was the claim made that Isaac actually died. However, while it may be argued that the '*Aqedah* does not mandate animal substitution for child sacrifice, it is clear that the story teaches such a substitution was believed permissible by Abraham.[70] Thus no single typological function of the Genesis story can be made to match a later interpretation in every detail. On the one hand, an obedient son Isaac carrying wood may appear to foreshadow the obedient son Jesus carrying his own cross to be crucified. But since Isaac did not die, the ram offered as a substitute for Isaac must also prefigure Jesus. It is important to note that such typological interpretation does not withdraw historical meaning from the original event, but adds a secondary or "filled" layer to its chronologically prior meaning. In this sense, typology in the NT is close to the form of exegesis we observed in Philo, reading into authoritative texts meanings that were not originally intended.[71]

To conclude this section, we need only mention that numerous other OT types are appropriated by NT authors, some of which we will also examine in detail in chapter 6. But here we may note three of special significance because of their methodological pattern: 1) The church may be seen as a new creation of God, the spiritual descendants of Abraham, the new (true) Israel, or even the new temple; 2) The great universal flood can serve as a type of the final cosmic judgment, or it could also be a type

---

67. Josephus, *Antiquities*, 1.13.1–4.

68. Philo, *De Abrahamo* ("About Abraham"), 32–36. The first-century BCE *Book of Jubilees* adds very few details to the Genesis account, except to certify that Mount Moriah was Mount Zion (18:13).

69. For the two opposing positions, see Vermes, *Scripture and Tradition in Judaism*, who argues for a pre-Christian kerygma, contra which are Davies and Chilton, "The Aqedah," 514–46.

70. See Levenson, *The Death and Resurrection*, 111–12.

71. This is especially the case for Paul, whose views on Isaac and the '*Aqedah* we will consider in detail in chapter 6.

of baptism into the Christian faith (baptism could also prefigure both circumcision and the crossing of the Reed Sea); 3) proclamation of the gospel to the entire world had been prefigured by the promises of God to Abraham and by various prophetic predictions of worldwide salvation.[72]

Allegory

In chapter 1 we spoke briefly of allegory as exemplified in the works of Philo of Alexandria. Here we observe that the earliest interpreters of the NT writings included allegory as one of the principle methods of explaining the Bible they shared with the rabbis, their Old Testament. On one side, strong advocates of gnosticism denied the reality of the physical and human experiences of Jesus, including his birth, death, and resurrection. On the other side, Jewish Christians looked for ways to underscore a sense of continuity between the Old and the New, and some of their number continued to insist on at least some attempt to keep Jewish law (specifically circumcision and *kashrut*) as a condition of conversion to Christianity. In dealing with such ideas, a literal OT was more a problem than a solution for the new faith. However, once it was accepted that Scripture required free-ranging interpretation, at issue was whether that interpretation should lead in every case to a single point of view that was unchanging in every circumstance. Articulated first by Origen (185–254 CE), four levels of meaning, the last three stemming from the broad category of allegory, came to be widely used by the early church fathers. The ways in which each came to be used is instructive:

1. The first of these was the plain or literal sense of the words in the text. But giving lip service to the literal sense of the OT was one thing, and accepting as divine truth a single meaning quite another. Inevitably, just as the rabbis had turned from the *peshat* to seek meanings that spoke to the real life situations in which they and their people lived, so the early Church fathers quickly found in Paul justification for abandoning the literal sense (*grammatos*) in favor of the spiritual (*pneumatos*) one.[73] Because the Bible was believed to have been ultimately authored by God, it was not like other (human) literature. Thus in addition to its literal (or "plain sense") meaning, there must also be a spiritual meaning not im-

---

72. For NT citations of these types and a comprehensive list of other examples, see Gundry, "Fulfill," *ISBE* 2:366–69.

73. 2 Cor 3:6 contains the phrase: "the letter kills, but the spirit gives life."

mediately signified by the literal words themselves. And Paul himself had exemplified such a dual level of meaning in 1 Corinthians 10:6, showing that events that had happened to the Jews were to be used as examples to teach Christians not to crave evil things.[74]

2. By the end of the second Christian century, the church fathers began to think of a second part of Scripture, a New Testament[75] to be added to the Old. And as Jews and Christians drifted ever farther apart, Christianity had to decide once again whether it would renounce its Jewish heritage altogether. Following once again the lead of Paul,[76] the church fathers turned to allegory in the effort to keep intact the link between Judaism and Christianity. By allegory, the literal sense of OT passages that appeared to apply for all time could be traded in for an application to Jesus or otherwise fitted into Christian clothing. Thus the need to use the OT as a witness to Jesus became the driving force behind the move to transvalue the Jewish Scriptures and reconstitute them as Christian. "The allegorical sense became a common device for changing questionable [OT] stories into acceptable moral and doctrinal precepts and examples."[77] As it had done for Philo, the allegorical method allowed commentators to invest biblical narratives with meanings that fit the presuppositions with which they had approached the text at the outset, and it is perhaps fair to say that allegory provided a way for Christianity to save the Old Testament for the church. The example of allegory given by Bellarmine is that of "Abraham, who indeed literally had two wives, one a free woman and the other a servant, and two sons, Isaac and Ismael [signifying] God as the author of two testaments and as the father of two peoples."[78]

---

74. Robert Cardinal Bellarmine, the seventeenth-century opponent of Galileo, included an especially insightful description of this phenomenon and its acceptance within the Catholic Church in his "Disputations on the Controversies Over Christian Faith Against the Heretics of the Day." The full text is available in Blackwell, *Galileo, Bellarmine, and the Bible*, 187–93. His essay treats all four levels of meaning under discussion here and in the following paragraphs.

75. The expression "New Testament" in reference to a collection of writings was used for the first time by Irenaeus (ca. 180 CE), Bishop of Lyons, in his work, *Against Heresies* (4.9.1). Paul used the phrase in Corinthians 11:25 and 2 Cor 3:6, not with reference to a body of literature but to describe a new pathway to God made possible via Jesus.

76. Whose allegorical treatment of Abraham, Isaac, Sarah, Hagar, and Ishmael we will consider in chapter 6.

77. Marius, *Martin Luther*, 91.

78. Blackwell, *Galileo, Bellarmine, and the Bible*, 188–89. Bellarmine's basis for this interpretation was the teaching of Paul in Galatians 4, which we will consider in detail

3. A third level of early Christian biblical exegesis was the *tropological*, which laid greatest stress on the figurative or metaphorical sense of the words of the Bible. As was the case with allegory, so also with *tropology* could an interpreter tease out of a passage virtually any meaning that he had brought to it. The only limits *to tropological* exegesis were the boundaries of the imagination of an individual expositor. Here Bellarmine's example begins with Deuteronomy 25:4:[79] "Do not muzzle an ox treading corn."[80] To Bellarmine, these words, obviously about an actual ox, "signify spiritually that orators should not be prohibited from accepting food from the people."[81] Again Bellarmine justified his interpretation by turning to Paul, who had cited Deuteronomy 25:4 in 1 Corinthians 9:9 to argue that those who offered spiritual service were entitled to receive material remuneration for it. This is a clear example of using a figurative interpretation as an inducement to righteous actions, and is quite similar to the way the rabbis employed Midrash or *haggadah* to underscore examples of the ways in which the faithful should live.

4. Anagogical interpretation ultimately became the goal of Christian treatment of the Bible, seeking not merely a figurative but specifically a *mystical* application of seemingly plain words of Scripture.[82] The final example from Ballarmine involves Psalm 95:11: "Concerning them [people with erring hearts], I [God] have sworn angrily, 'They shall never come to My resting-place.'" The literal meaning of Psalm 95:11 Bellarmine took as a reference to physical space, land. He then interpreted "resting-place" (*mənûḥah*) as a reference to eternal life, turning to the book of Hebrews 4:3 (which he attributes to Paul) for his authority.[83]

We cannot but be struck by the similarities between the rabbis and early Christian interpreters.[84] Whereas the rabbis had included minority

---

in chapter 6.

79. Which, very much like the *Tanna'im* had done in their Mishnaic arguments, he does not bother to cite.

80. The Hebrew text reads: "You shall not muzzle an ox while it is threshing."

81. Blackwell, *Galileo, Bellarmine, and the Bible*, 189.

82. We will note use of this method by Paul when we examine his explanation of the resurrection in chapter 6.

83. Here it is important to note that this fourfold division of exegetical meanings was borrowed by mystical branches of Jewish interpretation late in the twelfth or early in the thirteenth century CE, and given the name *pardes*: *peshaṭ* (plain meaning), *remez* (allegorical), *derash* (the Talmudic use of Midrashic forms), *sod* (a mystical, sub-surface meaning).

84. Remember that Bellarmine, although writing in the seventeenth century, bases

opinions in their published works, attesting to the fact that more than one interpretation was possible, Christian interpreters followed suit by creating four separate levels on which a particular passage might be interpreted. This meant that for both groups, we should speak of the meanings (plural!) of Scripture, rather than *the* meaning (singular!). Once again, Bellarmine made the point explicitly: "No one doubts that the Old Testament has allegorical, tropological, and anagogical meaning."[85] Bellarmine then added, "And many think the same thing about the New Testament, and rightly so."

Parables[86]

Closely related to the allegorical method is the "parable" (*parabole*), an extended metaphor or simile.[87] In 1935, C. H. Dodd offered what has become the classic definition of a parable: "a metaphor or simile drawn from nature or common life, arresting the hearer by its vividness or strangeness, and leaving the mind in sufficient doubt about its precise application to tease it into active thought."[88] The Hebrew Scriptures attest numerous examples of parables, among the most interesting of which is the story told to King David by the prophet Nathan about a rich man who owned numerous animals and a poor man who had only one tiny ewe lamb (2 Samuel 12:1–4). When the rich man seized the lamb of the poor man to provide supper for a guest, David immediately indicted the man, unwittingly indicting himself in the process. A second famous parable in Judges 9:8–15 forms the basis for an antimonarchic lesson. In succession, an olive tree, a fig tree, and a vine, all of which are productive and useful, declined kingship, opening the way for the useless bramble to seize office, an obvious reference to the dangerous and equally useless Abimelech. These two parables about David and Abimelech were easily understood, while a third, Isaiah's parable about the "Vineyard of YHWH" (5:1–7), came complete with an internal and explicit interpretation at the end.

---

his essay on the examples of interpretation that had come to him via the early church fathers.

85. Blackwell, *Galileo, Bellarmine, and the Bible*, 189.

86. A good basic article on the subject is Crossan, "Parable," *ABD* 5:146–52. Crossan has included a short but helpful bibliography.

87. Cited by Blomberg, *ISBE* 3:657.

88. Dodd, *The Parables of the Kingdom*, 5.

Similarly, post-biblical rabbinic parables were often self-explanatory. As one example, we may cite the story of a king who invited guests to a banquet with instructions that the invitees bring whatever they desired to sit on for the meal. When those who brought rough pieces of wood or stone complained about seating discomfort, much to the annoyance of the king, the moral of the tale was clear: in the next life, complaints about being assigned to Gehinnom ("hell") will fall upon deaf ears because those who are there will have determined their own destiny by their conduct in this world.[89]

A parabolic explanation about the centrality of Abraham received an internal explanation that offers a striking parallel to the famous words of Jesus spoken to Peter (Matt 16:18): A certain king wanted to build and to lay foundations. He dug deeper and deeper, finding only a swamp until finally he dug deep enough to strike a rock.[90] Then he said, "On this spot I will build and lay the foundations." The parable then explains that God had chosen Abraham because, "I have found a rock on which to build and establish the world."[91]

Scholars often classify as parabolic another Hebraic form of comparison, the *mashal*,[92] a proverb which contrasts two common items or concepts using short, pithy language. Thus we learn that "wisdom . . . is more precious than jewels" (Prov 3:13–15) or that "a wise son makes a father happy, but a son who is a fool is grief to a mother" (Prov 10:1). Such short comparisons need no internal explanation.

In the NT, Jesus frequently used parables in brief narrative form to tell a story with a double meaning. Most of these parables were self-explanatory, but some appear complete with interpretations either from Jesus himself or from the gospel author.[93] Such parables seem to have been used most often to illustrate the character of the kingdom of God. For example, three parables in the Synoptic gospels testify to the remarkable growth of the kingdom from small beginnings: the sower (Mark 4:1–9), the mustard seed (Mark 4:30–32), and the leaven (Matt 13:33). Other parables show that the kingdom of God is so valuable that a wise person would abandon everything in order to possess it. Here fall the de-

---

89. *Ecclesiastes Rabba*, 3.9.1.
90. Aramaic *petra* ("rock") is a loanword from Greek.
91. *Yalqut* to Numbers, 766.
92. The Hebrew title of the book of Proverbs is *mišlei*, the plural of *mašal*.
93. The standard work on NT parables is Jeremias, *The Parables of Jesus*. Also useful is Crossan, *In Parables*.

pictions of the pearl of great value (Matt 13:44–45) and the dragnet (Matt 13:47-50). Close in form and in meaning, but with the added dimension of divine care for the outcast and dispossessed, were the parables of the lost sheep (Luke 15:4–7), the lost coin (Luke 15:8–10), and the lost (prodigal) son (Luke 15:11–32).

An interesting sub-form of the longer parable employs the rabbinic principle of *Qal va-Ḥomer*, from lesser to greater, with the words "how much more?" Here we may cite the importuned friend who helps his troubled neighbor, leading to the knowledge of "how much more" God will give to those who ask of him (Luke 11:2–13). In similar fashion, the examples of the unjust judge (18:1–8), the unjust steward (16:1–13), the unprofitable servants (17:7–10), the tower-builder (14:18–33), and the animals in the well (14:5) all point to the sharp contrast between human reactions and the dependability of God.

These formal characteristics notwithstanding, the parables used by the *Tanna'im* are significantly different in function from those of Jesus. For the rabbis, parables were employed to illustrate a biblical text that was mentioned explicitly either in the introduction or the conclusion of the narrative record of a rabbinic debate. In the mouth of Jesus, parables were used to reveal the new age of the kingdom of God, not merely to expound a written text from the Bible.[94]

Ecclesiastical Politics and Biblical Interpretation

From the outset, Christianity acknowledged openly the seventy-five year span of time, the existence of numerous alternative textual traditions, and the multiple human writers necessary for the composition of her New Testament, and embraced the fact that there was an additional three-hundred-year lapse before the church officially declared its canon

---

94. Among post-NT Christian interpreters, the link between parable and allegory became explicit. One of the most famous examples occurs in Augustine's view of the parable of the Good Samaritan (Luke 10:25–37), where virtually every detail of the story is given allegorical significance:

of sacred Scripture.[95] During these three centuries, numerous Christian writers composed gospels comparable to the four now included in the New Testament and epistles comparable in style and content to many things that came from the hand of Paul the Apostle. But the church acted with conscious precision to declare certain books "in" and all others "out" of her sacred canon.

Two facts emerge. First, in making the decision to include certain books and exclude others, Christianity demonstrated its conviction that the Bible was created by the church; the process did not work the other way around. This conviction became the first fundamental principle of interpretation honored in early Christianity. Since the church had created the Bible, only the church could shoulder its ongoing responsibility to interpret, and to reformulate what it had created.[96] Its initial and most significant act of reformulation involved the wholesale acceptance of the Old Testament as its own, accompanied by an authoritative guide to its transvaluation, the New Testament, which provided the true meaning of the Old.

Second, in addition to its classic reformulation of the "old" into the "new," the church also developed its own ideas of oral tradition. In fact, major parts of the New Testament gospels portray Jesus offering his personal oral interpretation of Jewish law and customs, as we have seen. Just as the rabbis had done with their reformulation of the Bible in the Talmud,

NT Detail	Symbolism
Man traveling down from Jerusalem	Adam exiting the city of heavenly peace
The robbers	The devil and his angels
Priests and Levites	The Law and the prophets
The good Samaritan	The Christ
Oil and wine	Comfort and Exhortation
The beast	The body of Christ
The inn	The church
The innkeeper	The Apostle Paul

95. The Council of Carthage (394 CE) reaffirmed the twenty-seven-book NT canon of Athanasius, but debate over the parameters of the OT was not settled.

96. Vatican II resulted in an actual change in the lectionary readings for Passion Week, a change necessitated by the sad history of Jewish deaths at the hand of Christians whose own passions were aroused to violence by the words of the NT itself!

the church ultimately came to define and accept a Christian oral tradition that was equally authoritative with the written Scriptures of the Old and the New Testaments. That is, alongside the Old and New Testaments, the church asserted early on the value of oral interpretations offered by her teachers, bishops, and scholars, only some of which ultimately were put into written form. The best of these opinions acquired the name "tradition," and came to symbolize the results of corporate debates by councils, which the church could follow with confidence.

While The Council of Trent did not create the idea of the authority of tradition *de novo*, to it goes the honor of providing the classic, and simplest, expression of the concept. The stated purpose for calling the council was to deal with the splitting of the Church into factions following Rome and factions following Luther. "The initial occasion for convening the Council of Trent was Martin Luther's break with Rome in 1519."[97] But the actual topics treated by the Council over an eighteen-year span (1545–1563) were far broader.

The first order of business for the Council was to determine which books properly belonged in sacred Scripture, clearly in dialogue with the positions of Luther. By denying authoritative status or "canonicity" to the "deutero-canonical" books,[98] Luther had excised from the Catholic Old Testament all texts not in Hebrew,[99] slashing the number from forty-six to thirty-nine (= twenty-four in Hebrew). Luther also had problems with the book of James in the NT, calling it "a right strawy epistle without any evangelical sense"[100] because of its support for righteous deeds and action alongside faith. This had the effect of *de facto* if not *de jure* excision. In addition, because of a single statement implying that after one had been baptized to become a Christian, any further sin would result in eternal damnation (6:4–6), Luther also distrusted the letter to the

---

97. Blackwell, *Galileo, Bellarmine, and the Bible*, 5.

98. As discussed in chapter 2, these were 1 and 2 Maccabees, Sirach, Baruch, Tobit, and Judith plus the additions to Daniel (the stories of Bel, Susanna, and the Dragon) and LXX expansions of Esther.

99. This was a slippery problem for Luther, however, as virtually all of the OT texts he excluded had been composed originally in Hebrew and only subsequently rendered into Greek as part of the LXX. What he really intended was to deny the authority of the LXX in favor of what he considered the original, and thus inspired, Hebrew. One major problem with such a stance, is that virtually all of the quotations of the OT in the NT are from the LXX, a fact that Luther never addressed.

100. *WAB* 6:10. Yet for all this, Luther translated James into German and included it in the NT proper, not in the appendix for Apocryphal works.

Hebrews. He also spoke negatively about the book of Revelation, which he found impossible to interpret literally, and excised the short Epistle of Jude as well. The net effect was that Luther effectively operated as if there were three canonical components: an OT that differed from that of the Catholic Church, a NT some of whose contents he excised, and a biblical corpus of his own favorites from which he actually read and preached. "This selective reading shows in sharpest focus in the boldness with which Luther asserts his own canon of scripture within the larger corpus of the New Testament.[101] He tells us that the Gospel of John, Paul's epistles—especially Romans—and 1 Peter are central to all the rest and ought to be read daily by Christians. These books, he says, are to be prized above even the Gospels of Matthew, Mark, and Luke."[102] In direct opposition to Luther, the Council of Trent reaffirmed the complete canon of the Roman Church by accepting the formal statement of the Council of Florence dating to February 4, 1441.[103]

The second concern of Trent was to explain the role and authority of tradition alongside of Scripture. Luther had argued that the Bible alone (*his* canon!) constituted the only authoritative source for all Christian doctrine. He had also pressed for individual interpretation of the Bible, giving his infamous word picture of the farmer with one hand on the plow and the other holding the word of God as more powerful than all the popes of Rome. Yet for all of his lofty rhetoric about the plain sense of the Bible, Luther's use of allegory and typology to force the Old Testament into conformity with his idea of Christian truth was overly broad and excessive. His idea of *sola scriptura* is a theological method, not a method of interpretation, and his dismissal of Roman tradition is unique in this regard. Luther did not seek a plain sense, merely a Lutheran [sic!] sense that lent support to his own ideas about theology, faith, and the church.[104]

---

101. In fact, Luther's canon of the Bible contained thirty-nine OT books and twenty-seven for the NT, some of which he regarded as theologically central, others of which he appeared to dislike personally.

102. Marius, *Luther*, 354–55.

103. As a doff of the cap in the direction of the concerns of Luther, the church also continued to develop its idea of penance, which it taught was necessary to counteract the effects of sin committed post-baptismally.

104. Examining Luther's commentary on Psalm 85, Marius notes wryly: "Even when Luther provides what seems to him to be a 'literal' interpretation, his work is not literal exegesis at all. . . . The words [of the Psalms] inspired his pious imagination to find signs of Christ in every line" (*Luther*, 92).

When the Catholic Church challenged Luther, it did not object to his use of allegory or typology, or to his efforts to transvalue the sacred text of the Bible, it merely insisted that its own transvaluations were correct and those of Luther were not. In other words, the dispute was over *conclusions*, not about hermeneutical *methodology* that was common to both sides. As a result, when the Catholic Church responded to Luther at Trent, it issued not only a re-affirmation of its broader canon, but also published its official statement on tradition.

> The Council also clearly maintains that the truths and rules (for the church) are contained in the written books *and* in the unwritten tradition which, received by the Apostles from the mouth of Christ or from the apostles themselves, the Holy Spirit dictating, have come down to us, transmitted as it were from hand to hand. Following then the examples of the orthodox Fathers, it receives and venerates with a feeling of *equal piety and reverence* both all the books of the Old and New Testaments, since one God is the author of both, *and also* the traditions themselves, whether they relate to faith or to morals, as having been dictated orally either by Christ or by the Holy Spirit, and preserved in the Catholic Church in unbroken succession.[105]

Here the Council not only rejected Luther's shrunken canon, but included as authoritative an oral tradition quite similar to that noted for Judaism.[106] There is more. Neither written Scripture nor unwritten revelation ("tradition") could be subjected to private interpretation alone: "Furthermore, to control petulant spirits [none more petulant than Luther himself!], the Council decrees that, in matters of faith and morals pertaining to the edification of Christian doctrine, no one, relying on his own judgment and distorting the Sacred Scriptures according to his own conceptions, shall dare to interpret them contrary to that sense which Holy Mother Church . . . has held and does hold."[107]

Here, of course, the Catholic Church differed from Judaism, which lacked a single central authority. To the contrary, we have noted often that rabbinic literature bears eloquent witness to numerous "petulant spirits" whose minority opinions are found therein. As we have seen repeatedly, the results of rabbinic debates over doctrinal and *halakhic* matters regularly included multiple minority or individual opinions alongside the

---

105. Blackwell, *Galileo, Bellarmine, and the Bible*, 9, emphases added.
106. This is quite similar to the response of the rabbis to the Karaites!
107. Blackwell, *Galileo, Bellarmine, and the Bible*, 11–12.

record of what the majority of the rabbis had ruled. Catholic Christianity, now under pressure from Luther, sought for a single expression that would be accepted universally as "true" because it was *the* opinion of the church. At the same time, much as it had done centuries earlier when faced with a myriad of competing "gospels," the Catholic Church continued to suppress minority opinions once the majority vote of an official council had marked them as unsuccessful.[108] In other words, the Trent statements given above were not about dogma or canon, but about authority. Who has the *authority* to interpret and publish "*the* truth?"

We should also note that the creation of untold numbers of Protestant variations of the true faith began almost immediately to testify to the inability of the Catholic Church to suppress alternative theological positions as successfully as it had once suppressed alternative gospels. This was a situation about which Luther had been warned by the Dutch scholar Desiderius Erasmus (1466–1536), with whom he had carried on an extensive dialogue via letter. Both were members of the Catholic Augustinian order, and both were keenly interested in biblical exegesis. Erasmus was in fact the celebrated editor of the first printed edition of the Greek New Testament published in 1516, only one year before Luther nailed his ninty-five theses to the door of the church in Wittenburg, an edition to which Eramus appended copious notes in Latin containing many positions close to those of Luther.[109] Luther badly wanted Erasmus to be his ally, and many Catholics perceived the two scholars as standing shoulder to shoulder in an assault against the church.[110] But despite his agreement with Luther on numerous issues, and although he had attacked many of the abuses that Luther himself castigated,[111] Erasmus wanted no part in a break with Rome.

The issue that separated the two men was Luther's call for action that Erasmus perceived was certain to lead to violent division within

---

108. A classic early case in point is the debate over original sin between Augustine and Pelagius.

109. This led to his branding as a heretic by the Council of Trent!

110. Note the proverb, "Erasmus laid the egg that Luther hatched," cited by Marius, *Luther*, 247. Erasmus, of course, replied with his usual flair: "Yes, but the egg I laid was a hen, whereas Luther has hatched a gamecock." Cited by Durant, *The Story of Civilization VI*, 429.

111. Two books on Erasmus investigate his influence on and relationship with Luther and document his opposition to many of the excesses in Catholicism that bothered Luther. See Bainton, *Erasmus of Christendom*; Krueger, *Humanistische Evangelienauslegung*.

Christendom. Erasmus also believed that Luther's movement was a direct threat to reason and the humanism of the Renaissance, only one aspect of which was Luther's use of Scripture. While Erasmus shared Luther's longing for common people to be able to read the Bible for themselves, he could not share equally Luther's selective canon within a canon, discussed above. Nor could he accept Luther's cavalier dismissal of all Catholic tradition and authority.

As biblical exegetes, Erasmus and Luther both accepted the validity of the four principle methods introduced centuries earlier by Origen, and Erasmus praised Luther's commentary on the Psalms for his employment of these four. In other words, both as biblical exegetes and as critics of ecclesiastical excesses, Luther and Erasmus shared very similar points of view. The greater issue for Erasmus was his pacific nature. He longed for his church to reform itself, and spoke clearly about the areas in which reformation was needed. In the interim, "I endure the Church till the day I shall see a better one."[112] So he would not join with Luther in an all-out attack on the church he loved. In his own words, "Sedition I have always abhorred, and would that Luther and all the Germans had felt the same abhorrence,"[113] a statement that prompted an acerbic response from Luther: "Whenever I pray, I pray a curse upon Erasmus."[114]

Addenda

Biblical Interpretation and the Struggle with Science

Luther's clash with Erasmus pales by comparison to his angry attack on the scientists who forced the church into another debate that was to have a lasting impact on biblical interpretation. For centuries, no one had questioned the accuracy of the Bible not only with respect to theological matters, but equally on points of history and science. Some interpreters, like the fifth-century North African Bishop Augustine, had understood that the Bible was not intended to support or deny any specific theory of physical science.[115] Saint Thomas Aquinas, writing in the thirteenth century, had articulated the view that the Bible used human speech to ex-

---

112. Cited by Durant, *Reformation*, 436.
113. Cited by Mangan, *The Life, Character and Influence of Desiderius Erasmus*, 2:165.
114. Ibid., 2:255.
115. See Langford, *Galileo, Science and the Church*, 65.

press ideas that ordinary people could understand. Thus when it speaks of physical or scientific matters, the Bible limits itself to "the common conceptions and modes of speech in use" in the era of the biblical writers.[116] In short, both Augustine and Aquinas understood that the Bible was not a textbook of science.

But their view faded in the light of an intense debate sparked by the theories of Copernicus and Galileo. When the astronomer Nicholas Copernicus initially published his theory of a solar-centered universe in 1530, his system was received with favor by no less than Pope Clement VII himself.[117] Despite such papal favor, clearly the majority of Christian priests and biblical expositors still believed that the Bible was "true" in all matters, including the scientific and the historical. Copernicus was not a priest, but he was loyal to the Church and concerned not to be attacked with scorn and ridicule. Luther's reaction to him proved that his concern was well founded. "This fool wishes to reverse the entire science of astronomy; but Sacred Scripture tells us that Josue [Joshua] commanded the sun to stand still, and not the earth."[118]

Luther was joined in his objections to the new theory by other scholars of Scripture. As the seventeenth century dawned, Galileo took over the task of refining and demonstrating the truth of the Copernican hypothesis to Scriptural literalists, and it soon became apparent that "Scripture could be a more effective silencer than their attempts at reasoning had been."[119] It became ever clearer that the majority opinion among church interpreters followed a path that Augustine and Aquinas had rejected, and assumed that the Bible was scientifically accurate in every detail. With such a starting point, a clash between science and Scripture proved inevitable. When we recall the statement from the Council of Trent regarding private interpretation of the Bible and the need to control petulant spirits, it was perhaps also inevitable that the idea of a scientist, a layman no less, telling biblical scholars how to interpret the holy Book, would give rise to the fear that such private interpretation teetered close to the edge of undisciplined and unruly Protestant exegesis.

116. Ibid.

117. Langford's chapter on "Theories of the Universe" (ibid., 23–49) sets forth the details of this issue clearly and concisely.

118. Ibid., 35.

119. Ibid., 50. See also Langford's entire chapter on "Scriptural Objections" (50–78).

The theory of Copernicus was officially condemned by the church in 1616, and Galileo was forbidden to teach it. In spite of this ruling, he published his Magnum Opus in 1632, titled *Dialogue on the Great Systems of the World*.[120] As a result, the now ailing scientist was summoned to Rome early in 1633, where after a long and tedious formal hearing, his book was banned and Galileo himself placed under house arrest until his death.

On January 8, 1642, the year in which Isaac Newton was born, Galileo died. The great scientist was buried in the church of Santa Croce in Florence. Later, his remains were moved next to the tombs of two other famous Florentines, Michaelangelo and Machiavelli, in the same church. When the Grand Duke petitioned for permission to place a monument over the tomb of Galileo, he was refused and told that this would not be fitting since Galileo had given rise to the "greatest scandal in Christendom."[121]

Biblical Interpretation after Vatican II

This state of affairs reigned within Catholicism for three hundred years, not to be ameliorated until the encyclical *Divino Afflante Spiritu* of Pope Pius XII in 1943, the declaration that would serve as "a Magna Carta allowing Catholics to use literary and historical criticism that had long been suspect."[122] In the interim, Christian biblical scholarship outside the Roman Church developed in several important ways. Although a complete analysis of these issues is impossible here,[123] at least the following may be noted. First, archaeological recoveries throughout the world of the Bible came into prominence and provided background material that was invaluable in assessing the world of the Ancient Near East in which the Bible had been created. Perhaps the most interesting discoveries were of non-biblical literature that made possible the comparison of numerous foundational narratives of the Bible with those from Babylonia, Egypt, Anatolia, Ugarit (later Phoenicia), and the Holy Land itself. Closely related to these new data were the discovery and decipherment of previously

---

120. de Santilla, *Galileo*.
121. Langford, *Galileo*, 158.
122. Brown et al., *The New Jerome Biblical Commentary*.
123. For reasons of length, I have omitted discussion of the modernist controversy in Catholicism and the rise of fundamentalism among Protestants, both in the early twentieth-century.

"lost" cognate and related languages from the world of the Bible, adding greatly to our understanding of Hebrew, Aramaic, and Greek. Recovered also were several important manuscripts of biblical texts themselves, some (like the Dead Sea Scrolls) copied hundreds of years earlier than the best texts previously available for study.

A second line of development has been the long struggle to examine the Bible using methods of analysis and criticism applied to secular literature. As a result, the messages of the Bible are now routinely interpreted using scientific methods in a struggle for objectivity that was never possible as long as scholars were forced to approach the Bible with the responsibility of proving what a particular theological system asserted was already true.

A third point of emphasis is quite recent, as scholars over the past thirty years have paid more attention to the final form of the Bible, its canonical form, to analyze its function in church and Synagogue.

We will see in chapter 6 that one tool has remained firmly in the hands of Christian interpreters from NT times until the present, and that is the freedom to transvalue. Whether claiming fidelity to the plain sense of Scripture or complete freedom to use the latest methods of critical analysis, Christian biblical interpretation shares with Jewish interpreters the fundamental goal of understanding time-bound, event-specific narratives from long ago in the context of a constantly morphing modernity.

5

Jewish Transvaluation

"God spoke one thing. I heard two [things]"—Psalm 62:12

*Miqra' 'eḥad yôtze' ləkamah ṭə'mîm və-'eyn
ṭa'am 'eḥad yôtze' mi-kamah miqra'ôt.*[1]

IN CHAPTER 1 WE surveyed the sacred and some of the authoritative literature of classical and rabbinic Judaism. Chapter 3 furnished a tour of the principles used by Jewish sages over the centuries to interpret that literature. In this chapter we turn to specific examples of Jewish transvaluation, beginning with inner-biblical examples before turning to post-biblical texts that use the hermeneutical principles followed by the rabbis to produce results that are often surprising.

Inner-Biblical Transvaluation

The Ten Commandments

In chapter 1 we noted briefly that numerous parallel accounts of the same story are included in the biblical record. Here we examine some additional examples of the broader application of this phenomenon, beginning with a look at one of the more well-known passages in all of sacred

---

1. "One verse conveys several meanings, but one meaning is not conveyed by numerous verses" (*San.* 34a), attributed to Abbaye.

Scripture. One list of the Ten Commandments is found in Exodus 20, while a second list occurs in Deuteronomy 5. Although the two versions are quite similar, several important differences are noteworthy.

First, according to Exodus 20:8–11, the Israelites were commanded to "remember" (*zakhôr*) the day of Shabbat in honor of the fact that God had rested on day seven following the six days of creation.[2] This ties the commandment neatly to the creation narrative of Genesis 2:2–3,[3] and instructs ancient Israel to "cease" [*shabbat*] from their weekly work as God had ceased following His task of creation. It further enjoins humans to "make holy" their day seven as God had made his holy.

In Deuteronomy 5:12–15, both the wording of the commandment and its rationale are changed. "Remember" becomes "observe" (šamôr), not a serious difference taken alone, for to "remember" a special day connotes an act of recalling it from the past and bringing it into the present. In order to "observe" Shabbat, or course, it would be necessary first to "remember" it.[4] But the basis for a human Shabbat in Deuteronomy is not simple recall and imitation of the actions of God in creation. Instead, *observance* of the Shabbat is enjoined as an act of thanksgiving for the historic act of divine deliverance from Egypt. To "observe" such a day implies its celebration by means of generally accepted and prescribed religious procedures.[5]

Second, justification for the Shabbat is offered in general terms by Deuteronomy: "just as YHWH your Deity has commanded." This phrase is absent from Exodus.

Third, Exodus 20:11 also notes that God had "rested" (not merely "ceased") on the first Shabbat, a specific description lacking in the Genesis link. It is one thing to cease from work, quite another to "rest." However, not only was the concept of "resting" expanded by Deuteronomy, it was also tied to the story of the exodus (consistent with the deuteronomic link to the exodus as contrasted with the act of Creation). Whereas the book of Exodus simply notes that God had "rested" (*va-yanaḥ*) following creation,

---

2. This and the following commandment about honoring parents are the only two of the ten that are positive as opposed to negative. Both of them are given extended justification as well.

3. As well as to numerous other biblical passages. See for example Exodus 31:16–17.

4. Thus the liturgical formula in the hymn, "*Lekha Dodi*," sung at the opening of the Friday evening service, notes that "Observe and remember are a single command" (šamôr və-zakhôr ba-dibbûr 'eḥad).

5. Šamôr is used this way in Deuteronomy 29:8, as also in Exodus 12:17 and 23:15.

Deuteronomy 5:14 demands that all humans "rest" (*yanûaḥ*) on Shabbat, owners along with male and female slaves, at the same time allowing work animals to stop their labor as well. Once again, the rationale is not the imitation of God, but a reminder of Israel's own ordeal of slavery.

Fourth, another subtle difference illustrates the "general" and "particular" distinctions that would later become a major concern of the post-biblical rabbis. The listing of those eligible to remember the Shabbat in Exodus 20:6 includes simply "your animals." Deuteronomy 5:14 begins with the particular mention of oxen and donkeys before picking up the general "animals" from Exodus.

Fifth, the fifth commandment in Deuteronomy 5:16 contains a justifying statement absent from Exodus 20:12. Not only does the honor of (or "respect for") parents portend a long life, as in Exodus, but also a "good life."

Sixth, most English translations of the Bible render the ninth commandment (Exodus 20:16; Deuteronomy 5:20) employing the same wording: "You shall not bear false witness against your neighbor." In so doing, modern translators are following the example of the LXX, which reads the same in both places. However, the traditional Hebrew text attests two different words. Exodus uses the Hebrew word *šeqer*, a "lie," while Deuteronomy chooses *šav'*, which is akin to meaningless or worthless speech in an otherwise serious situation. While both versions forbid the offering of false testimony in a legal proceeding, the broader wording of Deuteronomy appears to be an attempt to make the restriction more far-reaching.

These variants may seem insignificant, especially in light of the fact that the basic instructions are essentially the same. But an interesting statement from Moses in Deuteronomy 5:19 (English 5:22) emphasizes the fact that YHWH had spoken "these words . . . and no more," before personally inscribing them on tablets of stone to ensure their permanence. Thus even slight variations in detail must be considered noteworthy. In the words of Mark Brettler:

> they teach us that the ancients did not transmit biblical texts like we transmit modern texts, using photocopiers and "cut-and-paste" word-processing programs. Rather, all biblical texts changed during their transmission. They were updated, expanded, and made to fit their broader context. If this happened to the Decalogue—which is ascribed directly to God—then it

certainly happened to other texts, which would have been even more fluid.[6]

This brief look at the Ten Commandments illustrates that when the rabbis attempted to interpret biblical texts in their era, they had at hand clear precedents of the fact that even biblical authors and editors themselves had not been bound to a wooden standard of literalism. And this was a precedent that they used freely, expanding biblical concepts as they believed appropriate and necessary. Thus when specific commandments from one context were considered elsewhere in biblical narrative, they were modified by expansion and clarification. The simple statement, "You shall do no work," was fleshed out elsewhere in the Bible with additional, specific examples designed to define "work". Considered broadly in passages outside the Ten Commandments proper, "work" was seen to include agricultural labor (Exodus 34:21), the gathering and preparation of food (Exodus 16:23), the gathering of firewood (Numbers 15:32–36), the kindling of a fire (Exodus 35:3), carrying a load (Jeremiah 17:21–24), or normal business activities (Amos 8:5; Nehemiah 13:15–21).

Extending this inner-biblical clarification of work even further, the rabbis built upon the principle of context, noting that the instructions for the building of the portable shrine in which to house the original stone tablets containing the Ten Commandments (Exodus 25:1—31:11) were concluded with a repetition of the prohibition against doing work on the Shabbat. This biblical juxtaposition led the rabbis to infer that all thirty-nine categories of labor involved in the construction of the Ark were to be included with the other activities noted above and specifically banned on Shabbat.[7]

Isaiah and Jeremiah

Our second example involves messages given by Isaiah and Jeremiah. Late in the eighth century, the prophet Isaiah advised his king that Jerusalem would be defended against a force of almost 200,000 professional Assyrian soldiers.[8] God, he said, would defend Jerusalem in order to protect the honor of His own reputation, and in order to fulfill a promise he had

---

6. Brettler, *How to Read the Bible*, 66 and 299 n21.

7. See the extended discussion in *Mishnah Shab* 7:2-4 and the Gemara in *Shab.* 49b

8. Isaiah 37:35. The episode is chronicled both in Isaiah 36–37 and in 2 Kings 19.

made more than two centuries earlier to King David through the prophet Nathan.[9] The biblical text notes that Isaiah was 100 percent correct in his prediction. Following Isaiah's pronouncement, "that very night, the messenger of YHWH went out and struck dead 185,000 in the Assyrian camp, so the following morning, all of them were dead corpses."[10]

But while the Assyrians were the imperial terrorists when Isaiah lived, the prophet Jeremiah lived in the era that witnessed the demise of Assyria and the rise of a new bully in the Mediterranean sphere. More than one hundred years after the Assyrian siege about which Isaiah had spoken, Jerusalem was once again besieged by an overwhelming enemy force, this time the Babylonians. And the historical fact is that the Babylonians accomplished in 587 BCE what the Assyrians had failed to accomplish in 701. Many of the smaller Judahite towns were devastated by the rampaging Babylonian army, and Jerusalem herself was besieged for approximately eighteen months,[11] before being captured in August 587. The results were disastrous: large sections of the city were burned, most notably the Temple and the royal palace complex; the Judahite King Zedekiah was taken into captivity; thousands of Jews were marched into exile; and Judah was constituted a province of the Babylonian Empire rather than an independent nation, and was headed by a governor rather than a king.[12]

During the sixth-century advance of the Babylonians, two different prophetic perspectives were heard in Judah. Many prophets in Jerusalem doubtless took great comfort in repeating the sentiment if not the actual words of Isaiah to the frightened people in their own audiences. This led Jeremiah to complain to God: "Look, the prophets are telling them (the people), 'you will not see the sword nor will you have famine, but I will give you true peace in this place'" (14:13). But this time, the divine instructions to Jeremiah were not what Isaiah had heard from the Lord

---

9. Recorded in 2 Samuel 7:16.

10. Compare Isaiah 37:36 and 2 Kings 19:35.

11. The siege was apparently lifted briefly when the Egyptian army approached, but the Egyptians did not engage the Babylonians, and retreated to allow the siege to continue.

12. The new governor was Gedaliah, a member of one of the most highly respected families in Jerusalem. But after five short years during which he followed Babylonian orders, he was murdered by Ishmael, a member of the former royal family. The Jews who still remained in Jerusalem feared a reprisal by the Babylonians, and fled to Egypt, taking an unwilling Jeremiah with them. Tradition holds that he was finally stoned to death in Egypt by some of his own countrymen who hated his messages.

in the eighth century. Rather, because they assumed that what Isaiah had said in the late eighth century BCE would always be true, specifically in the early sixth century during which they were living, prophets other than Jeremiah made the fundamental mistake of assuming that an older prophetic narrative would remain valid regardless of changes that had occurred in time and circumstances. Only Jeremiah dared to disagree with the famous Isaiah, asserting that, "The prophets are prophesying falsehood in My name" (14:14).[13] Although his message clearly links back to that of Isaiah, employing one of Isaiah's own words, the fearful "siege mound" (*solelah*) that brought terror to cities under siege by the Assyrians, he presents a message in polar opposition to that of his predecessor.

Isaiah	Jeremiah
This is what YHWH of the Hosts has said concerning the King of Assyria: "He will not come to this city or shoot an arrow there. He will not come before it with a shield, nor throw up a siege mound (*solelah*) against it" (37:33).	This is what YHWH of the Hosts has said: "Cut down her trees, and cast up a siege mound (*solelah*) against Jerusalem. This is the city being punished" (6:6).

There is wide scholarly agreement that the earliest messages of Jeremiah were delivered during the reign of King Jehoiakim (609–598), oracles delivered in the context of an impending and then an actual Babylonian invasion. But Jeremiah opposed the majority prophetic opinion that linked back uncritically to Isaiah's message cited above, the idea that Jerusalem, no matter how sinful, could not be destroyed because she was the holy city of God. Jeremiah alone believed that King Nebuchadnezzar of Babylonia was a "servant" of the Lord who was being used to punish the sins of the Judahites.[14] Because he saw no way for Judah to escape this punishment, he openly advised capitulation to the Babylonians as a means of avoiding total devastation of the city and countless deaths to

---

13. The concept of "false" prophets/prophesying occurs *passim* in the book of Jeremiah.

14. Jeremiah 27:6.

her citizens.¹⁵ And while his messages were widely interpreted as treason, Jeremiah apparently believed that God had to punish sin in order to maintain his faithfulness and dependability. As blessing was a covenantal promise for obedience, even so was punishment an equally sure promise for disobedience.

It is important to remember that Jeremiah was warning about something early in the sixth century that Isaiah had said simply could not happen late in the eighth century, not to Jerusalem! Clearly Jeremiah believed that Isaiah's message was no longer valid in the sixth century, and the story of the life and career of Jeremiah cannot be told apart from this background. Of even greater significance is the fact that this incident illustrates from within the biblical text itself the necessity and the legitimacy of transvaluing sacred texts from one generation to the next. For Jeremiah, the fact of widespread sinfulness within sixth-century Judah and Jerusalem, sinfulness in direct violation of the Ten Commandments,¹⁶ brought Judah under the provisions of the Sinaitic Covenant that was even older and more venerable than the covenant God had made with King David to which Isaiah had appealed.¹⁷ Jeremiah trumped the eighth-century word of Isaiah based on the tenth-century prophetic promise of Nathan that a son of David would always reign in Jerusalem. Thus it is critical to note that the prophet Jeremiah not only disagreed with the majority prophetic view of his own day, he specifically preached that the message of Isaiah more than one hundred years earlier was no longer relevant or true.

Elijah, Elisha, and Hosea

A third example of prophetic transvaluation is found in the book of Hosea. According to the narrative offered in Second Kings, the ninth-century dynasty of Omri had been ended violently and the new dynasty of Jehu had begun at the direction of God, with the prophetic approval and backing of both Elijah and Elisha.¹⁸ More than a century later, Hosea had to deal with a member of that same Jehu dynasty, Jeroboam II, and Hosea's evaluation of the dynasty differed radically from that of Elijah and Elisha.

15. Jeremiah 27:8, 11, and especially verse 12.
16. His views are summarized in 7:1–15.
17. This concept was developed by Raitt, *A Theology of Exile*.
18. See especially 2 Kings 9–10.

One of the ways in which he expressed his disapproval stemmed from his own personal life. In his own private marriage we are told, Hosea's wife had born three children, to each of whom the prophet assigned names symbolic of a particular aspect of his ministry to the nation. The first child he named "Jezreel," "God will sow" (1:4). The name was obviously chosen to remind national leaders of the great slaughter that had been perpetrated by Jehu near the Valley of Jezreel, for it had been with this slaughter of all members of the Omride Dynasty that Jehu had begun his own reign over one hundred years earlier. As we have noted, the king reigning at the time of Hosea was a member of that violently established dynasty of Jehu. Yet despite the fact that the actions of Jehu in the ninth-century BCE had received the backing of Elijah and Elisha, who regarded the destruction of the evil Omrides as God's own punishment,[19] Hosea was certain in the eighth century that Jehu's successor could no longer escape divine punishment due for those crimes, even though they were over a century in the past.

The important fact is that the Bible has preserved both messages in each of these two cases, clear testimony to the understanding that no single message was valid for all times and in every situation. This may be said another way. While it may be true that God does not change, it was equally apparent to the framers of the Bible that people, problems, and political forces do indeed change from era to era. Just as a medical Doctor must alter his diagnosis to fit the malady of a particular patient, well aware that another patient suffering a different illness will need a different diagnosis, even so could a spiritual doctor (prophet) offer a message that served as a cure for the spiritual cancer of his era, while a later prophet would judge that message to have little effect on the spiritual maladies of his own time.

Job and Ecclesiastes

In addition to these three specific instances of prophetic transvaluation, two additional examples may be noted, both of which pertain to the concept of theodicy or divine justice in a general rather than in a specific sense. For centuries, the normative position of those who created the literature of the Torah and the Prophets was that obedience and righteousness would always be honored and blessed by God, while disobedience

---

19. 2 Kings 19:15–17; 2 Kings 9:1–10; 10:10.

and unrighteousness would lead inevitably to punishment. But the biblical story of non-Israelite Job offers a spectacular dissent from the standard view. Job was a man of unquestioned righteousness to whom no sin could be imputed. Still, according to the normative view, his horrible losses of wealth and family, followed by his own personal physical illness, could only mean that he was guilty of some sin. In the book that bears his name, four "orthodox" friends argue vociferously that Job need only admit his sin and cry for forgiveness in order for God to reverse his terrible misfortune. Since Job could not admit to sin that he had not committed, the human actors in the story reached an impasse. To bridge this gap between them, the book concludes with an appearance of God to Job, making the argument that some things are simply beyond human ability to comprehend them. Thus the book makes clear that not all righteous people are rewarded. That such an alternative to standard theology could become an important part of the sacred canon is stark testimony that even the most basic biblical teachings could be brought under the harsh light of scrutiny when facts and circumstances demanded.

The book of Job not only made the point that some righteous people suffer, but also implied that people who are not righteous do sometimes prosper. And even though the author could not explain the reasons why, he remained convinced that it was indeed true. The book of Ecclesiastes emphasizes this second point implied in Job, calling into question the unexamined majority view that there was a radical difference between the fate of the righteous and the unrighteous.

Prophecy and Apocalypticism

The final example of inner-biblical dynamic tension leading to the necessity of transvaluing older points of view is seen in the rise of apocalyptic literature. One cannot understand the biblical prophets without grasping their view of history, specifically their belief that God is the Sovereign of all events in the world. So whenever difficult times came upon ancient Israel and Judah, the prophets assumed that the hand of God could be discerned. Even when the two states of Israel and Judah were defeated, the prophets announced that no outside power had won a victory over the people of God. Rather, it was their conviction that God had brought *momentary* defeat to his own people in an effort to punish them for misdeeds and even more, to call them back to the holy path of obedience to him.[20]

But there came a time when such a viewpoint proved to be too simplistic. The nation of Israel passed off the screen of human history in 722 BCE, and then tiny Judah was carted off into exile by the powerful Babylonian Empire 135 years later. And even though many of the Jewish exiles eventually found their way back to Jerusalem (Judah), the political reality was that independence was gone; although mighty Babylon fell in 539 BCE, Jews remained a subject people for centuries—to Persians, to Greeks, to Syrians and then to Romans.

In the context of subjugation to these great world powers, it became clear that the rubric of the prophets had to be revised. Their simple idea that obedient people would be blessed and protected by God no longer held true in a world that denied both the Israelite and the Judahite people any semblance of political independence. It had been fine to tell children of earlier eras that God would always honor obedience, but children of these later eras saw with their own eyes another truth. Sometimes God did not protect even righteous people in the way that the old stories of the prophets had promised. Ultimately, the undeserved suffering of numerous Jews at the hand of a godless madman demanded an explanation that the preaching of the prophets could not give. This madman, known as Antiochus Epiphanes (175–163 BCE), executed Jews who owned copies of the sacred Torah, forbade religious rites like circumcision, and set forth on a campaign to exterminate Judaism from the face of the earth.[21] Many of the Jews who died by his hand were among the most obedient to God, the most observant, in the community. To the contrary, those Jews who seemed likely to survive were those who submitted to the program of Antiochus and assimilated, essentially abandoning Judaism. The simple formula of the past no longer worked in the harsh context of insanity.

In this context, a new kind of visionary arose, people who were not prophets of the old school, but who created a new kind of message that came to be known as apocalypticism.[22] The purpose of apocalyptic writing and preaching was not to call people to repentance as the prophets had done, in the hope that repentance might turn the hand of God from punishment to blessing once more. Rather, apocalypticism was a new

---

20. See my "From Yahwism to Judaism."

21. Cf. 1 Maccabees 1:57–61.

22. Apocalyptic teachings in the Bible include much of the book of Daniel, Zechariah 9–14, Isaiah 24–27, and numerous other shorter passages.

method of interpreting history, not by affirming merely that God is the Sovereign of all events, but by the assertion that the final outcome of history had already been predetermined. While the prophets had carefully drawn a direct link between faithfulness to God and national survival, the apocalyptic visionaries upped the ante. Of course God is just. And certainly he will reward the faithful and punish the wicked. But rewards and punishments may not be doled out in this life! We may need to wait until a future, better world to see the justice of God defended in a final settling of accounts with appropriate punishments and rewards. And this day of final settlement may be delayed until the end of all time.

The prophets had preached that the results of their belief system could be tested in the fires of history. A just society would be blessed, a wicked people would be punished. One had only to look and see what had happened to the evil Pharaoh, to the idolatrous Canaanites, even to the monstrous Assyrians. So the preaching of the prophets was filled with a sense of urgency: repent today so the punishment from God could be lifted and divine blessing ensured. But when people believed the prophets and reformed their ways, and the punishment still did not end, what then? The visions of the apocalypticists provided an answer to precisely this question. Righteous people may never see the true results of their actions. This alternate answer meant that the key questions needed to be changed as well. Can people continue faithfully to live moral and obedient lives even when they cannot reap the rewards? Is righteous living worthwhile simply because it is the right thing to do? Believing the answer to be in the affirmative, the apocalypticists urged their listeners to remain faithful even without seeing the reward for their efforts, all the while waiting patiently for God to intervene in the world, bring an end to all of history, and exhibit in his own way the full truth of his justice. This was a vision that people could not test for themselves, for "history" could not ratify a victory that remained to be won outside of time and space. They had to choose to live lives of obedience and create moral and just communities while realizing all the while that it might not pay off for them in concrete terms.

The following chart indicates six basic differences between prophecy and apocalypticism. Once again we note that the Bible unabashedly includes both types of teachings.

Prophecy	Apocalypticism
Language is pointed, direct, clear, challenging a present day human audience to repentance.	Language is symbolic, mystical, to avoid death at hands of evil leaders.
Focus is the present world, human history.	Focus is the future world, divine activity, the end of history.
Goals are discipline, repentance, correction, and restoration.	Goal is faithfulness, whether rewards are reaped or not.
Appeals to "history" as proof of God's power and essential character.	Appeals to eschatology (the end of time), outside of time (history).
God and righteousness appear to be losing, but can win via repentance.	God and righteousness soon to win openly, victory shared by the faithful.
The battle with "evil" must be joined in time and space.	The battle has *already* been won, outside of time, awaiting confirmation.

The idea that many people have about "prophets" is really more about an apocalyptic vision of the end of the world than it is about biblical prophets who offered spiritual advice during political, military, or theological crises of their own day. No one knows the end of time except God. No one can prove that morality is preferable to immorality. Even the greatest apocalyptic figures of the Bible did not live long enough to know whether they had been correct. So the realities of defeat and occupation forced people to decide whether to live faithfully or unfaithfully because they believed one alternative was morally correct and the other was not. For the apocalypticists, "to be faithful to the end" was more important than being faithful for the moment in the hope for quantifiable rewards.

People for whom the Bible was an authoritative book found in the apocalyptic vision of reality a source of encouragement as well as a guidebook for life. Some things are always the right thing to do. For the great prophets, true religion implied the necessity of creating a society of fairness for everyone from king to commoner, building systems of justice that protect the powerless, and respecting the rights of all individuals, including those who are unable to speak for themselves. Even when such things were not actually done, no one doubted that they should be done. In other words, the tradents who transmitted the sacred canon of prophetic literature to the world believed the prophets were theologically correct even when people did not obey their call for repentance and reformation. But apocalypticism extended the authority of the prophet out beyond the scope of history, outside the boundaries of time, giving God a second chance to reveal his absolute justice. The prophets had taught that repentance and righteousness would yield tangible results that could be measured, and their call for repentance was based on this premise. The apocalypticists knew all too well that tangible results were not *pro forma*. Their call was not for repentance, but for faithfulness to God in spite of all evidence indicating that no reward might be earned in the present world.

Rabbinic Transvaluation of Biblical Texts

In chapter 3 we noted the process of transvaluation attested in the translation of Scripture into Greek and Aramaic, the attempt to harmonize biblical values with Greek philosophical ideals, and the urge to fill out biblical stories with greater detail in the Pseudepigrapha. We have surveyed briefly the evidence that similar transvaluation occurred within the pages of the Bible itself, as older texts were challenged and updated to meet changing circumstances. Now we turn to specific examples of biblical teachings that were radically transformed by the rabbis in the post-biblical era.

Capital Punishment

Our first example of the rabbinic system of transvaluation involves the question of capital punishment. Biblical legislation prescribes capital punishment for a variety of offenses, and provides various methods of carrying out a death penalty.

Crime or "Sin"	Punishment
apostasy (Lev 20:2; Deut 13:11; 17:5)	Stoning
blasphemy (Lev 24:14, 16, 23; 1 Sam 21:10)	
sorcery (Lev 20:27)	
violation of Shabbat (Num 15:35–36)	
misappropriation of חרם (ḥerem) (Josh 7:25)	
a disobedient son (Deut 21:21)	
adultery (Deut 22:20–24: both man and woman!)	
rape (Deut 22:25)	
incest (Lev 20:14)	Death by Fire
fornication by the daughter of a priest (Lev 21:9)	
the perceived adultery of Tamar (Gen 38:24–26)	
an apostate city (Deut 13:15, and cf. 1 Kgs 18:40)	Death by Sword
homicide (Num 35:9)	

If one is limited to a literal interpretation and allows the debate about capital punishment to be determined by the Bible alone, the biblical position plainly champions the view that capital punishment was an acceptable and necessary aspect of criminal procedure.

jewish transvaluation 159

In the literal sense, of course, this view is correct, for the Bible not only favors but *commands* the death penalty in more than a few places, as the chart above indicates. However, when the death penalty came under discussion among the Talmudic sages, an interesting shift began to occur. Numerous places in the Mishnah refer to the death penalty as if it were taken for granted by the *Tanna'im* as it had been by the biblical authors. Thus in *Makkot* 1:10 (*Sanhedrin* 7:1), we read: "The court has power to inflict four kinds of death-penalty: stoning, burning, beheading, and strangling."[23] Both preceding and following this summary statement are a series of paragraphs describing exactly how each of these methods was to be carried out. But one short paragraph of this intriguing Mishnaic debate about capital punishment sheds light on the whole process, and exemplifies the method of transvaluation that we are attempting to demonstrate.

In *Makkot* 1:10: (7a), a general principle is enunciated and placed on the docket for discussion. "A Sanhedrin (Jewish High Court) that votes a death penalty one time in seven years is called reckless." Reactions among the rabbis to this broad statement are instructive. First, Rabbi Elazar the son of Azaryah says, "One time in seventy years" would also be reckless. Then Rabbi Tarfon and Rabbi Akiva weigh in: "If we were on the Sanhedrin, it would never impose the death penalty." This opinion is especially significant in light of the fact that a unanimous vote of all Sanhedrin members was necessary for a death penalty. So even one member, thinking as did Tarfon and Akiva, could indeed ensure the fact that no death penalty would ever be issued. But the matter does not end there, for Rabban Shimon the son of Gamliel opined: "Well then, we would multiply capital crimes [literally, "the shedding of blood"] in Israel."

This was a debate carried out during the era of Roman hegemony, when Jews did not have the legal authority to execute a death penalty for any reason. In other words, the entire discussion could not have been simply about when or whether to apply a death penalty, but served as an exercise intended to instruct scholars about the complexity involved in the taking of a human life even with appropriate biblical justification. Thus in this brief report of what surely must have been a heated debate, virtually every position represented in the modern debate is found:[24]

---

23. According to 2 Sam 21:9, impalement is also a possibility in certain cases. MT *yoqi'um*, Hiphil of the root *y-q-'*, can mean either "to impale" or "to expose."

24. The discussion of this paragraph in the *Gemara* is brief, and concerned only to ensure that witnesses were adequately cross-examined.

- The death penalty is necessary only in exceptional cases (Elazar).
- The death penalty is an improper sentence in every case (Tarfon and Akiva).
- The death penalty is necessary as a deterrent to crime (Shimon).

Following the setting forth of these various points of view, the Mishnah makes no attempt to declare which position was determined to be correct. The point of such an example is clear. There was no central agency dictating *the* Jewish view of capital punishment. As their discussion of the issue demonstrates, men who were both learned and honorable disagreed among themselves about capital punishment so sharply that they were unable to arrive at a consensus, and thus no student of the Mishnaic masters could simply hide behind blind acceptance of a specific rabbinic opinion endorsed uncritically. Whatever an individual Jew might decide about the death penalty, he would have to face the fact that credible and serious rabbinic scholars had disagreed with his conclusion. No one could read their debate, vote "I agree," and be relieved of the responsibility of personal reflection and involvement in a complex moral issue. Both in the Mishnaic era and in all subsequent periods, the biblical information had to be transvalued, i.e., subjected to interpretative decisions that moved beyond the Bible from the outset.

"An Eye for an Eye" (*'ayin taḥat 'ayin*)

Our second example of rabbinic reconstruction and transvaluation pertains to the famous "eye for an eye" rule found three times in the Bible (Exodus 21:22–25; Leviticus 24:17–22; Deuteronomy 19:18–21). This law of equivalency[25] or retaliation (*lex talionis*) has often been perceived in the popular mind as an adequate summation of biblical law, with no thought given to the context in which it occurs or the way it was interpreted within Judaism from earliest times. In fact, from within the Bible itself comes the first indication that a strict rule of physical mutilation was not always (and perhaps never) followed. Exodus 21:22 deals with the question of appropriate punishment in the case where two men were engaged in a fight during which one of them accidentally struck a pregnant women hard enough to cause a miscarriage. If this happened, the guilty man was to be fined an amount of money to be determined by an appro-

---

25. Cited in Matthew 5:38.

priate court of law. Arguing from this text, and with spirited expressions of their own personal feelings about harsh corporal punishment, the rabbis created an elaborate system of monetary compensation for bodily injuries that stood in opposition to the clear teaching of Scripture in numerous places.

As was the case with respect to capital punishment in the Bible, the rabbis were keenly aware that biblical legislation sometimes demanded corporal punishment for non-capital offenses. And yet, following an undeniably apologetic line of interpretation, and influenced by their own sensibilities of conscience, harsh measures of corporal mutilation were set aside by the *Tanna'im*, and their decisions were ratified and justified by the *'Amoraim*. The relevant Mishnaic ruling begins: "If a man injures another, he becomes liable to him on five counts: for injury, for pain, for healing, for loss of time, and for the indignity inflicted."[26] To determine the appropriate compensation, the courts "make an assessment of how much he [the injured man] *was* worth [before the injury] and how much he *is* worth [after the injury]." The discussion then extends to the possibility of a wound becoming worse, or recurring after having appeared to be healed, and states that the guilty party "is under obligation to pay medical expenses" also in such cases.

When we examine the five bases for compensation, we note that the first four pertain to actual physical injury inflicted upon a victim or its aftermath of pain and medical costs. However, the fifth basis for compensation pertains not to an injury but what we might call an insult, i.e., "a wrong done to you as an affront to your pride."[27] And the rabbinic basis for ordering pecuniary compensation for an insult was not grounded in the eye-for-an-eye texts.[28] To the contrary, a separate passage from Deuteronomy 25:12 was appropriated. This verse provides for the severing of the hand of a woman who has seized the genitals of a man involved in a fight with her husband, a stipulation whose clear intent cannot be dodged. So we may well ask how the rabbis argued from such a verse to the subject of an insult. They did it by making a verbal link between the biblical verse and their own belief that "insults" should be compensated monetarily. In Deuteronomy 25:11, the Hebrew word referred to above as "genitals" is

---

26. This and the following citations are from Mishnah *Baba Kamma* 8:1 and the accompanying *Gemara* in *M. Baba Kamma* 83b–84a.

27. Daube, *The New Testament and Rabbinic Judaism*, 259.

28. Would "eye for an eye" payment for being insulted have meant the right to offer a responding insult?

mevušav, literally "his shameful (parts)." The rabbinic word for "insult" is *bošet*, literally "shame," which is formed from the same verbal root (*bûš*). Since actual situations of a woman seizing a man's genitals during his fight with her husband were surely extremely rare, the rabbis apparently saw no reason to push for its literal enforcement. This meant that they had at their disposal a verse they were free to requisition for other situations that did indeed occur with some frequency in all societies.[29]

In the Gemara, the *'Amoraim* realized that the plain meaning of Scripture had been set aside by the ruling of the Mishnah, forcing them (or leaving them at liberty!) to find a solution using the principle of *Qal va-Ḥomer*: "Just as in the case of smiting a beast monetary compensation is to be paid, so also in the case of smiting a man monetary compensation is to be paid."[30] A little later in the discussion, when the objection is raised once again that such a general softening of the eye-for-an-eye principle was not strictly defensible biblically, three intriguing examples were cited to show that a literal application of biblical law would be impossible in some cases and thus should be transvalued in all cases except murder. An initial example was given: "What then will you say where the eye of one was big and the eye of the other little, for how can I in this case apply the principle of eye for eye?" This example proved to be unsatisfying to the majority, and required a more explicit justification after the plain sense of Scripture was once again invoked. "What then would you say when a blind man put out the eye of another man, or a crippled man cut off the hand of another, or a lame person broke the leg of another? How can I carry out 'an eye for an eye' in such cases?"

It is necessary to notice in this discussion that two things occur, both of which were central in importance to the rabbis. On the one hand, the biblical plain sense was not ignored or treated as if it did not exist. Throughout the discussion a rigorous defense of the clear biblical intention of physical retaliation was presented by some, who were bothered

---

29. Although Roman Law can scarcely be demonstrated to have had an appreciable effect on either the rabbis or on Jesus, it is interesting that the Twelve Tables of Canonized Law in Rome spoke of three things that required reparation from an offender: a broken limb (*membrum ruptum*), a fractured bone (*os fractum*), or an injustice (*iniuria*). The first two involve physical damage, while the third corresponds to an "affront," and is used often in Cicero specifically of an insult. See Simpson, *Cassell's New Latin Dictionary*. We will take up this theme again in our examination of Jesus' treatment of the "eye for an eye" principle in chapter 6.

30. Here they cite Leviticus 24:18 as their justification. "One who takes the life of an animal shall make it good, life for life."

that movement beyond the *peshaṭ* of the Bible might be occurring without adequate hermeneutical justification. But on the other hand, even in the light of this objection and in spite of the plain biblical teaching, the majority ruling advanced reasons that were not biblical, but an outgrowth of the sensitivity of the rabbis to painful and harsh punishment. In some cases, imposition of comparable bodily injury would not be equitable, and in other cases such a punishment was simply deemed too harsh. A modern authority on Talmudic and biblical law has summarized this tension as follows, noting that the Talmudic masters whose discussions we have been considering, "thought that mutilation was unconscionable as a punishment. This testifies to their own sensibilities; they resorted to hermeneutic interpretation in a humane cause. This does not, however, alter the realities of biblical law in its original context, the realities of which the Talmudic sages may well have been aware."[31]

The Talmudic discussion then extended the principle of pecuniary compensation to include injuries of all sorts, building a system of monetary payments to be made for cases involving a wide variety of injuries. Each payment amount had to be determined with reference to specific facts that varied from injury to injury: the age and health of the injured party, the loss in economic earning power, the probable medical costs to be incurred, the intention of the guilty party, the social embarrassment of the injured party, etc. The long history in ancient Near Eastern law favoring monetary compensation over physical punishment[32] should serve as an indication that the rabbis did not create from nothing their system of monetary compensation for personal injury, but merely codified what had been long in practice throughout the ancient Mediterranean world. In particular, there is no evidence that eye-for-an-eye punishment was ever followed literally among Jews with the single exception of capital punishment cases. And it is also significant that one biblical passage discussing these laws of equivalency concluded with the following adjuration: "There shall be a single standard for you. It shall be for the resident alien as well as for the native" (Leviticus 24:22). This is the verse cited several times during the rabbinic discussion, sure testimony to their concern that an equitable system must be established. Still, their discussion shows how willing they were to move beyond a strictly literal sense, and

---

31. Levine, *JPS Leviticus*, 270.
32. See *Sarna, JPS*, 125–27.

highlights their commitment to the necessity of making classical sacred texts appropriate and relevant to their own day.

Homosexuality

The Talmudic view of homosexuality presents a third example of rabbinic transvaluation of clear biblical teaching. The biblical legislation regarding homosexuality is based upon Leviticus 18:22 and 20:13, where male-with-male sex is considered "abhorrent," and the penalty of death is prescribed for its practice. An early rabbinic commentary on Leviticus employed the rule of *Binyan 'Av*[33] to extend this prohibition to lesbianism, linking its argument to the general warning not to indulge in the abhorrent practices that were well known among the Egyptians and the Canaanites.[34] This concern is also reflected in the Gemara,[35] where the Rabbis rule that the Egyptian Potiphar purchased Joseph "for himself," a phrase which Rashi interpreted to mean that he wanted Joseph for purposes of homosexual activity.

An interesting Mishnaic discussion[36] records Rabbi Judah forbidding two bachelors to sleep together under one blanket, although the majority view of the *'Amoraim* appeared to be that there was no need for such a safeguard against homosexuality[37] because Jewish males were considered unlikely to engage in its practice.

Elsewhere in the rabbinic writings, various reasons are advanced for the strict ban on homosexuality. In one Talmudic discussion, the ban was regarded as a universal law included among the "Seven Commandments of the Sons of Noah."[38] Much later, homosexuality was also considered to be an unnatural perversion according to *Sefer ha-Ḥinnukh*,[39] 209, where the reasoning is that homosexual acts frustrate the procreative purpose of sex, just as do all other forms of "spilling the seed in vain."[40] According to

33. Rule number three of Rabbi Ishmael, discussed in chapter 3.
34. *Sifra* 9.8.
35. *Sotah* 13b.
36. *Kiddushin* 4:14.
37. *Kiddushin* 82a.
38. *Sanh.* 57b–58a.

39. A thirteenth century work by an anonymous scholar in Spain, who listed and explained the 613 "Commandments" believed by the rabbis to be contained in the Torah.

40. I.e., by masturbation or early withdrawal to prevent pregnancy.

yet another view, a homosexual man was believed to be likely to abandon his wife,[41] again circumventing the appropriate purpose of marriage.

It is with the question of the specific sin of the men of Sodom that two biblical prophets, followed by the rabbis, turned the discussion of homosexuality in completely new directions. In Genesis 19:5, the male citizens of Sodom demanded that Lot allow them to commit homosexual rape against his visitors, and were only prevented from carrying out their intentions by the miraculous intervention of the visitors themselves, who turned out to be divine messengers. Yet even so specific a phrase as that found in Genesis: "Bring them out to us so we may have sex with ["know"] them," received two interesting treatments from the biblical prophets Jeremiah and Ezekiel. Jeremiah 23:14 identified the sin of Sodom with adultery, false dealing, and refusal to turn evil-doers from their evil ways. Ezekiel 16:49–50 argued that "this was the iniquity of Sodom your sister: arrogance! She and her daughters had plenty of food and untroubled tranquility. Yet she did not support the poor and the needy. They became haughty and committed an abomination in My presence, so I removed them when I saw it." Thus already within the Bible, there was a movement to transvalue the plain wording of the Genesis text, or at the least, to ignore the implications of the homosexual demands made by the citizens of Sodom in an effort to focus on the more serious sin of inhospitality. And yet the observation of Ezekiel could be justified contextually in light of the fact that the narrative preceding the destruction of Sodom described the almost excessive hospitality of Abraham (Genesis 18) to the visitors who later appeared in Sodom. Whereas Abraham had sought to serve their needs for food and shelter during a journey, the people of Sodom reacted to them only as sexual objects that could be co-opted to satisfy their own lusts. Visitors to Abraham were treated with respect and civility. Visitors to Sodom not only were not treated graciously, they became the objects of intended rape.

This focus upon the social issue of hospitality was continued by the rabbis, with two Talmudic references of significance. The first occurs in the course of a discussion about a rigid attitude taken by some people who firmly held to the letter of the law in an attempt to avoid doing a positive and good (and thus more valuable) *mitzvah*. Such an attitude, taken

---

41. *Tos. Ned.* 51a.

regarding a variety of religious obligations totally unrelated to homosexuality, is defined as *middat Sedom,* or "[acting in] the manner of Sodom."[42]

The second passage that deals with the rabbinic or Talmudic perspective on Sodom is *Sanhedrin* 109a–b, where an extended and complex discussion is recorded. The Mishnaic discussion lists certain individuals (Jeroboam, Ahab, Manasseh, *inter alia*) and groups of people who have "no share in the world to come." Included in this latter category are "the generation of the Flood" and "the men of Sodom." In the Mishnah, the men of Sodom, called "wicked and great sinners against YHWH" (citing Genesis 13:13), were equated with the "sinners" who will not "stand . . . in the assembly of the righteous" (Psalm 1:5). The Gemara attached to this Mishnah interprets the description in Genesis 13:13 to refer both to sins of the body and to sins involving money. Then the rabbis linked the physical sin of the body to the predicament of Joseph described in Genesis 39:9, where the biblical reference is clearly to heterosexual adultery. Finally they linked sinning with money to Deuteronomy 15:9, where reference is made to the withholding of financial assistance from the poor.

In a further explanation, and almost as an aside, the *'Amoraim* equated Joseph's refusal to sin "before YHWH" as a reference to blasphemy, and linked the bloodshed of Manasseh to the specific word "exceedingly." Then they added several stories (*haggadot*) as further illustrations of the sinful activities of the men of Sodom. None of their *haggadot* pertained to homosexuality, but all of them portrayed a ruthless and crooked society that trampled the civilized standards of hospitality to strangers. To illustrate their conclusion, the rabbis recounted specific examples of thievery by trickery, bloody assault, unjust sentences by perverse judges, mistreatment of orphans and other powerless folk. The attitude underscored was the denial of food, sustenance, and protection to strangers.

In one instance, we are told, a young woman who was discovered bringing food in secret to a starving traveler was herself severely beaten. But the parade example of Sodomite wickedness was their custom of offering bricks of gold to strangers instead of food. After the death by starvation of the stranger, each individual could retrieve his own gold bricks because their names had been inscribed on them in advance to prepare for just such an eventuality.

---

42. *Ket.* 103a; *B. Bat.* 12b. Subsequently in the same discussion (*B. Bat.* 12b), it is argued that this phrase is being used to describe a man who refuses to confer a benefit, which costs him nothing.

It is clear that the rabbis were far more concerned about the general bloodiness and violence, the perversity of justice, etc., which they perceived in Sodom than merely about sexual deviation. In addition, as we have shown, they took what appears in the Bible as a sexual deviation and used it as an object lesson about the necessity of civilized treatment of strangers in a just society, drawing a sharp contrast between the destruction of Sodom in Genesis 19 and the warm hospitality to strangers exhibited by Abraham in Genesis 18. This should not be taken to imply that homosexuality was acceptable to the rabbis, but should certainly serve to illustrate its relative importance when weighed against injustice and bloodshed. Apropos of our subject, we observe once again that the rabbis did not hesitate to go beyond the Bible in order to teach truths that seemed to them more applicable to their own era and to their own personal moral code than the original biblical legislation.[43]

The Law of Prozbol

A fascinating passage in Deuteronomy opens with a blanket statement: "At the end of seven years, you must make remittance" (*shemiṭṭah*, literally, "dropping," "remitting"; Deut 15:1). The following verses clarify the exact nature of the remittance being commanded, specifying that every sabbatical year, unpaid *loans* were to be cancelled (15:1–2). But the biblical teaching was also aware that such a provision might trigger a negative result if people with capital refused to make risky loans in the latter years of the sabbatical cycle for fear that not enough time for repayment remained. And so an additional stipulation was added, admonishing lenders: "you must not harden your heart or close your hand to your poor brother; you must freely open your hand to him and lend him generously enough for his need, whatever he lacks" (15:7–8).

These provisions were clearly designed to make capital available to those who would not make a lender's "A" list, or who had "bad credit," as we might say. And yet, as a matter of practicality, exactly what Deuteronomy anticipated became the order of the day in post-biblical times. Early in the era of the *Tanna'im*, loans for the poor did in fact become unavailable, and people with money became reluctant to lend to the poor near the end of the recurring seven-year cycle. Into this difficult situation entered Rabbi Hillel, a great early *Tanna'*, seeking a legal way to

---

43. See my "Homosexuality, the Bible, and the Rabbis."

circumvent the apparently airtight biblical rule. His reasoning exhibits many of the classical examples of rabbinic hermeneutics.

First, Hillel noted that the context[44] of the biblical teaching involved loans to people who were virtually insolvent, people to whom it would be considered an act of charity to lend in the first place. In other words, the kinds of loans enjoined by the Bible were not sound business. With prospects of repayment so uncertain, and since such loans were acts of charity from the outset, Hillel ruled that cancellation of these debts should be viewed as an extension of the original charitable act instead of a business decision.

Second, Hillel appealed to the plain wording of Deuteronomy, the *peshat*, with the observation that the biblical law pertained only to *personal* debts, and did not apply to debts owed to the courts.[45] Therefore, if lenders transferred a personal loan to the courts that would then act as their legal agents, those loans would not fall under the biblical rule of cancellation.

Third, Hillel demonstrated that he was guided by concern for the greater good of the community as a whole, and sought a way to create the *result* at which the biblical teaching had aimed originally. While Deuteronomy had intended to make capital more widely available, practical considerations of money and business had turned its teaching into the exact opposite result: money became tighter and loans harder to obtain. In order to accomplish in fact what the Bible had prescribed in theory, Hillel instituted a simple legal procedure whereby a lender was required only to notify the court of his intention to continue collecting an outstanding debt, thereby making himself an agent of the court rather than a personal lender. This procedure was given the name *prozbol*, an abbreviation of the Greek phrase *proboule/bouleuton*, "searching for a decision." In the Mishnah, *prozbol* became a technical term used with reference to this innovation by Rabbi Hillel whereby registration of a loan with the courts exempted it from automatic cancellation in the Sabbatical year. Here is the Mishnaic wording:

"A *prozbol* is not cancelled. This is one of the things that Hillel the Elder ordained. When he saw that people stopped giving loans to each other and transgressed what is written in the Torah ("Beware that you do not harbor in your heart the base thought, 'the seventh year, the year of

---

44. Hermeneutical rule 13.

45. Note the words "neighbor" (twice) and "brother" in 15:2. By contrast, 15:3 stipulates that a lender could seek repayment from "a foreigner."

cancellation, is approaching,' so that you are hostile to your needy brother and give him nothing."), Hillel ordained the *Prozbol*."[46]

Following this simple explanation, the Mishnah gives the exact and legally binding wording composed by Hillel that must be used in making a formal declaration of *prozbol* before a court (10:4); a ruling about a post-dated *prozbol* (not legal) and an ante-dated one (legal) (10:5); and a decision about the way in which collateral must be handled (10:6). Lest it be argued that such a ruling was merely a tricky legal move aimed at dodging responsibility, we should emphasize the practical effect that the rule of *prozbol* was designed to produce. Few rulings produce benefit for all sides in a legal transaction, but the law of *prozbol* both benefited the rich by securing their capital, and helped the poor because it enabled them to borrow. A modern rabbi has answered the objection sometimes made by modern scholars, that Hillel need not have circumvented the Torah, but could simply have quoted the Bible to insist that people make loans to the poor because they needed help, whether they could repay or not. "Hillel wished to assist the poor, not to preach ineffectual sermons!"[47]

The lengthy Gemara discussing this ruling of Hillel is difficult to follow.[48] But several notable points of clarification are made by the 'Amoraim in their effort to justify the ruling of Hillel.

1. The reason that a *prozbol* debt may be collected after the seventh year was that a court has the power of expropriation. So an agent of the court (the actual lender) is not guilty of extortion when he acts to collect a debt legally owed to the court rather than to him as an individual.

2. Orphans may be lent money stretching past the seventh year without the formal declaration of *prozbol*. The interesting rationale for this ruling is that one of the leading *Tanna'im*, Rabban Gamaliel, was the adopting parent of an orphan.

3. Collateral liens may be placed on virtually worthless property, including a flower pot, or even one branch of a carob tree. While it might seem unusually pedantic to take as collateral something with no monetary value, the legal point being protected was that only a secured loan was eligible for *prozbol*. This also underscored the

---

46. *Shevi'it* 10:3.
47. Telushkin, *Jewish Literacy*, 121.
48. *Gittin* 36b, 37a–b.

fact that the rules of lending to the poor were not designed to cover superfluous loans or loans for non-essential purposes. Rather, the kinds of loans in question were those to a farmer who needed seed or provisions, to a person who had lost a job and needed to support his family, or to someone who faced a crisis of illness or disability.[49]

4. A bond for debt could serve as collateral for a *prozbol* loan, but because a bond is not a loan, it did not come under the provision of *shemittah*. Therefore, a bond serving as collateral for a loan that had to be cancelled was not itself cancelled as a result. This final provision kept open the possibility that a more well-to-do relative or friend might allow a bond to be used as collateral for a loan to a poor person who lacked even a small amount of property or any other form of the collateral that would qualify that loan for *prozbol*.

Divine Mercy and Retribution

Exodus 34:6–7[50] attests the most complete formulaic statement of the attributes of God in the Bible. In the immediate context, the formula was offered in response to the request of Moses to God in the aftermath of the sinful golden calf episode: "If I have found favor in Your eyes, please make me know Your ways" (33:13). Very early, Rabbi Yohanan argued[51] that "God's recital of His moral qualities was intended to set the pattern for Israel's future petitions to God,"[52] leading to a prominent role for the oral recital of the formula in liturgy.[53]

Clearly the biblical formula contains both a positive (divine compassion, forgiveness, faithfulness, etc.) and a negative (punishment and

---

49. See the discussion by Tigay, *The JPS Torah Commentary*, 145.

50. "The Lord! The Lord! A God compassionate and gracious, slow to anger, abounding in kindness and faithfulness, extending kindness to the thousandth generation, forgiving iniquity, transgression, and sin; yet He does not remit all punishment, but visits the iniquity of parents upon children and children's children, upon the third and fourth generations" (*JPS*).

51. *Rosh ha-Shanah* 17b.

52. Sarna, *Exodus*, 216.

53. Most notably during the High Holy Days and as part of the *Seliḥôt*, the penitential prayers recited on days of trouble (including fast days), especially during the month of *Elul* and the first days of the month of *Tishri* leading up to Yom Kippur. The formula is also recited aloud when the Torah scroll is taken from the ark on festivals and holy days, except Shabbat.

retribution) category. Yet the wording chosen for the liturgy omitted all reference to the negative, an idea integral to any fair reading of the biblical formula. In fact, the liturgical wording actually changes a biblical negative ("[God] does *not* remit [punishment]") into a positive ("[God] *does* remit"). This transvaluation, achieved only by reading into the Bible a meaning it clearly does not bear, was so radical as to appear shocking, leading the scholar Jacob Milgrom to ask: "What has given the rabbis such audacious, indeed scandalous, license?"[54] To be sure, as Milgrom notes, the rabbis had in hand ample biblical precedents[55] for the citation of only that part of the full Exodus formula that underscores the mercy of God.[56] Yet for our purposes, the rabbinic transvaluation of this classic biblical formula of divine attributes, even based upon inner-biblical precedents, serves as a clear illustration of the stunning freedom with which the rabbis approached biblical exegesis. Their transvaluation was not based upon grammatical exegesis, or a *peshat* reading, but upon their view of the liturgical needs of the community at worship.

Conclusion

Additional examples of rabbinic transvaluation could easily be adduced. But the samples chosen above are sufficient to indicate the spirit and the methods that governed rabbinic discussion and exegesis. The rabbis believed that their interpretations were faithful to the biblical text. But in their hands, teachings that had originated in a specific context and for particular purposes were shaped to address their generation with its changing political and religious climate. The examples just cited should not be taken as evidence that one or more of the thirteen principles of Rabbi Ishmael were always used slavishly in every examination of a biblical passage. What is significant is rather that the thirteen are illustrative of the wide-ranging freedom arrogated by the rabbis to themselves. All of the examples cited indicate that underlying all hermeneutical rules was the principle that their own common sense, ideological needs, and spiritual sensitivity not only could but should be brought to bear on the

---

54. Milgrom, *Numbers*, 393.

55. Num. 14:18; Jer. 32:18; Joel 2:13; Jonah 4:2; Nah. 1:3; Pss. 86:15, 103:8; Neh. 9:17 (the form chosen for the *Vidduy* prayer on Yom Kippur).

56. Milgrom's full treatment of the biblical formula and its transvaluation (*Numbers*, 392–96) is masterful.

text. They were often influenced by social or political reality that could make a plain-sense reading impossible or simply undesirable. But they appear to have been guided by the conviction that to abandon the text to a single meaning that had become outdated or that violated acceptable cultural norms was not to honor but to dishonor the sacredness of their source book. Respect for the text of the Bible and their belief that it was somehow timelessly true never meant for them that Scripture was inflexible and unbending.

6

New Testament and Early Christian Transvaluation

IN THIS CHAPTER WE will examine specific examples of the fact that just as the Jewish rabbis did not view the Bible as an abstract, static deposit of truth given by God from the outset in full and complete form, neither did the New Testament writers. It is important to note that the influence of the LXX, the Pseudepigrapha, and writers like Josephus and Philo extended to the early interpretative work done within Christianity, affecting it much as it had rabbinic Judaism. It also bears repeating that Christian sages were interpreting the same Bible that had formed the starting point for rabbinic exegesis.

The examples below show clearly that just as the rabbis created reformulations of ancient biblical principles, so too did the NT writers. It will also become apparent that just as the rabbis accorded to their own work in the Talmud the status of authority equal to that of Scripture, the church ultimately elevated the writings of the NT authors to a status fully equal to that of the Bible they had adopted as their own, their "Old" Testament.[1] In other words, neither group accepted the idea that they might be inventing truth not already contained in the standard sacred text revered by them both. As we saw in chapters 3 and 5 that the rabbis thought of their work as "repetition" of biblical truth in modern terms, so now we will see that the NT went to great lengths to tie itself firmly to the same Bible the rabbis sought to honor, both groups employing the principle of

---

1. See especially Hebrews 1:1–2.

transvaluation freely and without apology. That is to say, although both the rabbis and the NT authors were aware of the radical nature of some of their conclusions, both remained convinced that they were articulating what the Bible had taught all along. In their minds, they were not inventing truth; they believed they were recovering meaningful teaching from the deep layers of their biblical repository, interpretations that had been there all along. In their respective arenas, the rabbis and the NT writers believed that they were the ones who "saw" them for the first time.

Additionally, the examples cited throughout this chapter will raise awareness of yet another similarity between the rabbis and the NT authors, namely the dynamic interaction between their personal convictions and the varied circumstances in which they lived and wrote, circumstances that were time- and event-specific in the post-biblical world of both groups. Finally, we will note that both groups believed deeply in *universal* principles that were necessary to interpret *particular* expressions of their beliefs, especially when those expressions were demanded by historical developments beyond their control and beyond the reach of plain truth biblical statements.

General New Testament Transvaluations

The Virgin Birth

The treatment of the Virgin Birth serves as a primary example of transvaluation flexibility, and testifies to the freedom that NT authors granted themselves to reconstruct the Bible in a way that served their special ideological needs. To deal with the burning question of how Jesus became God, one can scarcely imagine a more powerful tool than a biography founded upon a birth narrative designed to explain the deity of Jesus by means of the patrimony of the divine Holy Spirit. Yet here, for all its desire to base itself upon the Hebrew Scriptures, the need for early Christianity to articulate a Virgin Birth concept ran into a solid roadblock. There is nowhere in the Hebrew Scriptures, or indeed anywhere in Second Temple Judaism/Judaism, anything that may serve as justification for what appears in Matthew and Luke as unambiguous doctrine.

The Hebrew Bible indeed has its own miraculous birth narratives relating especially to Isaac (Genesis 18:1–20; 21:1–3) and later to Samuel (1 Samuel 1:1–20). But the natural birth credited to a one-hundred-year-old father and a ninety-year-old mother does not address the question of the *divinity* of the child thus produced. What is more, the very idea of sexual union between divine and human beings is bluntly denounced by the same book of Genesis in which we learn about Abraham and Sarah and Isaac,[2] a denunciation greatly expanded in the First Book of Enoch, composed only slightly earlier than the NT. This may explain why the concept of a son born from Mary, "conceived from the Holy Spirit" (Matthew 1:20) did not become a major topic for all writers of the NT narratives about Jesus. Neither the earliest gospel, Mark, nor the latest one, John, appears to know anything of a virgin birth. In fact, while Mark was silent on the question of the virginal birth of Jesus, implying that the idea was unknown or at the least unimportant to him, John contravened the idea of divine impregnation directly, reporting that Philip testified to Nathaniel about "Jesus of Nazareth, the son of Joseph" (1:45).

Peter does not mention the Virgin Birth in any of his sermons recorded in Acts, and Paul authored two statements that directly contradict the idea of a virgin birth, describing Jesus in Galatians 4:4 as "born of a woman,"[3] and in Romans 1:3 as "born from the sperm of David,"[4] before noting in the following verse that this person born by entirely natural means "was appointed to be[5] the Son of God ... via the resurrection from the dead." In other words, the resurrection, not a miraculous birth, made Jesus unique and *divine* for Paul.

We are left with the books of Matthew and Luke to puzzle out the NT presentation of a virgin birth for their messiah. In Luke, the wording in the birth narrative proper (1:34) is not only clear but includes the traditional expression used often in the Hebrew Bible to emphasize virginity, quoting the recently pregnant Mary asking, "How can this be, since I have not known a man?"[6] So it is doubly surprising to read elsewhere in Luke of "his father and mother" (2:33), to hear Mary describe Joseph to Jesus as "your father" (2:48), and to note the description of Mary and Joseph as "his parents" (2:41). While such references may simply reflect Luke's citation of a source from which he was working to compile his gospel, his decision to include them surely detracts from the weight he gave to his own virgin birth narrative.

2. See Genesis 6:1–9.

3. The operative phrase in Greek is *gegomenon ek gynaikos*, avoiding the *parthenos* of Matthew 1:23.

4. *gegomenou ek spermatos David*.

5. *oristhentos* from *oristhein*, "to constitute, appoint."

6. I have discussed many of these matters in "Does the Gospel of Matthew," 18–52.

This leaves the Gospel of Matthew, whose birth account contains several details of note. First, the name of the mother of Jesus is hellenized from *Miryam* (Miriam) to Mary. The *Miryam* of the Bible did not derive her fame as the consort of a powerful male, but was a powerful and assertive character in her own right. She was given credit for lightning-quick thinking that saved the life of her infant brother,[7] and later opposed Moses at the height of his power.[8] What is more, she received the referentially powerful title "prophetess" in a passage that includes an ancient poem, at least part of which she herself had composed (Exodus 15:20–21). If a powerful woman were needed as a role model for the mother of Jesus, it is hard to imagine a more attractive candidate than *Miryam*. Perhaps Matthew may have been influenced by the need to avoid any confusion between the mother of Jesus and the favorite wife of evil Herod the baby-killer. But his depiction of Mary has the result of pushing the woman, even the mother of God herself, into the background in favor of the men in her life.

This leads to a second point. Not only was Jesus more important than Mary, even her husband Joseph, who played no role in the conception of Jesus, was given the significant title "a righteous man"[9] elsewhere (Matthew 1:19). By contrast, Mary herself is deemed by Luke to be "favored" or "blessed,"[10] a far less rigorous term than "righteous."

Still, this one-time-only title for Joseph hardly compensated for the way he was treated otherwise in the gospel narratives. Mark (6:3) left out all reference to him in describing Jesus and his siblings, having Jews who were astonished at his wisdom pointedly call Jesus "the carpenter [*ho tekton*], Mary's son." Such a designation indicated the tendency on the part of some to question the legitimacy of the birth of one whose human patrimony was unknown. Accordingly, Matthew deftly amended Mark's words to have the Jews who were astonished at the wisdom of Jesus describe him as "the carpenter's son" (*ho tou tektonos huios*) in 13:55, despite the fact that the human patrimony of Joseph undermined his own account of the birth of Jesus from Mary and the Holy Spirit. On the other hand, that Matthew seemed here to call Jesus the son of Joseph, as both Luke and John did, was consistent with the carefully crafted genealogy

---

7. See my "The Feminine Touch."

8. Unsuccessfully, to be sure. See Numbers 12.

9. Greek *dikaios* is used often in the LXX to translate the powerful Hebrew word *tzaddiq*.

10. *kecharitomene* in Luke 1:28.

designed to highlight the Davidic ancestry of Jesus traced through the family of Joseph (Matthew 1:1–17).[11]

Third, regardless of how one views Matthew and Luke, whether they were Hellenized Jews or merely Gentiles conversant with the LXX, the remarkable fact here is this. The freedom felt by these two gospel writers to create a text that was either unknown to or deemed insignificant by other early Christian writers (Paul, Mark, John), and one that bears no connection to the Hebrew Bible itself, falls squarely within the same referential field we have observed functioning among the rabbis who created Judaism from biblical Yahwism/Judahism.

And yet even this radical teaching sought its link with the Bible, when Matthew cited a text from Isaiah detailing the birth of a biblical child whose significance Isaiah had witnessed amidst the eighth-century BCE morass of Assyrian, Syro-Israelite, Judahite politics.[12] By linking the passage from Isaiah with the birth of Jesus, Matthew both created a new text and avoided a prickly problem with a single brilliant stroke. Surely Matthew did not believe that the birth described by Isaiah had been virginal, for that would have required two virgin births, thereby undermining the unique claim to divinity for Jesus. Rather, Matthew was doing what the *Tanna'itic* rabbis did routinely in their creation of the text of the Mishnah, and more explicitly what the later *'Amoraim* would do in linking individual *mishnayot* to biblical authority. Using an isolated word from Isaiah, Matthew transvalued an ancient text to provide the basis for his ideological needs, operating with the same assurance of authority that informed the rabbis. In order for the ancient text to achieve and maintain meaning and relevance to people of a new faith in the first century CE, it needed to be reformulated and radically reconstructed for a new and specific context of which eighth-century BCE Isaiah could never have dreamed.[13]

---

11. Although the genealogy leading to Joseph would certify Jesus as a Davidide, the following paragraph in Matthew asserting that Joseph had played no role in the conception of the son of Mary (Matthew 1:18–25) is impossible to square with such a fact.

12. As has been shown repeatedly, his appropriation of Isaiah 7:14 does not bear the weight of an argument that Mary was *virgo intacta*. See my, "Does the Gospel of Matthew," and the references there.

13. Matthew's version does not address the fact that the language of Isaiah 7:14 is not a predictive future tense, but refers to an impregnation that had already happened when Isaiah spoke to King Ahaz. Hebrew *ha-'almah harah və-yoledet ben* is clearly a past tense statement: "The young woman has [already] become pregnant, and is [in

The Resurrection of Jesus

The virgin birth that begins the life and the resurrection that follows the death of Jesus are the two trickiest issues in the NT, and it is significant that both topics fail to receive a singular unified theological explanation among all the writers of the NT. The earliest NT treatment of the resurrection is that of Paul, found in 1 Corinthians 15, an authentic Pauline epistle composed well before the destruction of the Jerusalem Temple. As we have noted above, for Paul, the divinity and power of Jesus were certified by the resurrection rather than by the virginal birth. Thus it is of great significance that in dealing with what he perceived to be the central event of the Jesus story, Paul never indicated in any of his writings a belief in the *physical* resurrection of Jesus. For him, the resurrection was a mystical, spiritual event. In general terms, that is, not limited to Jesus alone, the physical body of even the average person, "is sown as a natural body, but it is raised as a spiritual body" (1 Cor 15:44). This led naturally to the conclusion Paul reached at the end (15:50): "flesh and blood cannot inherit the kingdom of God." That the term "spiritual body" is difficult to imagine was admitted freely by Paul: "Look, I am speaking a *mystery* to you" (15:51).[14]

This Pauline perspective on the spiritual aspect of the resurrection of Jesus is mirrored in three of the gospels. Mark assumed that Jesus was capable of morphing into an alternate form and materializing at will among his disciples (16:12). Luke described Jesus as capable of invisible movement (24:15–16), and reported in Acts that Jesus levitated into the air (1:9). In a similar vein, John described Jesus as a disembodied spirit that could pass through locked doors (20:19).

But the gospels also contain another perspective, one lacking in Paul. Mark described an empty tomb (16:8), clearly implying that the physical body of Jesus was now absent. Matthew, who omitted references to a spiritual dimension of the resurrection, described a physical Jesus who could be detained when his feet were grasped (28:9). Luke described the order of Jesus to his amazed disciples: "Handle me and see. A spirit does not have flesh and bones as you see that I have" (24:39). And John portrayed Jesus offering the ultimate proof of his physical resurrection to

---

the process of] bearing a son."

14. Akenson (*Surpassing Wonder*, 254) sees a link between Paul's view of the spiritual resurrection of Jesus and the fate of Enoch and Elijah in the Hebrew Scriptures. The link is not obvious to me. Neither Enoch nor Elijah was reported to have died!

Thomas by instructing him to insert his fingers into the nail holes in his hands and the spear hole in his side (20:19).

It is beyond the scope of our investigation to seek to harmonize these two different views of the resurrection of Jesus. Surely the gospel accounts of Jesus having raised three dead people physically[15] were designed to illustrate his power over physical death. And biblical precedents for such miracles were available from the lives of Elijah (1 Kings 17:21–23) and Elisha (2 Kings 4:32–37).[16]

In short, by arguing for the physical nature of the resurrection of Jesus, the gospel writers could find adequate precedent in their own textbook, the "Old" Testament.[17] But Paul clearly has the better of the argument here, for the first time that a Christian believer died without being raised again physically, the gospel emphasis on physical resurrection would have lost much of its appeal. Only a spiritual resurrection (which could be neither proved nor disproved) could serve as a universal paradigm offering hope to believers in the new religion that they too could experience a similar fate. Here too we find a point of similarity with Judaism. Paul, himself a Pharisee at one time, and the rabbis shared this perspective about the doctrine of resurrection, which neither he nor they expected immediately upon death. Although the rabbis seem not to have anticipated an imminent eschatological judgment, as did Paul, and offered no discussion about how soon after death such a judgment might occur, their conviction that an eschatological judgment followed by resurrection was congruent with what Paul expressed.

The Ten Commandments

As we saw earlier in our discussion of Matthew's Sermon on the Mount, the NT treatment of the Ten Commandments provides a textbook example of the general nature of NT flexibility in transvaluation, demonstrating again that the freedom and authority the rabbis had arrogated to

---

15. The twelve-year-old daughter of Jairus (in all three synoptics), the adult son of a widow who lived in Nain (only Luke 7:12–15), and Lazarus, a member of his inner circle from Bethany (John 11:43–44).

16. In fact, Elisha had retained his power over physical death long after his own burial (2 Kings 13:20–21)! Of course, neither of these two great Hebrew prophets were resurrected, and neither became the pattern by which their disciples could hope for their own resurrection.

17. Except perhaps in the late book of Daniel (12:2), which they do not cite.

themselves in their reconstruction of the Bible also devolved to interpreters of the new faith.

The New Testament does not include a listing of the Ten Commandments in their complete form, following either Exodus or Deuteronomy. "However, the individual precepts of the decalogue are more frequently cited in the NT than they are in the OT."[18] Further, in addition to the changes suggested by Jesus in Matthew 5, the NT citation of the Hebrew Ten often contains subtle variants. As we saw in examining the variants between Exodus 20 and Deuteronomy 5, it is not that these variants are substantive but that they occur at all that is significant. In Matthew 19,[19] Jesus responded to a question about how to inherit "eternal life" (16) with a short answer, "If you wish to enter into life, keep the commandments" (17), which he then proceeded to list. Five of the commandments mentioned by Jesus are part of the biblical Ten, but a sixth is not. "You will love your neighbor as yourself" is a citation from Leviticus 19:18.

Paul, who elsewhere argued the impossibility of fulfilling the Torah, stated in Romans 13:8 that "he who loves his neighbor has fulfilled the Law," and noted in 13:10 that, "love is the fulfillment of the Law." In this short pericope, Paul also mentioned four of the Ten Commandments specifically, three of which he shared with those chosen by Jesus (adultery, murder, stealing). He then added a commandment not mentioned by Jesus (coveting), before citing Leviticus 19:18 as Jesus had done.[20]

The book of James is yet a third NT source that juxtaposed Leviticus 19:18 alongside the biblical Ten Commandments, sounding quite Pauline in the assertion that loving one's neighbor as oneself actually "fulfills the royal Law" (2:8). Clearly, not only Jesus, but Paul and James as well, arrogated to themselves the freedom not only to cite some but not all of the Ten Commandments, but to interpret their overall meaning as well.[21]

18. Collins, "Ten Commandments," *ABD* 6:386.

19. See also Mark 10:17–31 and Luke 18:18–30.

20. Jesus included the honoring of parents and the bearing of false witness, which Paul omitted. In Ephesians 6:1–4, Paul cited the honoring of parents from Deuteronomy, but included the phrase, "that it may be well with you," absent from Exodus.

21. Following the path hinted at in the NT itself, our own day has witnessed an Alabama judge making a federal case [sic!] out of his insistence that the "Ten Commandments" should be posted in a building dedicated to the search for justice in "Christian" America. Yet in none of the discussions about the issue has anyone addressed the fact that Christians, including the judge himself, have radically altered the meaning of the words of "Moses" to ancient Israel, fitting them into modern clothing, transvaluing them to fit the context and social needs of the Christian faith.

Post-New Testament Christianity undertook the transvaluation of the Ten Commandments in four distinct ways. First, all of Catholicism and virtually all of Protestantism hold dear the divinity of Jesus, despite the unmistakable meaning of, "There will be for you no other gods in My presence," and despite the examples of prophets like Elijah on Mount Carmel[22] that demonstrate how radically this commandment worked when read literally.[23]

Second, a visit to any Catholic and almost any Protestant church will show how often transgressed is the absolute prohibition against creating an "image" of the deity who gave the Ten Commandments (again, assuming that deity to have been Jesus).

Third, Christianity shows no regard to statements scattered throughout the Bible about the eternally binding force of Shabbat observance.[24] With neither a biblical ("Old" Testament) nor a New Testament warrant for it, the biblical Shabbat became Christian Sunday, which Christian worshippers around the world still call "Sabbath," assuming as they worship on that day that they are keeping one of the Ten Commandments.

Fourth, the Hebrew commandment, "Never commit murder" (*lô' tirtzaḥ*) is not a generic reference to all killing, but the specific prohibition of willful murder.[25] This raises the important question as to whether the

22. See 1 Kings 18, especially verse 40!

23. Note the following statement from Martin Luther: "If I had power over the Jews, I would assemble the best and most learned among them and, under penalty of having their tongues cut out, would force them to accept the Christian teaching that there is not one God, but three Gods." Cited in Ozick, "The Modern 'Hep! Hep! Hep!'" "Hep" stands for *Hierosolyma est perdita*. Ozick does not cite the original reference in the works of Luther.

24. For example, in Exodus 31:16–17, there is an apodictic injunction, included in all versions of Jewish prayer books: "The children of Israel must guard the Sabbath, observing Sabbath throughout their generations as a covenant forever. This is a sign forever between Me and the children of Israel."

25. The Alabama judge doubtless knows the modern American legal distinctions that must be drawn to delineate murder in the first degree, second degree, vehicular homicide, involuntary manslaughter, and even accidental homicide, etc. Yet in the version of the Ten Commandments that he wished to post publicly, the Hebrew text that prohibits murder without stipulating its penalty is simply transvalued into English "thou shalt not kill." Such a translation, which misses the point of the Hebrew text, can be, and indeed has been, used to argue against everything from abortion to participation in a war. All finer legal distinctions, so well known and so necessary to the American system of justice, must be drawn from outside the biblical text of the Ten Commandments, and cannot be linked to biblical authority. Thus it is that a Christian judge sincerely reads the words of Exodus 20, hearing as he reads not

NT reformulation of the biblical Ten Commandments can be defended. And the answer must be in the affirmative. We need only remember the numerous examples of the rabbis going beyond a clear biblical statement in order to communicate with people of their own day—abandoning corporeal punishment because of its harshness, transferring debts from an individual to a lender, etc.—because they believed such teachings no longer applied in the context of their world. When the NT writers extended and amplified specific commandments, they disclose a similar perspective. If Jesus was divine yet visible in human form, offering an artistic depiction of him does not run the risk that the biblical injunction seeks to avoid. For the NT writers and their later interpreters, Jesus was not a false idol, worship of whose image would lure people away from the one true God. He was/became God.

Similarly, the concept of setting aside one day in seven for spiritual renewal and worship need not be tied to the story of an exodus to freedom provided by God for a group of people with whom increasing numbers of new Christians had no connection. Day seven could thus be switched to day one, in the process making a clear connection to an event with which all Christians easily identify. It was "on the first day of the week" (Matthew 28:1 and parallels) that the empty tomb was discovered in witness to the fact of the resurrection of Jesus. If Christians were to be "grafted in" (Romans 10:17) and thus included in the universal plan of God for salvation, it is only natural that they should have availed themselves of the new history of divine deeds on their behalf. The conclusions of the two groups were different, but the path followed to reach those conclusions was very much the same.

Manna

After the death of Jesus, the metaphorical or spiritual dimensions of the teachings of Jesus came to be underscored by the early Church. A passage

---

an ancient Israelite context, but his own twenty-first-century understanding of the Christian meaning of those words. Whether this Christian reading of Moses is "true" or not is beyond the scope of our discussion here. The point is simply that this particular reading of the Ten Commandments is a transvaluation that serves the needs of the church, while the interpretative freedom called upon to meet those needs goes unnoticed and undiscussed in one of the most public debates of our day. Indeed, we suspect that the judge and his backers have convinced themselves that they are reading the Bible literally.

in John 6:48–51 quotes an oral teaching of Jesus to illustrate this new mode of interpretation: "I am the bread of life. Your fathers ate the manna in the wilderness, and they died. This is the bread which comes down out of heaven, so that one may eat of it and not die. I am the living bread that came down out of heaven; if anyone eats of this bread, he shall live forever; and the bread that I give for the life of the world is *my flesh*."

That this was an incomprehensible position to the average Jew of the day is indicated by the following verses: "The Jews argued with each other, saying 'How can this man give us flesh to eat'?" (6:52), eliciting the following response: "So Jesus said to them, 'I tell you the truth, unless you eat the flesh of the son of man and drink his blood, you have no life in yourselves. Whoever eats my flesh and drinks my blood has eternal life, and I will raise him up on the last day'" (6:53–54). Few modern NT scholars believe that Jesus spoke the words here ascribed to him by John, especially the accusation that the Jews believed he was advocating eating human flesh and drinking human blood. The role of the Jews in this passage was created by John as a parade example of the ways in which "Jews" consistently failed to grasp the true meaning of the teachings of Jesus. In John, Jesus routinely spoke on a metaphorical, spiritual level, but those around him, including his own disciples, took his words literally and repeatedly failed to understand his true intention. We note for example, the dialogue between Jesus and Nicodemus (John 3) about the concept of becoming "born again" (literally "from above"), or his dialogue with the Samaritan woman (John 4) on the subject of "living water."[26] That his own disciples failed to grasp the spiritual dimension of his teachings is illustrated graphically in Acts 1:6. Even after the dramatic death and resurrection of their master, and after having been in dialogue with him in his resurrected form, his closest followers still wondered when he planned to restore *political* independence to Israel, apparently with no thought of a kingdom that was "not of this world" (see John 18:36).

The manna episode to which John alludes is in Exodus 16:12–36, a story centered around the fact that the food sent miraculously by God to the people was a substance that no one recognized and whose identification was unknown: "When the Israelites saw it, they said to each other 'What is it' [*man hû'*], because they did not know what it was."[27] For John

26. My colleague Delbert Burkett suggested these two examples.

27. In fact, *man hu'* may be either standard biblical Aramaic spelling of "what" (*man*); or a dialectic variant of classical Hebrew *mah hû'*, used here as "folk etymology" to explain the following phrase. In either case, it is clear that the escapees from

to have Jesus offer a specific explanation of *man hû'* (manna) radically reformulated the biblical story that describes a substance so miraculous as to be impossible to identity. Taking the Exodus story at face value, the identification of manna as any specific substance was surprising, and to equate manna with the physical body of Jesus was indeed incomprehensible to a Jewish audience. But it was the eating of manna in the wilderness that had sustained the ancient Israelites, making possible a later entry into the land of promise. The New Testament interpretation here identifies Christian participation in the Eucharist as the guarantee of resurrection in the future. A "particular" from the biblical story yields a "general" principle in the NT. A one-time event in the wilderness leads to a general premise about the providence of God in this life and the hope of resurrection in the next. Thus the story of manna is given new life by John, taking advantage of a well-established principle to stretch it well outside its original boundaries in the book of Exodus, a principle used often by the rabbis living in the same time frame.

Jesus and "An Eye for an Eye"

In chapter 5, we examined the rabbinic transvaluation of the "eye for an eye" concept in Scripture, noting that rather than brutal bodily punishment in kind, monetary compensation became the accepted legal response of the rabbis to physical injuries. We also saw that the rabbis delineated five different gradations for which a victim could claim compensation, noting that while the first four of these grades dealt with actual physical injury, the fifth concerned insult. These rabbinic distinctions prepare us to re-examine the view of Jesus about the *lex talionis*.

In the fifth of his six reformulations of OT principles ("You have heard that it was said . . . but I say to you") discussed in chapter 4, Matthew offered the teaching of Jesus about the "eye for an eye, tooth for a tooth" principle. His interpretation is only partially related to the "eye for an eye" idea, because he made no comment about the rules concerning actual physical injury, that is, four-fifths of what had concerned the rabbis. Instead, he went straight to the issue of insult. His examples in verses 39–41 (a slap in the face, granting a coat as well as merely a shirt, or going two miles instead of one) do not involve physical injury. They are all three insulting, all three violate an individual's "rights" and sense of

---

Egypt had no clue as to the identity of the substance they were eating.

personal space, and all three are calculated to provoke an angry response. But they do not involve physical damage.[28] As we saw, the rabbinic ruling provided that monetary compensation could be sought for such insults as well as for actual injuries. The opinion of Jesus offered by Matthew was also known to the rabbis, and had been advanced by Gamaliel II, the grandson of the rabbi who had been Paul's teacher according to Luke: "if you are struck, you must forgive the offender even if he does not ask your forgiveness."[29]

In sum, since the three examples mentioned by Matthew[30] all focused upon the aspect of insults that are personally degrading or humiliating rather than upon physical injury, the gospel principle attributed to Jesus achieves broad application. Paul, writing to Christians in 1 Corinthians 6:1–7, speaks specifically about "brother against brother" lawsuits that must not be aired in the presence of "the unrighteous" (vs. 1) or "unbelievers" (vs. 6). For Paul, such an incident was a defeat for everyone involved. But Jesus may have had something different in mind. In his day, the presence of Rome was underscored in numerous ways. With soldiers stationed throughout the region and Roman judges deciding cases according to Roman law, Jews were vassals who had little chance of winning in a clash with a Roman authority. Thus while Jesus may have wished to have Jews avoid seeing their personal disputes dragged into a foreign court, he may also have deemed it foolish to strike out against a foe whom one could not defeat under the circumstances. And while he did not mention forgiving those who act to insult or humiliate a person, as Gamaliel had done, his counsel was probably intended to forestall the possibility of a spiral that, beginning with a small insult, might end in violence or a Roman court.

The New Testament Treatment of Isaiah 40:3

John the Baptist is quite an enigmatic figure in the New Testament. The descriptions of his activities within the gospels themselves indicate someone of no little importance, and this impression of John is buttressed by the fact that he is also mentioned favorably in the writings of Josephus,

---

28. Unless, of course, a "slap" became a punch intended to injure.
29. My paraphrase of *Tosephta Baba Qamma* 9:29.
30. And Luke in 6:29–30.

outside the pages of the New Testament.[31] In fact, it is not pressing the evidence to assert that in his day, John was more famous than Jesus, and the fact that Jesus submitted to a public baptism at the hands of John doubtless posed a problem for the later gospel portrayals of Jesus as the divine messiah. Accordingly, it is not surprising that each gospel writer sought for some way to subordinate John to Jesus. To this end, all four gospels[32] identified John with Elijah, the biblical prophet whose role was to prepare the way for the coming of "the great and fearful day of the Lord" (see Malachi 3:23, English 4:5).

Luke employed the most detailed accounts about John and Jesus together, each detail serving to underscore the subordination of John to Jesus. 1) While the birth of John was miraculous, yet his conception was "normal" (1:24), compared to the miraculous virginal conception of Mary with Jesus (1:34–35); 2) when Mary greeted the mother of John, Elizabeth, the fetus soon to be born as John leapt for joy in the womb of his mother (1:41, 44); 3) while John was a prophet in the great tradition of Elijah (1:17, and see also 1:76), Jesus was "the son of the most high God" (1:32). But while Luke included the most details, the Gospel of John was no less clear that Jesus outranked John, and ultimately offered the plainest expression of all from the mouth of John himself: "It is necessary that he must increase but I must decrease" (3:30).

Now the persistent linkage of John the Baptist with Elijah is quite odd in light of the Baptizer's specific denial in John 1:21. When asked by Jewish priests and Levites, "Are you Elijah?" John answered simply, "I am not." But all four gospels agree that in responding to other questions about his identity, John quoted from Isaiah 40:3: "[I am] the voice of one crying in the desert, 'Prepare the way of the Lord, make his paths straight.'"[33] Placing this particular verse in the mouth of John the Baptist created a clear link with the gospel depictions of John exercising his prophetic role in the wilderness of Judea, showing him to be radically alienated from normal society by wearing odd clothing and eating exotic foods (see Mark 1:4–6 and parallels).

It should be noted that the Hebrew text of Isaiah 40:3 does not describe a voice in the wilderness, but rather a voice (presumably the Babylonian "Isaiah" himself) beseeching the exiles to prepare for the Lord an

---

31. The pertinent passage is his *Antiquities*, 18.5.2, paragraphs 116–19.
32. Mark 1:6; 9:11–13; Matthew 11:7–15; 17:9–13; Luke 3:16; John 1:8.
33. Mark 1:3; Matthew 3:3; Luke 3:4; John 1:22.

appropriate highway in (or through) the wilderness over which a return to Jerusalem could be undertaken. However, no such problem exists in the LXX rendition of Isaiah 40:3, which may be read either as the Hebrew text indicates or exactly as the NT writers understand it. Still, identifying John, the forerunner of Jesus, with a famous text from Isaiah prepared the way for the single most noteworthy link in the gospels between Jesus and the Hebrew Scriptures, again a concept located in the book of Isaiah. To this link we now turn.

The New Testament Messiah and the Suffering Servant of Isaiah

Some of the most elegant poetry in the entire Hebrew Bible is found in chapters 40–66 of the book of Isaiah, written by an anonymous author who was probably a member of the "school" of the great eighth-century Isaiah of Jerusalem.[34] Scattered within this larger corpus, sometimes placed seemingly awkwardly, are four poems dealing with the "servant of the Lord" (*'eved YHWH*).[35] While the NT made extended use of the "servant songs," it did not do so with reference to the main theme of chapters 40–55, the encouragement of the Judean exiles in Babylon. This encouraging message of the prophet was accomplished with close reference to the policies of Cyrus of Persia, who supported a Judean return to Jerusalem and furnished Persian financial support for the rebuilding of the Temple. As a result, the poet/prophet quotes YHWH himself as having granted to the foreign Emperor the title of "messiah" (45:1).[36] The granting of such a title to Cyrus underscored two significant points.

First, the Hebrew Scriptures employ the term "messiah" with reference to high priests, prophets, and above all to kings. But "messiah" in the Bible does not refer to anyone offering himself as a sacrifice that redeems other people. In the Hebrew Bible, the basic term for "sacrifice" is *zevaḥ*, which falls into four distinct categories.

1. An *'ôlah* was a burnt offering totally burned on the altar; the smoke and scent ascend to the heavens, to God, attracting the attention

---

34. On the concept of prophetic schools in general and the Isaiah school in particular, see my "The *Limmûdîm* in the Book of Isaiah," 99–109.
35. 42:1–4; 49:1–6; 50:4–9; 52:13—53:12.
36. Fried, "Cyrus the Messiah?" 373–93.

of the deity, whose presence was sought for a ritual act.[37] The ʿōlah could also imply a gift to the deity, although the Bible is clear that God does not need a sacrifice.[38]

2. "Peace" offerings (šəlamîm) included three subdivisions: 1) Tôdah: the thank offering; 2) Neder: the sacrifice ratifying a vow; 3) nədavah: the free-will offering. These had nothing to do with atonement for sin; the salient feature of peace offerings was their function in ceremonies of religious celebration. The ʿōlah might have been perceived as being consumed by the deity, but the peace offerings were food shared with deity by humans, and the rites for slaughtering animals for all food occasions are part of the rules for their consumption.

3. A "sin" offering (ḥaṭaʾt) is based on the root meaning of ḥaṭaʾ ("to miss the mark"), but it was not a sacrifice that dealt with *intentional* transgressions. Its referential field in biblical literature involves a process of purification more than an act of sacrifice. An example of this emphasis occurs after the presentation of the sin offering by a person suffering from an inappropriate bodily discharge. "Thus [i.e., via the purification function of the ḥaṭaʾt] you shall keep the people of Israel separated from their uncleanness. Otherwise they might die in their uncleanness by defiling My tabernacle in their midst" (Lev 15:31). In other words, the ḥaṭaʾt was not offered by a sinful person hoping to achieve pardon, but by someone who had repented of a sin or had cleansed himself ritually after a physical illness or bodily discharge. To offer a ḥaṭaʾt *before* having repented or having undergone a cleansing process would have been improper. It should be noted above all that a "sin" offering was not an acceptable substitute either for repentance followed by a changed lifestyle or for ritual cleansing after an illness or a bodily discharge.

4. If the emphasis of the ʿōlah was on attracting the deity to ritual, of the šəlamîm on celebration, of the ḥaṭaʾt on purification, the emphasis of the fourth category of sacrifice, the "guilt" offering (ʾasham) centered on the concept of reparation. "Unlike other sacrifices which one 'offers' [hiqrib], the ʾasham could be converted into a

---

37. Note Job's custom of offering ʿōlôt for his sons each morning, just in case one of them *might* have sinned (1:5).

38. Note 1 Sam 15:22; Isa 1:11; Jer 7:22–23; Amos 5:21–24; etc.

monetary equivalent and simply paid."³⁹ It is with specific reference to the *'asham* of Isaiah 53:10 that the gospels depicted the relationship between Jesus and the suffering servant of Isaiah. But if the servant offers his own life as reparation in exchange for the sins of other people, it is difficult to explain how he can then look forward to a future with children and a long life. Only if the "servant" is the people of Israel/Judah collectively, can such a passage acquire meaning. The generation of the exile in fact did suffer horribly, many did die, and they might accurately be called a lost generation. But their faithfulness even in exile made possible a return for the following generations. The *zeraʿ*, or offspring ("seed," the nation collectively) of this exilic generation have lengthened their days, to date, from the middle of the sixth century BCE until now. From a Jewish perspective, this is the heart of 53:12, the inheritance or reward for the faithfulness of the servant, Israel.

The second issue highlighted by designating Cyrus "messiah" is that the enigmatic "servant of the Lord" in Second Isaiah never received this exalted title. The NT claim that the *ʿeved YHWH* in Isaiah is the prefigurement of Jesus relied on the fact that the collective Hebrew noun *ʿeved* ("servant") has become a singular (*pais*) in the Greek language of the LXX quoted in the gospels.⁴⁰

This identification of Jesus as the servant of the Lord in Isaiah was made most explicitly in the book of Acts (8:26–39). An Ethiopian high court official (national treasurer?) traveling along the desert road leading from Jerusalem to Gaza, happened to be reading from the fifty-third chapter of Isaiah when he was approached by Philip, and asked whether he understood what he was reading. Admitting that he could not grasp the text without a guide, the Ethiopian invited Philip into his chariot, where the two of them examined Isaiah 53:7–8 together. When the Ethiopian official inquired of Philip into the meaning of the text, his question was framed as a false dichotomy. That is, by asking to which *individual* the text referred (the prophet himself or some other person), Phillip's answer sidestepped the clear implication of the Hebrew text

---

39. See Anderson, "Sacrifice and Sacrificial Offerings," *ABD* 5:880.

40. See Matthew 12:18. The basic meaning of *pais* is "child," a nice connection with numerous biblical references to the people of Israel as the "children of YHWH." But it is only in a secondary sense that *pais* can mean "servant." It is so used contextually in Matthew 8:6–13.

with its *collective* reference to the people of Israel as a group.[41] The same poem also noted that the servant had been "formed from the womb to be [YHWH's] servant," a reference to the prophet Jeremiah 1:5.[42] On the basis of such statements, one rabbinic view held that Jeremiah was the "suffering servant." In addition to this womb reference, Jeremiah's suffering also suggested to some rabbis that he was the figure described in Isaiah 53. Thus Luke was not breaking new ground in seeking a specific individual who could be identified as the "servant." This is a transvaluation quite similar to that performed by Matthew, identifying Jesus as the "son" (singular) called out of Egypt, citing Hosea's reference to all Israel collectively exiting Egypt.

Nowhere in the gospels is there discussion of whether the Hebrew collective in Isaiah had become invalid with the arrival of Jesus. Whenever the rabbis made similar shifts from the plain text to a conclusion they wished to reach, someone in the group regularly expressed concern about the original sense, leaving us with a clear picture of the steps involved in the process of updating an ancient text and bringing it to bear on a current issue. In the NT, the gospel writers simply moved beyond a plain sense reading of Isaiah to the significance of the passage for their day without discussing what they were doing or how. Nevertheless, such a shift has clear precedent in rabbinic disputation. Both groups indicated their belief that while a particular text may have *meant* one thing originally, their interpretation was a fair representation of what it had come to *mean* to them. In both cases, all new interpretations were carefully based upon the text that was held sacred by everyone involved.

The Transvaluations of Paul

Paul and the Torah

Recent New Testament scholarship has been divided in its assessment of Paul's attitude to the Jewish Torah. But taken as it stands, Paul's view of the Torah ("Law") in the book of Galatians[43] created several fascinating new definitions of significance for the emerging Christian faith. In general terms, Paul was quite rabbinic in *methodology*, particularly in

---

41. See for example Isaiah 49:3, where clearly the servant is all Israel.

42. Evidently a stock phrase Paul also chose to refer to himself in Galatians 1:15.

43. Unless otherwise noted, subsequent chapter and verse references are to Galatians.

the way in which he appears to use the LXX translation of the Hebrew Scriptures as his point of departure for whatever issue he discussed. But when he moved to his own personal specific definitions and explanations to plough new and unfamiliar ground, he reached *conclusions* that can only be described as radical.

Paul's quotation of and subsequent explanation of Deuteronomy 27:26 is a case in point. What Deuteronomy enjoins as a sacred obligation upon Israelites to keep the teachings of the Torah carefully, Paul simply asserts meant the opposite. So "Cursed is everyone who does not abide by all things written in the book of the Law, to perform them" Paul took to mean that everyone who was attempting to live according to the teachings of the Torah was under a curse (3:10). He offers no specific reason why the verse should mean the exact opposite of what it says,[44] but from statements made elsewhere, it is apparent that the Law was a curse for Paul because of his own professed inability to keep it in every detail. This is the position he spelled out in some detail in Romans 7, arguing that although he did not do what he wanted to do (7:15), he was not personally at fault. Rather, "sin that dwells in me" (in verses 17 and 20) was the culprit. Here, of course, Paul departs from the rabbinic position that sin is a wrong action, and sets the stage for what would become the Christian conception of sin as a "condition" from which sinful actions were derived. Since Paul "would not have been aware of sin except for the Law" (7:70), the Law for him was nothing more than a "body of death" that made him "wretched" (*talaiporos*) (7:24).[45]

When we attempt to discover the source from which such a perspective on the Law could have arisen, Paul's autobiographical reflections are of little assistance. "Advancing in Judaism beyond many of [his] contemporaries, being more extremely zealous for [his] ancestral traditions" (Gal 1:14), Paul could assert that he had been "blameless with respect to righteousness that is in the Law" (Phil 3:6). Yet he longed for a greater righteousness, not found in the Law, but only in Christ (Phil 3:9). Here Paul deviated from the rabbinic perspective on two counts. In the first place, the rabbis never imagined the possibility that any individual could or would fulfill every requirement of the Torah perfectly at all times, as we noted in chapter 5.

---

44. We must recall here the similar rabbinic overturning of the clear meaning of Exodus 34:6–7 discussed in chapter 5.

45. Even if we recall the earlier distinction between divine law and the law of Moses, we must also note that the Mosaic Law was at least in part a reflection of God's law.

But Paul's second deviation from the rabbis about Torah was his concentration only on the keeping of commandments, ignoring in the process a major component of that Torah that provides specific remedies for failures of personal performance. The rabbis understood not only that every individual Jew would fail in the attempt at perfect compliance, but also that the Torah itself provided for repentance, forgiveness, and reconciliation at the very junction of non-compliance. For the rabbis, the moment of failure was not the time to abandon the Torah, but the time to turn to the legal correctives that were an integral part of the Torah itself. The heroes of rabbinic faith were not those who had kept the Torah perfectly, but were those who, in the moments of their failures, had sought and acquired reconciliation through the Torah.[46]

It is not our purpose is to determine who was correct, Paul or the rabbis. It remains only to examine the method by which Paul derived his position. And each step in his process was rabbinic. First, as we have seen, Paul began by citing the Torah, clearly implying that any successful refutation of the common rabbinic view of Torah must be taken from it. Second, Paul chose a single word from Genesis 15:6 ("believed") and linked it with another word from Habakkuk 2:4 ("faith"), setting in opposition the concepts of "doing" and "believing."[47] But while the rabbis understood *'emunah* in the Hebrew sense of "faithfulness," that is, the keeping or doing of the Torah, Paul latched on to the Greek sense of *pisteuein*, "to believe," or even "to be convinced" of a propositional truth.

Paul turned next to a historical argument, noting that Abraham could not have been "righteous" as a result of keeping the Torah, which was received more than four centuries after he lived (3:17). In other words, for Paul, Abraham was not the first Jew, whose keeping of Torah earned him righteous status before God, but the first Christian, whose belief in God merited that status. And that means others who followed in the footsteps of Abraham (and Paul!), that is, those who believe as Paul did, were "the children of Abraham" (3:7), not those who keep Torah.

Yet Paul did not simply ignore the Torah, he addressed what he believed to be its incorrect *interpretation*, basing his entire argument for the setting aside of Torah on the Torah itself. Accordingly, the fourth step

---

46. This was the case for Abraham, Jacob, Moses himself, and even the great King David.

47. Both in Hebrew and in Greek, the verb from Genesis and the noun in Habakkuk derive from a common root (*he'emin* and *'emunah* from '-m-n, *episteusin* and *pisteos* from *pisteuein*).

of his argument was linked to another important word in Genesis 13:15 ("seed"). In Hebrew, singular *zera'* is a collective noun referring to the innumerable descendants of Abraham who will inherit the land promised to the first patriarch. Paul, arguing from the Greek text, noted that the promise to Abraham had not been made to plural seeds (*tois spermasin*), but "to one" (*'eph' henos*), who was none other than Jesus (3:16). In other words, the promise in the Torah was not invalidated, but it needed to be re-interpreted. The original promise may have been about Abraham's numerous offspring who would inherit a physical territory, but in light of the life and teachings of Jesus, it needed to be understood as a promise about a single "seed" (Jesus) and his spiritual kingdom. The common rabbinic conception of the Torah may have been correct originally, but new times and circumstances demanded from Paul a reformulation of the Genesis promise. In other words, the rabbinic interpretation of Genesis 13:15, while not incorrect, was *incomplete* because the singularity of Jesus ("the seed") was a concept that could not have been grasped until the advent of Jesus (3:19). "Before faith" (3:23), the Torah served temporarily as a "tutor" (*paidagogos*) leading inexorably to Jesus (3:24). "But now that faith has arrived, we are no longer under a tutor" (3:25).

These four steps in Paul's argument about the Torah lead to a truly innovative fifth step. Not only was Abraham the progenitor of Christian faith, but his son Isaac was also an integral link in the chain leading from Abraham to Jesus to Paul. Abraham, Paul recalled, had fathered two sons, "one by a slave woman and one by a free woman" (4:22). For Paul, "these things are allegorical utterances" (4:24). The promise to Abraham was about a single son only, and that son was clearly Isaac. But just as Abraham was not a true link to Torah Judaism (having become righteous centuries before the Torah existed), neither was Isaac. He was, in fact, the first child of promise, even as Paul and his Galatian readers were to be considered later children of promise (4:28). The Torah, far from traveling through the "seed" (Isaac) promised to Abraham, actually had developed through the slave line of the descendants of Ishmael. Thus Jews who follow the Torah are slaves, as was their progenitor Ishmael, while Christians who accept the new meaning of Torah are the children of promise, as were Abraham and Isaac. In short, Christians, not Jews, are the descendants of Isaac. Jews descend from Ishmael. And Jews, again following the example of their progenitor, persecute Christians, as Ishmael had once persecuted Isaac (4:28–31).

This link between Ishmael and the Torah depends upon the relationship between Ishmael and the woman presented in the Genesis narratives as his mother, Hagar. "The equating of Hagar with Sinai is suggested either by the location of Sinai in Arabia . . . or by the linguistic similarity of an Arabian word *hajar* ("rock" or "cliff"), with which certain place names on the Sinaitic peninsula seem to be related."[48] Whereas the biblical link between Abraham and Moses (the Torah) is established by Exodus 6:2–3 (and see also Exodus 3:6), Paul's argument depended upon negating any relationship between the two men, which he accomplished by reference to the wide gap of centuries between their two lives.

The contrast between the rabbinic and this Pauline view of Ishmael and the Torah could not be sharper. A Midrash found in the second (or early third) century CE *Mekhilta deR. Ishmael*[49] relates the following:

> Before Israel was asked, the nations of the world were asked in the presence of God to receive the Torah, so that they could not have an opportunity to say: If we had been offered the Torah we would have already accepted it upon us. In fact, they were asked and they did not accept the Torah upon themselves, as it is said: "The Lord came from Sinai and shone from Seir [homeland of Esau's descendants] for them" (Deuteronomy 33:2). This means that God revealed himself to the children of Esau the wicked [descendants of Seir] and said to them: Will you accept the Torah? They said to him: What's written in it? He said to them: "You shall not murder" (Exodus 20:13). They said: But this is the inheritance which our father bequeathed us, as it is said: "By your sword shall you live" (Genesis 27:40).
>
> God then appeared to the children of Amon and Moab. He said to them: Will you accept the Torah? They said to him: What's written in it? He said to them: "You shall not commit adultery" (Exodus 20:13). They said to him: All of us are born from adultery, as it is written: "The two daughters of Lot became pregnant by their father" (Genesis 19:36).[50] How can we accept the Torah?
>
> God then appeared to the children of Ishmael. He said to them: Will you accept the Torah? They said to him: What's written in it? He said to them: "Do not steal" (Exodus 20:13). They said to him: But this was the very blessing with which our father

48. Kittel, "Agar," *TDNT* 1:56.

49. BaḤodesh 5 (commenting on Exodus 12:1–20).

50. Lot's daughters gave birth to Amon and Moab. This was both incest and adultery, because according to Rabbinic tradition, Lot's daughters were engaged to be married, and in Jewish law engagement was equal to marriage. If a woman had sexual relations with another man while engaged, she committed adultery.

was blessed, as it is written: "He will be a wild man, his hand against everyone"[51] (Genesis 16:12).

When God came to Israel, "from his right hand was a fiery law for them" (Deuteronomy 33:2). They all opened their mouths and said: "All that the Lord has spoken we will do and will obey" (Exodus 24:7). And thus it says: "He stood and measured the earth, he looked and dismissed the other nations" (Habakkuk 3:6).

In sum, then, the Torah, which was a "tree of life" for the rabbis,[52] became "the body of this death" (Romans 7:24) for Paul. The blessing of rabbinic Judaism became a curse (Galatians 3:10), and salvation became the possession of non-Jews through acceptance of the Christian meaning of the Torah (Galatians 5:19–22). This was clarified by Paul's assertion that "Christ is the goal [*telos*] of the Law [leading] to righteousness for everyone who believes" (Romans 10:4).[53]

Paul, Christ, and Water in the Desert

We turn now to a final example of Paul's familiarity with rabbinic positions as well as his desire to go beyond them in search of a christological interpretation. In 1 Corinthians 10, drawing lessons from early Israelite disobedience, Paul reminded his readers of the corporate nature of the

51. I.e., he will make a living through theft.

52. A phrase attested in Proverbs 3:18, where it describes "wisdom;" 11:30, where it describes "the fruit of the righteous;" 13:12, where it symbolizes "desire realized;" and 15:4, where it characterizes "a healing tongue." In the liturgy, the Torah is celebrated as "a tree of life" during the ceremony of its return to the ark after it has been read to the congregation.

53. It is difficult to assess the motivation of Paul in arguing as he does in Galatians. Many scholars have noted his personal difficulty with the Jewish Torah, which he restricted narrowly to his own idea of "law." But clearly Paul was disillusioned about far more than Jewish law. In Galatians, he dismisses not just the Torah, not just circumcision or kashrut, but indeed the foundational story of the Old Testament in its entirety. In the context of the biblical narratives recalling the activity of God on their behalf— gracing them with the divine name of the deity who had appeared to Abraham, adopting them as his own "son" (Exodus 4:22), freeing them from Egyptian slavery, designating them as his "special possession" charged with the responsibility of becoming a "holy nation" (see Exodus 19:1–6)—nothing could sound more shocking to a Jew than the idea that Jews had never been and could never become anything but slaves because they are the offspring of the slave-child Ishmael. For Paul to denigrate virtually every aspect of Old Testament teaching can only be viewed as the first step in the process that led to the final break between Judaism and Christianity.

early events in Israelite history stretching from Egypt and the Exodus well into the time of wandering in the wilderness. "All of our Israelite ancestors were under the cloud, all passed through the sea, all were baptized into Moses in the cloud and in the sea, all ate the same spiritual food,[54] and all drank the same spiritual drink" (10:1–4). Even with these convincing experiences, Paul notes, most of the Israelites failed to please God (10:5). To what was Paul referring?

The Torah contains two different narratives chronicling the actions of Moses in striking a rock to draw water from it. The first event occurred at a place named Rephidim (Exod. 17:1–7), while the second was located at Kadesh (Num. 20:1–12). Because of the complaints of the people, Rephidim was renamed Massah ("test") and Meribah ("quarrel") in Exodus 17:7. The incident at Kadesh was specifically tied to Meribah in Numbers 20:13. This Meribah link between the well at Rephidim and the later incident at Kadesh, has led modern source critics to view the two narratives as alternate accounts of the same event, and attribute them to two different Pentateuchal literary sources.[55] Before the dawn of source criticism, however, the rabbis posited another theory, according to which the water-producing rock struck by Moses originally in Rephidim followed the Israelites in the desert to Kadesh, and may have supplied them with water on numerous occasions, not all of which are specifically chronicled in the Pentateuch. Paul seemed to have been aware of this rabbinic idea of a single rock following the Israelites, and assigned to it a figurative interpretation with which the rabbis would have had little disagreement: "they were drinking from a spiritual rock that followed them" (10:4b). But Paul's unique contribution to the rabbinic idea was his specific identification of the rock: "the rock was the Christ" (10:4c).

Addendum: The Rabbis on the Pharisees

It was peculiarly the province of the great writing prophets of Scripture to address the question of what constitutes an appropriate response to YHWH in the light of his demands. From at least the time of the eighth century BCE, the prophets rejected any external standard as a guideline for measuring society's acceptability to God. To preachers like Amos,

---

54. See above on "manna."

55. See Milgrom, *Numbers*, 448–56 for a masterful treatment of two accounts as duplicates.

Hosea, and Micah, no particular method of praying or *halakhic* precision in offering animal sacrifices could compensate for societal actions of injustice and oppression. How or even if people performed the national cultic liturgy, as well as when or how or if they celebrated special religious days also became secondary. The deity of Israel could not be controlled by his human partners simply through their forms of worship. What mattered to these prophets was exclusive human loyalty to YHWH and a partnership with God to create a society of justice and holiness. This alone, they believed, would produce appropriate conduct individually and corporately.

The opposition of the New Testament gospels against what they perceived as the spiritually meaningless *halakhah* of "the Pharisees"[56] is well known. Much less well known is an extended Talmudic discussion in which the rabbis themselves discuss the spiritual shortcomings of several different types of unacceptable Pharisees. Nestled in the middle of a long discourse on various difficulties between a man and a wife suspected of adultery lies a summarizing pearl of distilled Tannaitic wisdom of the type that is so familiar in Talmudic formulae, especially in *Pirkei 'Avot*: "These things wear out the world: a stupid *hasid*, a cunning rogue, a female Pharisee and the blows (or wounds) of the Pharisees." In the subsequent *Gemara* discussion, each of these phrases is defined.

The "stupid *hasid*" is a man who, when a woman is drowning in a river, refuses to look at her and thus rescue her from death. The "cunning rogue" may be one of several possibilities: 1) he "explains his case to a judge before the other party to the suit has arrived"; 2) he gives a poor person just enough money to tip him over the official poverty line, thus making it impossible for him to receive additional charity that he still needs; 3) he offers fraudulent advice about the sale of land to be inherited; 4) he induces gullible people to follow him by pretending to a level of piety that is false; 5) he interprets *halakhah* leniently for himself and restrictively for other people; 6) he studies *Tanakh* (Hebrew Bible) and Mishnah but does not seek a teacher for additional learning. The "female Pharisee" is a woman whose sexual or social mores are questionable.

The discussion then turned to "the blows of the Pharisees," stipulated as the final cause of the destruction of the world. The Gemara

---

56. Called variously "the tradition of the elders" (Matt 15:2; Mark 7:3, 5); "the tradition of men" (contrasted with "the commandment of God" in Mark 7:8 and with "philosophy and empty deception" in Colossians 2:8); "your [own] tradition" (Matt 15:6; Mark 7:9, 13); or "ancestral traditions" (Galatians 1:14).

explaining this phrase lists seven different types of Pharisee, and appends a description to each type:

1. A *shikhmi* Pharisee receives two alternate explanations. In the Babylonian Talmud [TB], such a person is like the citizens of the ancient town of Shechem, who were forcibly circumcised (Genesis 34). The Palestinian/Jerusalem Talmud (TJ) sees the word as a parody of those who exhibit great ostentation by carrying their *halakhic* obligations in plain view on their shoulders (Hebrew, *shekhem*).

2. A *niqpi* Pharisee is identified as one who "knocks his feet together" (*mənaqef*), attempting to affect a gait of exaggerated humility.

3. A *kiza'i* Pharisee may be either a "bleeder," or an "accountant," depending upon the derivation of its root. So TB appears to be describing a man who runs face-first into a wall, bloodying himself in the process, to avoid looking at a woman, while TJ views the *kiza'i* as a person who performs one bad deed for each good deed, carefully keeping track of both types.

4. A *medokhya* Pharisee receives his designation, "pestle," because he walks as if his head is bowed down into a "mortar," another apparent reference to false humility.

5. A *mah Hovati* ("what is my obligation?") Pharisee, we are told, is the kind who pretends to have fulfilled every possible religious obligation, and arrogantly runs around pretending to search diligently for something else to do in order to impress people with his piety.

6–7. To complete the number seven promised at the outset of the discussion, Pharisees "from love" and Pharisees "from fear" are listed. But immediately thereafter, the rabbis assert that these last two types "do not belong on this list at all." And we are also told why they do not fit. Study of Torah, and commandments, even performed for an unworthy motive (i.e., fear instead of love), must be encouraged. And we are also assured that "The Great Court" (דינא רבה—*Dîna' Rabbah*) will separate the true Pharisees from those who pretend to a piety that is false.

Before the discussion returns to the husband-wife disputes into which the listing of the seven types of Pharisee has been rather artificially inserted, a final "historical" reminder is appended to round out the Pharisee issue. King Alexander Jannaeus, we are reminded, advised his wife from his deathbed in the following way: "Do not fear the Pharisees or even the non-Pharisees, but [fear] the hypocrites who pretend to be Pharisees." It is difficult to imagine a Talmudic passage that is more "prophetic." And we must remember that all of the contributors to these definitions, these careful delineations of false pharisaical conduct, were themselves Pharisees! Many of them may have been aware of the New Testament polemic that tarred them with such a broad brush. Yet still they could not ignore the necessity of condemning false behavior, and specifically false behavior arising out of improper motives. With great skill and no little sarcasm they underscored the necessity of an appropriate scale of values. Life they placed above all else, followed closely by immersion in Torah and commandments. But false affectation, hypocrisy, exaggerated humility—these received their scorn, and they had no doubt that practitioners of such falsity would be unmasked and punished at the proper time. But one looks in vain for anything more than their careful delineation of the issues involved. There is no condemnation of specific opponents, no naming of a particular person guilty of any of the false types of Pharisaism, and no wholesale denunciation of an entire group based on the actions of some of their adherents. Even those whom they believed to be totally wrong in attitude and *praxis* were left in the hands of the Great Judge of all humanity.

Conclusion
Future Directions

OUR SURVEY OF THE hermeneutics of the early rabbis and first Christians has shown the dazzling freedom exercised by the earliest Jewish and Christian interpreters of their common sacred text. The claims of their modern counterparts notwithstanding, all subsequent interpreters arrogated to themselves a similar freedom whenever their sensibilities or ideologies so dictated. Some modern interpreters are, in the effective phrase of William Sloane Coffin, "selective literalists,"[1] who pick and choose small pieces of their (divinely authored!) Bibles, but the chosen pieces always miraculously conform to their own unexamined ideologies and prejudices.[2]

Christianity adopted the Jewish Bible, transvalued it, and thought of it as her own possession. It never rewrote the narratives of the Old Testament,[3] but re-interpreted, or reconstructed them by viewing them through its own special lens of faith so as to point them in the direction of Christology. In composing her New Testament, or covenant,[4] Christianity was doing something quite similar to what the rabbis of the same general epoch were attempting, that is, reformulating a sacred text and fitting it for a new world context. For the rabbis, the very title "Mishnah" testified both to their conviction that they had the authority to move in

---

1. A phrase proffered and defined in his excellent book, *Credo*, 159.
2. Only such a starting point allows one to argue that the wife of Lot was turned into a block of sodium chloride because the Bible says so, and then casually accept the statement of Jesus to his disciples ("You are the salt of the earth") as metaphorical.
3. As did Islam.
4. Adopting a phrase from Jeremiah 31:31.

radically new directions from the time-bound narratives of the Hebrew Scriptures, and that in so doing they were *not* inventing a *new* theology. For both Judaism and Christianity, the emphasis was upon shaping old and trusted *principles* into new formulations for *practice* that were relevant for their era.[5]

Judaism has its oral torah, that is, rabbinic exegesis that is essential to update and explain the basic text of the Bible. Christianity has ecclesiastical canon law and papal fiat to update and expand the original NT expansion of the Old Testament into Christian theology. Thus the cultural and theological gaps that exist between the two monotheistic faiths stemming from Abraham may not be traced to differences in the way the two have developed *methodological* machinery to interpret and appropriate their core texts, but must be sought elsewhere. Despite the radical differences in their *conclusions*, their *methods*, and, it may be added, their motivation, were essentially the same. This may be said another way. Popular perception to the contrary, post-biblical Judaism is not based exclusively on, nor is Jewish theological opinion derived from, the Bible. Instead, the first rabbis arrogated to themselves the authority to create a second holy book in order to explain and expand the meaning of the first holy book. Similarly the early Christians created their own second holy book as an interpretative guide to explain and expand the broader meaning of their adopted first holy book.

No modern rabbi can discuss the death penalty without reference to the discussions of the Talmud, no modern Christian adheres to the plain meaning of the Old Testament without his NT lens of faith close at hand, and no pious Christian reads the NT without reference to the teachings of the church. In both faith systems, no matter how hard a modern believer may pound his or her sacred text, it is clear that each holy book comes accompanied by authoritative interpretative keys: the Talmud, the rabbinic codes, the *responsa*, or the NT, ecclesiastical law, and church tradition. What each holy book *means* in each current era is often quite different from what it *meant* in its original context, and the distinction is determined by a methodological similarity in both Judaism and Christianity, not by blind adherence to a single meaning that was considered binding for all times and in every situation.

---

5. And the circumstances faced by the early rabbis and the authors of the NT are so similar that we must define rabbinic Judaism and nascent Christianity as sisters rather than forcing the old idea that Judaism is the mother and Christianity the daughter.

This fact offers the best hope for a way out of the difficult political situations created by the clash between one faith and another in modernity. Crucial here is the need for honest scholars to acknowledge what actually happens in the reading of a classical text, that is, exactly how it happens that an ancient text may be forged into a workable modern idea no matter how it appears in *the* book. Said another way, it is not the Bible that the world needs to fear but unrestrained and unacknowledged interpretation that calls itself literal no matter how boldly it has jumped from text and context into pretext. Employed negatively or polemically, biblical interpretation contains the potential for disaster. If the plain sense and original context of a classical text may be abandoned by the interpreter at will, it becomes quite simple to target each *opponent de jour* by dragging in an ancient text with which to cloak one's own designs and discredit everyone who disagrees. What ensues is harshness, a meanness of spirit that makes every opponent not only incorrect on a specific point of theology, but virtually an enemy of God. Having thus devalued all opponents, it becomes much easier to persecute or even seek to exterminate them. In other words, our analysis of the interpretative methods of early Judaism and Christianity indicates that the terror lies not in the holy texts themselves, but in the extreme *use* to which such texts may be put by recourse to hermeneutical scaffolding that has long been shared commonly by them both. Such action belies the exalted claims made by both religions about love, peace, and brotherhood, high-toned claims that surely sound hollow in the ears of those who are victimized or marginalized by persecution or terror in the name of God.

But freedom is a double-edged sword. On the positive side of the ledger, the freedom to transvalue can allow members of a group to retain what they perceive as universal and timeless *principles* of faith, while fashioning them into formulas that allow each successive generation to update its own *practices*. In this manner, successive generations not only link themselves with classical narratives that affirm their own identity, they can take refuge in the belief that they are exhibiting good stewardship by advancing the best possible expressions of the ancient narratives for their day. The famous question, "what would Jesus (or Moses) do?" can be answered honestly only by those who are willing to admit that modern personal interpretations are guided by what modern society and its interpreters need them to be, and cannot be foisted off on the world as the word of God or *the only* true teaching of the sacred book. Just as the rabbis, the Jesus portrayed in the gospels, and Paul were free to reshape classical texts for the modernity of their worlds, so their twenty-first-century followers can be free to become truly Jewish or Christian in sensible dialogue within the modern context of a global community unimagined by their founders. To hide behind a "God says" shield is not only utterly disingenuous, but also unfaithful to the spirit of those in whose names the shield is carried.

Let it be said with total clarity. The only reason for many interpretative positions is that they buttress the grasp for power and control. Throughout history, whenever a subgroup has lost control over its own *political* future, new *theological* rules have come into play. Two thousand years ago, sober Jewish leaders had to negotiate with Rome for the right to reconstruct a system of prayer and religious life without a Temple, a political structure, a king, a political state of any kind. Only this radical theological reconstruction of Judaism allowed for its survival once all Jewish political aspirations had been crushed by the superior Roman army. What emerged was a repetition of Scripture, a Mishnah, believed to be authoritative, but clearly transvaluing some of even the most fundamental biblical teachings.

Christianity likewise had to reconfigure what it adopted as its "Scripture" (the Old Testament) in order to achieve the self-portrait it sought during its formative years under intense pressure from Rome. Twenty centuries later, this self-portrait had to change even more radically when the church looked in the mirror and saw not only the faces of six million Jews who died in "Christian" Europe, but also millions of Christian eyes that had turned away while it happened. This reconfiguration compelled Christians to confront the truth about the ways in which key passages in the New Testament had been read for centuries, and to reinterpret some of its own NT texts in the process. Thus, in the fires of history, both Judaism and Christianity determined that extremist/literalist views needed to be ousted in order to make possible a new era of inter-faith dialogue and respect. In both cases, the methodology that permitted radical re-reading of sacred texts was close at hand to validate the new results.

The early interpreters on both sides understood that the Bible had not created them, but that their respective communities of faith had created a Bible fit for the social and theological needs of their own eras. With such an understanding, they opened the way for their successors in every subsequent generation to evaluate the applicability for their day of each part of the Bible as they themselves had done, even when it became necessary to abandon certain biblical teachings that were clearly wrong and harmful if they were taken uncritically and fashioned into a crude road map for life.[6]

It is unthinkable that in our modern world we should re-institute slavery because the Bible allows it. No one would argue seriously that a child who struck or cursed a parent should be executed (Exodus 21:15, 17). The idea of destroying anyone who prays to a different god (Exodus 22:20) must be categorically denounced. Persons with physical handicaps need no longer be denied the opportunity to serve as clergy (Leviticus 21:17-21), any more than we ought to continue to view males who experience a seminal discharge or menstruating females as "unclean" (Leviticus 15:13-33). Jews can no longer be called "a brood of vipers" (Matthew 12:34), nor can other non-Christians be dismissed cavalierly as mere "haters of the light/truth," as John would have it (3:18-20). No one should argue against homosexuality because the Bible condemns it, unless one is willing to take also the biblical view that homosexuals should be executed in order to keep the community of faith pure (Leviticus 20:13). Similar arguments can be made about adultery, disobedient children, or witches. We moderns cannot take only those parts of the Bible we choose. If we argue against the sin on biblical grounds, but cannot feel comfortable to argue in favor of the biblical punishment as well, perhaps it is time to reconsider our stance about the sin. It is precisely because the early *communities* of faith created the Bible in the first place that faithful modern Jews and Christians must accept the responsibility of re-formulating the meaning of that Bible for each generation, even to the point of changing its basic structure and clear original intention.

The similarities in the ways Judaism and Christianity have developed machinery to interpret and appropriate their core texts cannot explain many of the cultural and theological gaps that exist between them. But the fact that they have shared similar methods of interpretation for 2,000 years should indicate that given the will and the motivation to do so, the mechanism is in place for them to move away from the limitations and rigidity of their sacred texts to positions that will enable the children of Abraham in the faith to live together with an attitude of mutual respect for each other.

---

6. The radical scholar of early Reform Judaism, Samuel Holdheim expressed this viewpoint in 1844, at the first Reform rabbinical conference held in Brunswick: "The Talmud speaks with the standpoint of its time, and for that time it was right. I speak from the higher level of consciousness of my time, and for this age I am right."

Via close analysis of the methods by which Jewish and Christian scholars derived meaning from their respective texts for the worlds in which they lived, our research demonstrates two equally important facts. The centrality of the Bible in the intense conflict between early Judaism and Christianity points to the first of these facts by focusing on a fundamental perspective about biblical language. Over the objections of the famous Rabbi Akiva, the majority opinion among the second century CE *Tanna'im* was articulated by Rabbi Ishmael ben Elisha', who coined the pithy dictum: *dibra torah kilshon b'nei adam* ("the Torah spoke in human language"). This human language of the Hebrew Bible was translated into other languages at an early time with the clear purpose of allowing the opportunity for a greater number of people to read and understand its *ideas*. Two late biblical books (Daniel and Ezra) were composed partly in Aramaic, and Aramaic translations of the entire Bible began to be offered orally as early as 200 BCE, in an effort to make the sacred texts available to a wider audience of Jews. A translation of the Hebrew Bible into Greek was done almost two centuries before the time of Jesus with the exact same purpose in mind.[7]

Linguists know that it is impossible to give an exact, *literal* translation of any text from one language into another. As early as 132 BCE, the grandson of Ben Sira offered a classic apology for possible flaws in the translation of his grandfather's book from Hebrew into Greek for Egyptian Jews. "There is no equivalent for things originally written in Hebrew when . . . translating them into another language. What is more, the Law itself, the Prophets and the other books differ considerably in translation from what appears in the original text" (1:23–26). Still, the grandson notes, a Jew is duty bound, "not only to acquire learning by reading, but also, once having acquired it, to make oneself of use to people outside by what one can say or write" (1:4–7). The key phrase is "people outside."

The New Testament does not report the words of Jesus verbatim either, no doubt guided by the goal of spreading the new faith to "people outside." Although Jesus spoke in Aramaic, the New Testament texts were composed in Greek because far more people spoke Greek than Aramaic, and also because Aramaic was mostly limited to Jewish speakers, while Greek was the medium of expression for people of many nations

---

7. If one takes the story of Exodus literally, Moses surely composed the Torah in Egyptian rather than in the Canaanite dialect (Hebrew) that was spoken in the country to which he was denied access by God. This would imply that the Hebrew Torah is itself a translation!

throughout the Roman Empire. Similar motives underlay early projects to translate the Christian Bible into Latin and other important languages in the first few Christian centuries. Like their Jewish counterparts, the early Christians were seeking wider dissemination of core *ideas* rather than the slavish repetition of written texts.

A second point is also clear from the texts themselves: the methods used by both religions, methods that lead to radically different conclusions, are essentially the same. Acknowledgement that the accredited principles of interpretation used by both systems allowed such wide-ranging freedom offers current expositors the possibility of bringing classical sacred texts once again into the service of modernity and change, accompanied by a liberal dose of humility and respect for the others, who have so often been framed as the enemy.

Because it is methodologically unsound to argue any theological position from one literal text to the exclusion of other verses that moderate or disagree with the one chosen for a specific debate, several questions demand consideration. Should modern readers of the Bible employ the same flexibility in interpretation that was employed in obviating physical punishment (as the rabbis do because of their own sensibilities), setting aside Saturday for Sunday because of its importance in the developing story of Christian history, ignoring clearly imposed biblical punishments (i.e., the execution of homosexuals or disobedient children), and demanding specific conduct by extending Shabbat prohibitions well beyond the biblical text itself? The NT itself is clear on numerous issues that Christ (Christianity) sets aside "old" points of view! But the NT does not set aside the Shabbat. It does not overturn the death penalty. It does not say specifically that observance of *kashrut* is no longer mandatory. In fact, at the end of the only NT debate about *kashrut*, both sides agreed to *retain* the prohibition against eating meat killed improperly or with blood still in it![8] If Paul could simply decide on his own to ignore this agreement to which he had been a party, has he not thereby created the machinery for his modern followers to treat other objectionable *New* [sic!] Testament teachings in a similar fashion?

In at least one instance, Paul admits openly that he followed his own judgment,[9] acting in light of the needs of a specific situation. Because of his evident burning desire to convert as many Gentiles as possible

---

8. See Acts 15:20, 29.

9. 1 Corinthians 7:40.

with the fewest legal roadblocks in the way, this admission should not be surprising. But in so acting, does not Paul recommend to others the same *method*? And, as we have shown repeatedly, Paul was not alone in seizing for himself both the freedom and the *obligation* to make interpretative decisions in light of his own contexts, his own perception of current political and social needs, or his own personal moral judgment. Should such freedom now be abrogated? I believe the answer, shown by our examination of the long history of such interpretative freedom from the earliest moments of Judaism and Christianity, must be in the negative.

Bibliography

Akenson, Donald Harmon. *Surpassing Wonder: The Invention of the Bible and the Talmuds.* New York: Harcourt, 1998.
Alexander, Philip S. "Targum, Targumim." In *ABD* 6:320-31.
Anderson, Gary A. "Sacrifice and Sacrificial Offerings (OT)." In *ABD* 5:870-86.
Bainton, Roland H. *Erasmus of Christendom.* New York: Scribner, 1969.
Bamberger, Berhard J. *The Story of Judaism.* New York: Schocken, 1970.
Blackwell, Richard J. *Galileo, Bellarmine, and the Bible.* Notre Dame, IN: University of Notre Dame Press, 1991.
Blomberg, C. L. "Parable." In *ISBE* 3:655-59.
Breslauer, S. Daniel. *Understanding Judaism Through History.* Belmont, CA: Wadsworth, 2003.
Brettler, Marc Zvi. *How to Read the Bible.* Philadelphia: Jewish Publication Society, 2005.
Brown, Raymond E. *An Introduction to the New Testament.* New York: Doubleday, 1997.
———, et al., editors. *The New Jerome Biblical Commentary.* Revised. Englewood Cliffs, NJ: Prentice-Hall, 1990.
Charlesworth, James H. *The Old Testament Pseudepigrapha.* Two vols. New York: Doubleday, 1985.
———. "Pseudepigrapha, OT." In *ABD* 5:537-39.
Chomsky, William. *Hebrew: The Eternal Language.* Philadelphia: Jewish Publication Society, 1957.
Coffin, William Sloane. *Credo.* Louisville: Westminster John Knox, 2004.
Collins, Raymond F. "Ten Commandments." In *ABD* 6:383-87.
Crossan, John Dominic. *In Parables: The Challenge of the Historical Jesus.* New York: HarperCollins, 1973.
———. "Parable." In *ABD* 5:146-52.
———. *Who Killed Jesus?* New York: HarperCollins, 1996.
Dan, Joseph. "Hasidism." In *EJ*. No pages. CD-Rom.
Daube, David. *The New Testament and Rabbinic Judaism.* Reprint. Peabody, MA: Hendrickson, 1998.
Davidson, Herbert A. *Moses Maimonides: The Man and His Works.* New York: Oxford University Press, 2005.
Davies, P. R., and Bruce Chilton. "The Aqedah: A Revised Tradition-History." *Catholic Biblical Quarterly* 40 (1978) 514-46.

Delling, Gerhard. *"Pleres."* In *TDNT* 6:283–311.
Dimont, Max I. *Jews, God and History*. New York: Signet, 1962.
Dodd, C. H. *The Parables of the Kingdom*. New York: Scribner, 1961.
Durant, Will. *The Story of Civilization VI: The Reformation*. New York: Simon and Schuster, 1957.
Ehrman, Bart. *Lost Christianities*. New York: Oxford University Press, 2003.
———. *Lost Scriptures: Books That Did Not Make It Into the New Testament*. New York: Oxford University Press, 2003.
Eusbius. *Ecclesiastical History*. New York: Merchant, 2011.
Feldman, Louis H. "Josephus." In *ABD* 3:992–94.
———. *Josephus's Interpretation of the Bible*. Chico, CA: University of California Press, 1998.
Freedman, H. Translator: *Midrash Rabbah: Genesis*. Vol 1. London: Soncino, 1983.
Fried, Lisbeth S. "Cyrus the Messiah? The Historical Background to Isaiah 45.1" *Harvard Theological Review* 95:4 (2002) 373–93.
Friedman, Richard. E. "Torah (Pentateuch)." In *ABD* 6:605–22.
Gese, Hartmut. *Vom Sinai zum Zion. Alttestamentliche Beiträge zur biblischen Theologie*. Munich: Christian Kaiser, 1974.
Goldin, Judah. "The Period of the Talmud." In *The Jews: Their History, Culture, and Religion*, edited by Louis Finkelstein, 125–33. New York: Harper, 1960.
Goodenough, E. R. *An Introduction to Philo Judaeus*. 2nd edition. University Press of America, 1997.
Gundry, R. H. "Fulfill." In *ISBE* 2:366–69.
Harrington, Daniel J. *Invitation to the Apocrypha*. Grand Rapids: Eerdmans, 1999.
Hedges, Chris. *American Fascists: The Christian Right and the War on America*. New York: Free Press, 2006.
Hicks, L. W. "Isaac." In *IDB* 2:728–31.
Horgan, Maurya P. *Pesharim: Qumran Interpretations of Biblical Books*. Catholic Biblical Quarterly Monograph Series 8. Washington: Catholic Biblical Association of America, 1979.
Horsley, Richard A., and Neil Asher Silberman. *The Message and the Kingdom: How Jesus and Paul Ignited a Revolution and Transformed the Ancient World*. New York: Putnam, 1997.
Isbell, Charles David. "Confession." In *Encyclopedia of Religion, Communication, and Media*, edited by Daniel A. Stout, 86–89. New York: Routledge, 2006.
———. *Corpus of the Aramaic Magical Incantation Bowls*. Reprint. Eugene, OR: Wipf and Stock, 2009.
———. "Deuteronomy's Definition of Jewish Learning." *Journal of Biblical Literature* 31:2 (2003) 109–16.
———. "Does the Gospel of Matthew Proclaim Mary's Virginity?" *Biblical Archaeology Review* 3:2 (1977) 18–52.
———. "The Feminine Touch in the Legend of Moses." *Women in Judaism* (January 2000). No pages. Online: http://www.utoronto.ca/wjudaism/index.html.
———. "From Yahwism to Judahism." *Bible and Interpretation* (December 2008). No pages. Online: http://www.bibleinterp.com.
———. *God's Scribes: How the Bible Became the Bible*. Warren Center, PA: Shangri-La, 1999.

———. "'History' and 'Writing.'" *Bible and Interpretation* (August 2003). No pages. Online: http://www.bibleinterp.com.

———. "Homosexuality, the Bible and the Rabbis." *Bible and Interpretation* (November 2010). No pages. Online: http://www.bibleinterp.com.

———. "The Limmûdîm in the Book of Isaiah." *Journal for the Study of the Old Testament* 34 (2009) 99–109.

Jacobs, Louis. "Hermeneutics." In *EJ*. No pages. CD-Rom.

Jeremias, Joachim. *The Parables of Jesus*. Translated by S. H. Hooke. Revised. New York: Scriber, 1963.

Josephus, Flavius. *Antiquities*.

———. *Wars of the Jews*.

Kittel, Gerhard. "Agar." In *TDNT* 1:55–56.

Kolatch, Yonatan. *Masters of the Word: Traditional Jewish Bible Commentary From the First Through Tenth Centuries*. 2 vols. Jersey City, NJ: KTAV, 2006.

Krueger, Friedhelm. *Humanistische Evangelienauslegung: Desiderius Erasmus von Rotterdam als Ausleger der Evangelien in seiner Paraphrasen*. Tubingen: Mohr, 1986.

Kugel, James L., and Rowan A. Greer. *Early Biblical Interpretation*. Philadelphia: Westminster, 1986.

Lamberton, Robert. *Homer the Theologian: Neoplatonist Allegorical Reading and the Growth of the Epic Tradition*. Berkeley, CA: University of California Press, 1986.

Langford, Jerome J. *Galileo, Science and the Church*. 3rd edition. Ann Arbor, MI: University of Michigan Press, 1971.

Levenson, Jon D. *The Death and Resurrection of the Beloved Son: The Transformation of Child Sacrifice in Judaism and Christianity*. New Haven, CT: Yale University Press, 1993.

Levine, Baruch. *The JPS Torah Commentary: Leviticus*. Philadelphia: Jewish Publication Society, 1989.

Mahler, Refael. "HeḤasidut ve-Hahaskalah." In *Hadat ve-HeḤayim*, edited by Immanuel Etkes, 64–88. Reprint. Jerusalem: Merkaz Zalman Shazar, 1993.

Malter, Henry. *Saadia Gaon: His Life and Works*. Morris Loeb Series. Philadelphia: Jewish Publication Society, 1969.

Mangan, J. J. *The Life, Character and Influence of Desiderius Erasmus*. New York: Macmillan, 1927.

Marius, Richard. *Martin Luther: The Christian between God and Faith*. Cambridge, MA: Harvard University Press, 1999.

Martin-Achard, Robert. "Isaac" In *ABD* 3:462–70.

Maslin, Simeon J. "The Fury of Orthodoxy." *Reform Judaism*, Fall 1998, 19–24.

Mason, Steve. *Flavius Josephus: Life of Josephus*. Leiden: Brill, 2003.

———. *Josephus and the New Testament*. 2nd edition. Peabody, MA: Hendrickson, 2003.

Mielziner, Moses. *Introduction to the Talmud*. 5th edition. New York: Bloch, 1968.

Mowry, L. "Allegory" In *IDB* 1:82–84.

Neusner, Jacob. *Invitation to Midrash: The Workings of Rabbinic Bible Interpretation*. San Francisco: Harper, 1989.

———. *The Judaism Behind the Texts: The Generative Premises of Rabbinic Literature: II. Tosefta, Tractate Avot, and Earlier Midrash Compilations: Sifra, Sifre to Numbers, and Sifre to Deuteronomy*. Atlanta: Scholars, 1994.

———. *The Rabbinic Traditions about the Pharisees Before 70.* 3 vols. Leiden: Brill, 1973.

O'Keefe, John, and R. R. Reno. *Sanctified Vision: An Introduction to Early Christian Interpretation of the Bible.* Baltimore: Johns Hopkins University Press, 2005.

Ozick, Cynthia. "The Modern 'Hep! Hep! Hep!'" *The New York Observer*, May 7, 2004.

Philo of Alexandria. *De Abrahamo.* Paris: Editions du Cerf, 1966.

———. *Every Good Man is Free.* Loeb Classical Library. Cambridge, MA: Harvard University Press, 1941.

Pope, M. H. "Oaths." In *IDB* 3:575-77.

Porten, Gary. "Midrash." In *ADB* 4:818-822.

Raitt, Thomas M. *A Theology of Exile: Judgment/Deliverance in Jeremiah and Ezekiel.* Philadelphia: Fortress, 1977.

Rivkin, Ellis. *What Crucified Jesus?* New York: UAHC, 1977.

Roth, Cecil. *A History of the Jews from Earliest Times through the Six-Day War.* New York: Schocken, 1970.

Saldarini, Anthony J. "Pharisees." In *ABD* 5:289-303.

Samet, Moshe Shraga. "Moses Sofer" In *EJ*. No pages. CD-Rom.

de Santilla, G. Translator. *Galileo: Dialogue on the Great Systems of the World.* Chicago: Chicago University Press, 1953.

Sarna, Nahum M. *The JPS Torah Commentary: Exodus.* Philadelphia: Jewish Publication Society, 1991.

Schniedewind, William M. "Qumran Hebrew as an Antilanguage" *Journal of Biblical Literature* 118 (1999) 235-52.

Sefer haHinnuch. 3rd edition. Jerusalem: Feldheim, 1991.

Shulman, Yaacov Dovid. *The Vilna Gaon: The Story of Rabbi Eliyahu Kramer.* New York: C. I. S., 1994.

———. *The Chasam Sofer: The Story of Rabbi Moshe Sofer.* New York: C. I. S., 1992.

Sigal, Phillip. *The Halakhah of Jesus of Nazareth According to the Gospel of Matthew.* Atlanta: Society of Biblical Literature, 2007.

Simpson, D. P., editor. *Cassell's New Latin Dictionary.* New York: Funk and Wagnalls, 1959.

Sonsino, Rifat. "Shabbetay Zevi: The Fall of the False Messiah." *CCAR Journal* (Fall 1996) 71-83.

Sorkin, David. *Moses Mendelssohn and the Religious Enlightenment.* Berkeley, CA: University of California Press, 1996.

———. *The Transformation of German Jewry, 1780-1840.* New York: Oxford University Press, 1987.

Snijders, L. A. "*Male.*" In *TDOT* 8:297-307.

Steinsaltz, Adin. *The Talmud: A Reference Guide.* New York: Random House, 1989.

Strack, Hermann L. *Introduction to the Talmud and Midrash.* New York: Atheneum, 1972.

Telushkin, Joseph. *Jewish Literacy.* New York: William Morrow, 1991.

Thoma, C., and M. Wyschogrod, editors. *Understanding Scripture.* New York: Paulist, 1987.

Tigay, Jeffrey H. *The JPS Torah Commentary: Deuteronomy.* Philadelphia: Jewish Publication Society, 1996.

Trepp, Leo. *Judaism: Development and Life.* 4th edition. Boston: Wadsworth, 2000.

Vermes, Geza. *Scripture and Tradition in Judaism.* 2nd edition. Rome: Pontifical Biblical Institute, 1973.

Scripture and Other Sources Index

Hebrew Bible / Old Testament

Genesis

2:2-3	146
3:8ff	5n11
4:5-6	106
6:1-9	175n2
12:6	4
13:13	166
13:15	193
15:6	192
16:12	195
17	59
17:21	79
18	165, 167
18:1-20	174
18:22-33	5n13
19	167
19:5	165
19:36	194
21:1-3	174
22	78, 128
22:2	78, 79
22:12	79
27:40	114n26, 194
28:20-22	5n13
34	198
38:24-26	158
39:9	166

Exodus

1:22	125
2:1-10	4n10
3:6	194
4:19	124
4:22	124, 195n53
5	4n9
6:2-3	194
7:1	63
10:4a	196
10:4b	196
12:1-20	194n49
12:8-9	77–78
12:9	78n66
12:17	146n5
15	7
15:20-1	176
16:12-36	183–184
16:23	148
17:1-7	196
19:1-6	195n53
19:10-15	111
20	180, 181–182n25
20:6	147
20:8-11	146

Exodus (cont.)

20:11	146
20:13	105, 194
20:14	106
20:15	76
20:16	147
20:17	106
20:19-23:33	67n40
21:2	69
21:15	204
21:17	204
21:22-25	160
21:26-27	70–71
21:29-30	68
22:6-7	73
22:7-9	68
22:8	73–74
22:9	73
22:20	204
23:15	146n5
24:7	195
24:12	13n33
25:1-31:11	148
31:16-17	146n3, 181n24
32:9-14	6n14
33:13	170
34:6-7	170, 191n44
34:21	148
34:27	13n33
34:30-35	126n56
35:3	148

Leviticus

	122
1:2	73
15:13-33	204
15:31	188
16	69n45
16:29	69
17:13	75
18:22	164
19:11-13	77n63
19:12	110
19:14	11, 12
19:17	113
19:18	113, 180
19:19	111
20:2	158
20:10-14	107n11
20:13	164, 204
20:14	158
20:27	158
21:9	66n38, 158
21:17-21	204
24:14	158
24:16	158
24:17	105
24:17-22	160
24:18	162n30
24:22	113, 163
24:23	158
26:29	65

Numbers

12	63n28, 176n8
12:3	4
14:18	171n55
15:32-36	148
15:35-36	158
19:2	113n23
20:1-12	196
20:13	196
35:9	158
35:10-28	71n51

Deuteronomy

	109–116, 122
5	146, 180
5:12-15	146–147
5:14	147
5:16	147
5:19 (English 5:22)	76, 147
5:20	147
6:4	24
6:5	118, 119
6:7	29
8:2-3	69
9:11	106
13:2-6	63n28
13:11	158
13:15	158
15:1-2	167
15:2	168n45
15:3	168n45

15:7-8	167
15:9	166
15:12	69
16:7	77–78
17:5	158
17:8-11	55–56
18:18	63n28
19	71
19:4-6	71
19:11-13	106
19:18-21	160
21:21	158
21:22	110
22:1-3	75
22:11	72–73
22:20-24	158
22:25	158
24:1	108–110
24:6	70, 71n49
24:16	65–66
25:4	132
25:11	161–162
25:12	161
27:26	191
29:8	146n5
33:2	194, 195
34	4

Joshua

7:25	158

Judges

9:8-15	133

1 Samuel

1:1-20	174
6:7	113n23
15:22	127, 188n38
21:10	158

2 Samuel

	122
7:16	149n9
11:11	112
12:1-4	133
13:12	69n44
20:10	106
21:9	159n23

1 Kings

7:21-23	179
12	114n25
16:16-28	3
18:40	158, 181n22

2 Kings

4:32-37	179
9:1-10	152n19
9-10	151n18
10:10	152n19
13:20-21	179n16
19:15-17	152n19
19:35	148n8, 149n10
23:10	79

Isaiah

	59, 122
1:11	188n38
5:1-7	133
7:14	177n12–13
9:3	114n26
9:15	30n70
24-27	154n22
33:15-16	118
37:33	150
37:35	148n8
37:36	148n8, 149n10
40:3	185–187
40-66	187
42:1	187n35
45:1	187
49:1-6	187n35
49:3	190n41
50:4-9	187n35
52:13-53:12	187n35
53	190
53:7-8	189–190
53:10	189
53:12	189
56:1	118
58:3	69

Isaiah

	127, 189

Jeremiah

	122
1:5	190
2:20	114n26
5:5	114n26
6:6	150
6:16	115
7:1-15	151n16
7:22-23	188n38
14:13	149
14:14	150
17:21-24	148
20:7	6n15
23:14	165
23:29	55
27	114
27:2	114n27
27:6	150n14
27:8	151n15
27:11	114
27:11-12	151n15
27:12	114
30:8	114n26
31:15	125
31:31	200n4
32:18	171n55

Ezekiel

	122
16:49-50	165
34:27	114n26

Hosea

	122, 151, 190
1:4	152
11:1	124

Joel

2:13	171n55

Amos

5:4b	128
5:21-24	188n38
8:5	148

Obadiah

	47

Jonah

4:2	171n55

Micah

3:11	30n70
6:1-8	122
6:8	118

Nahum

1:3	171n55

Habakkuk

2:4	118, 128, 192
3:6	195

Zechariah

9:9	127
9-14	154n22

Zechariah

8-14	46

Malachi

1:2	47
2:7	30n70
3:23 (English 4:5)	186

Job

	6, 153
1:5	188n37

Psalms

	36, 59
1:5	166
5	122
10	122
14	122
15	118
16	122
22	43n16
35:13	69
53	122
59	122

62:12	145
85	138n104
86:15	171n55
89:35	79
90	6
95:11	132
103:8	171n55
140	122

Proverbs

1:8	28–29
1:10	28–29
1:15	28–29
2:1	28–29
3:1	28–29
3:13-15	134
3:18	195n52
4:1	28–29
4:10	28–29
4:20	28–29
5:1	28–29
10:1	134
11:30	195n52
13:12	195n52
15:4	195n52

Ruth

	31

Song of Songs

	31

Ecclesiastes

	31, 153

Lamentations

	31
1:14	114n24

Esther

	31, 36

Daniel

	6, 7, 36, 46, 61, 154n22, 205
4:28	127
4:30	127
4:31	127
12:2	179n17

Ezra

	61, 205

Nehemiah

8:1-8	61
9:17	171n55
10:35, 37	105n6
13:15-21	148
13:23-24	61n21

2 Chronicles

17:7-9	30n69
25:4	105n6
35:13	77–78

New Testament

Matthew

	40–41, 43, 44, 104–119, 123, 176
1:1-17	177
1:18-25	177n11
1:19	176
1:20	52, 175
1:23	124n56, 175n3
2:13	124
2:15	124, 124n56
2:16	124
2:17	125
2:18	124n56
2:19-20	124
2:23	124n56
3:3	186n33
3:7	44
4:15	124n56
4:23	40n9, 41
5	105, 180

Matthew (Cont.)

5:17	121n52, 128
5:17-19	116
5:20	116
5:21-22	105
5:21-48	116
5:27-30	106–107
5:28-48	123
5:31-32	107–110
5:33-37	110–112
5:38	160n25
5:38-42	112
5:39-41	184
5:43-48	112–113
6	116
6:2	116
6:5	116
6:7	116
6:16	116
6:32	116
7	116
7:5	116
7:15	116
7:24	116
7:26	116
7:28	116
8:4	125
8:6-13	189n40
8:17	124n56
8:19	117
9:18	117
9:32	108
11:7-15	186n32
11:29	115–119
12:2	117
12:18	124n56, 189n40
12:34	204
12:41	125
12:42	125
13:14	124n56
13:33	134
13:35	124n56
13:44-45	135
13:47-50	135
13:55	176
14:4	48
15:2	197n56
15:6	197n56
15:12-14	44
16:2	117
16:18	134
17:2-3	126
17:5	126
17:9-13	186n32
19:3	117
19:7-8	125
19:16-17	180
21:1-11	127
21:5	124n56
21:23	117
22:15	117
22:23	117
22:24	125
22:29	125
22:34-40	118n39
22:39	113n22
22:46	117
23:1	125
23:2-3	116
23:3	17
23:13	116
23:14	116n33
23:15	116
23:16	117
23:17	117
23:19	117
23:23	116
23:24	117
23:25	116
23:27	116
23:29	116
23:33	117
26:51	49n28
27:9	124n56
28:1	182
28:9	53, 178

Mark

	40–41, 43–45, 52n40, 175
1:1	40n9, 41
1:3	186n33
1:4-6	186
1:6	186n32

1:14	41	3:4	186n33
3:17	49	3:7	44
4:1-9	134	3:16	186n32
4:30-32	134	4:16-17	51n35
6:3	176	6:29-30	185n30
6:18	48	7:12-15	179n15
7:3	197n56	10:25-27	118n39
7:5	197n56	10:25-37	135n94
7:8	197n56	11:2-13	135
7:9	197n56	13:31	50
7:13	197n56	14:5	135
7:24	51	14:18-33	135
7:34	43n16	15:4-32	135
9:11-13	186n32	16:1-13	135
10:7-31	180n19	17:7-10	135
10:46	43n16	18:1-8	135
12:15-40	43	18:18-30	180n19
12:28-31	118n39	24:13-30	53
14:47	49n28	24:15-16	178
15:22	43n16	24:39	178
15:34	43n16		
15:43	50	*John*	
16:12	53		40–41, 45, 104, 138
16:18	178	1:8	186n32
16:22	178	1:9	48
		1:21	186
Luke		1:22	186n33
	37, 40–41, 43, 44–45, 49	1:45	52n40, 175
		3	183
1:1	103n2	3:1-10	50
1:17	186	3:18-20	204
1:24	186	3:22	48
1:28	176n10	3:30	186
1:32	186	4	183
1:34	175	6:48-54	183
1:34-35	186	6:52	183
1:35	53	8:19	51n34
1:41	186	11:43-44	179n15
1:44	186	11:45-48	49–50
1:76	186	11:48	11n27
2:2	44	14:6	116
2:33	175	18:10	49n28
2:41	175	18:36	183
2:41-51	117	20:11-15	53
2:46	27n60	20:19	53, 178–179
2:47	27n60	20:24-29	53
2:48	175	20:30	42, 104n3

scripture and other sources index

Acts — 40, 45, 175

1:6	183
1:9	178
5:34	119
5:34ff	50
8:26-39	189
9:2	116
11:26	13
15	51–52
15:5	50
15:10	115
15:20	206n8
15:29	206n8
15:30	52n38
18:25	116
22:3	119, 123
24:22	116

Romans

	40, 138
1:3	52, 175
1:4	53
3:9	122
3:10-18	122
4:1	122
6:1	122
7:7	122
7:12	123
7:13-8:11	121
7:14	123
7:15	191
7:17	191
7:20	191
7:24	191, 195
7:24-25	121
7:70	192
10:4	195
10:17	182
13:8	180
13:10	180
16:22	46

1 Corinthians

	40, 138
6:1-7	185
7:40	206n9
9:9	132
9:20-22	51
10:1-5	195–196
10:6	131
11:25	131n75
15	178
15:42-54	53
15:44	178
15:50-51	178
16:21	46

2 Corinthians

	40, 138
3:6	130n72, 131n75
3:7	121
3:9	121
6:14-18	122

Galatians

	40, 138
1:14	119, 191, 197n56
1:15	190n42
2	52n37
2:5	41
2:14	41
3:7	192
3:10	191
3:16	193
3:17	52, 192
3:19	193
3:23-25	193
4	131n78
4:1-7	121
4:4	52, 175
4:21-23	121
4:28-31	193
5:12	46
5:14	123
5:19-22	195
6:11	46

Ephesians

	40, 138
6:1-4	180n20
6:19	41

Philippians

	40, 119, 138

1:27	41	1:1-2	173n1
3:4-5	119	4:3	132
3:6	191	6:4-6	137–138
3:9	191	10:20	116

Colossians		James	
	40, 138		39, 45, 137
1:23	41	2:8	180
2:8	197n56		

1 Peter

40, 45, 138

1 Thessalonians			
	40, 138	5:12	46
4:13-17	53–54		

2 Peter

39, 40, 45

2 Thessalonians

40, 138

1 John

40, 45

1 Timothy

40, 45, 138

2 John

40, 45

2 Timothy

40, 45, 138

3 John

40, 45

Titus

45, 138

Jude

39, 40, 45, 138

Philemon

40, 45, 138

Revelation

46, 138

Hebrews

39, 45, 45n23

Apocypha / Deuterocanonical Texts and Pseudepigrapha

Apocrypha / Deuterocanonical Books

2 Maccabees

xviin4, 36, 137n98

1 Maccabees

xviin4, 36, 137n98, 154n21

Daniel (additions to)

36, 137n98

Esther (additions to)

36, 137n98

Judith

xviin4, 36, 137n98

Letter of Jeremiah

36

Psalms (additions to)

36

Sirach

xviin4, 137n98

1:4-7	205
1:23-26	205

Tobit

xviin4, 36, 137n98

Wisdom of Solomon

xviin4, 36

Pseudepigrapha

59–63, 157, 173

Baruch

137n98

Book of Jubilees

18:13	129n68

1 Enoch

xviin4, 60n15, 175

Dead Sea Scrolls

144

pesharim of Qumran

124n57, 126

Pesher on Habakkuk

2:1	126n62

Philo of Alexandria

58–59, 173

De Abrahamo

32-36	129n68

Every Good Man Is Free

12-13	111
13	112, 129

Josephus

47, 173

Jewish Antiquities

58

1.3.1-4	129n67
18.5.2 para. 116-19	186n31

The Jewish War

58–59

2	112n19
8:6-13	112n21
8:7	112n19

Vita

58

Mishnah, Talmud, and Related Literature

Mishnah
70, 82, 83, 86–88, 94, 95, 102–104, 108, 203

'Avot
197
1:1   125
2:21   120n45
3:6   114n29

Pirkei 'Avot
9, 15, 22n45, 197
1:1   107
1:6   29n68
4:15   29n65
5:18   29n67
6:3   30n72

Baba Kamma
8:1   161n26

Baba Metzia
2:5   75n60
9:13   70

Bekhorot
8n20, 13n33, 24n50
2:2   114n29
2:2, 4   115n30

Gittin
9:10   108n13, 109

Kiddushin
4:14   164n36

Makkot
1:10   159
2:1   71n52
2:2   72n53
3:14-16   120n46

Megillah
4:4   62n22
4:10   62n22

Sanhedrin
7:1   159
10:1   119n44

Shabbat
7:2-4   148

Shevi'it
10:3   169n46
10:4-6   169

Shevu'ot
110

Sotah
8n19

Yoma
1:1-8   112n18
8:1   70

Babylonian Talmud
83, 95, 159n24, 198

Baba Batra
12b   166n42

Baba Kamma
62b   74n58
83b-84a   161, 161n26

Baba Metzia
94b   68n43

Bekhorot
5a   13n33
2a   105n6
8a   105n6

Bekhorot (Cont.)

13b	114n28
31b	8n20
34b	120n46

Eruvin

60b	13n33

Gittin

6b	17n39
13b	17n38
36b	169n48
37a-b	169n48

Hullin

88b	75n59

Kiddushin

20b	23n48
24a	71n50
49a	62
81a	106–107
81a	107n10
82a	164n37

Ketubot

	109
103a	166n42

Makkot

23a	127
23b-24a	127, 118n38

Megillah

3a	61n20
9a	58n10
23b	62n25
74d	61n19

Pesahim

6b	81

Rosh ha-Shanah

17b	170n51

Shabbat

31a	121n51, 123n55
49b	148n7
63a	65n34, 81

Sotah

13b	164n35
16a	65, 125n58

Sanhedrin

27b	65
27b	65n35
34a	55, 145n1
51b	66n38
57b-58a	164n38
86a	76n61
109a-b	166

Yebamot

13b	65n34
24a	81

Yoma

9b	106n9
86a-b	120n47
87a	120n47
86a-b	120n47

Zevahim

84a	73n54

Palestinian / Jerusalem Talmud

	198

Other Rabbinic Works

Bamidbar Rabbah
13:15-16   55

inter alia
48:3   127n63

Karo, Joseph

"The Prepared Table"
                               34

Shulhan Arukh
                          34–35,
                      55, 96n102

Maimonides

commentary on the Mishnah
                               33

Repetition of the Torah (Mishnah Torah)
                           33, 89

A Teacher/Guide for the Confused
                        34, 89–90

Midrash
                  24–25, 80, 97, 132
161   63

Ecclesiastes Rabba
3.9.1   134n89

Mekhilta de R. Ishmael
                       67n40, 194

BaHodesh 5
                           194n49

Midrash Rabbah
                               31

Genesis, va-yera,' LVI, 8
                            79n67

Sifra
                            69n45
9:8   164n34

Sifrei Shoftim
161   62n24

Yalqut

Numbers, 766
                           134n91

responsa
                            31–32

Sefer ha-Ḥinnukh
209   164

Mitzvah 38
                              106

Tosephta (Ned)
51a   165n41

Tosephta Baba Qamma
9:29   185n29

Greek and Latin Works

Augustine
 135n94, 140n108, 141, 142

Copernicus
 142–143

Epistle of Barnabas
 41n10

Erasmus, Desiderius
 140–141

Eusebius

Ecclesiastical History
 39 40n8

Galileo

Dialogue on the Great Systems of the World
 142, 143

Irenaeus

Against Heresies
 39–40, 131n75

Origen
 130–133, 141

Thomas Aquinas, Saint
 85, 141–142

Catholic Councils and Papal Encyclicals

Council of Carthage (394 CE)
 136n95

Council of Florence (1441 CE)
 138, 162

Council of Trent (1545-1563 CE)
 137–140, 142

Pope Pius XII

Divino Afflante Spiritu
 143

Vatican II
 136n96, 143–144

Protestant Works

Martin Luther

Werke Briefwechsel
 6:10 137n100

Names Index

A

Aaron, 63
Abel, 57
Abimelech, 133
Abraham, 5, 52, 57, 59, 78–80, 128–129, 131, 134, 165, 167, 192, 193, 194
Agur, 6
Akenson, Donald Harmon, 38n3, 178n14
Akiva (rabbi), 18, 24n49, 66, 80, 108–109, 110, 159, 160, 205
Alexander, Philip S., 61n18
Alexander Jannaeus, 198–199
Alexander of Macedon, 22–23
Amon, 194
Amos, 196
Anan ben David, 81
Anderson, Gary A., 189n39
Antiochus Epiphanes, 154
Apollos, 116
Aristotle, 83, 85–90
Athanasius, 136n95
Augustine, 135n94, 140n108, 141, 142

B

Baal Shem Tov, 92–93
Bainton, Roland H., 140n111
Bamberger, Berhard J., 82n77, 91n87
Bar Kosiba, 90

Barr, James, xvii
Bellarmine, Robert Cardinal, 131, 131n74, 131n78, 132
Ben Sira, 205
Blackwell, Richard J., 131n74, 131n78, 132n81, 133n85, 137n97, 139n105, 139n107
Blomberg, C. L., 133n87
Breslauer, S. Daniel, 95n100
Brettler, Marc, 147–148
Brown, Raymond E., 43n17, 44n20, 45nn21-22, 143n121
Burkett, Delbert, 121n50, 183n26

C

Caesar Augustus, 44
Cain, 57
Charlesworth, James H., 59n12, 60n14
Chilton, Bruce, 129n69
Chomsky, William, 82n77
Clement VII (pope), 142
Coffin, William Sloane, 200
Collins, Raymond F., 180n18
Constantine, 19n42
Copernicus, Nicholas, 142–143
Crossan, John Dominic, 128n64, 133n86
Cyrus of Persia, 187, 189

D

Dan, Joseph, 92n89, 92n91, 93nn93-94
Daube, David, 161n27
David (king of the Jews), 3, 6, 59, 118, 133, 149, 151, 192n46
Davidson, Herbert A., 32n76
Davies, P. R., 129n69
Delling, Gerhard, 126n60
Dimont, Max I., 82n77
Dodd, C. H., 133
Durant, Will, 140n110, 141n112

E

Ehrman, Bart, 40n7, 41n11, 42n12, 119
Elazar ben Azaryah, 159, 160
El`azar ben Shamu`a, 29
Elijah (prophet), 126, 151, 179, 181, 186
Elijah ben Solomon, 91–93
Elisha, 151, 179
Erasmus, Desiderius, 140–141
Eusebius, 40, 40n8
Ezra, 6, 9, 61

F

Feldman, Louis H., 58n7, 59n11
Felix, 116
Fried, Liz, 92n91, 187n36
Friedman, H., 5n12

G

Galileo, 142–143
Gamaliel (defender of apostles), 50
Gamaliel (rabbi), 24, 114–115, 119, 123, 169
Gamaliel II, 18, 185
Gebiha the son of Pesisa, 23
Gedaliah, 149
Gese, Hartmut, xvii
Goldin, Judah, 46n25
Goodenough, E. R., 56n3
Greer, Rowan A., 39n5
Gundry, R. H., 126n61, 130n72

H

Hagar, 194
Harrington, Daniel J., 36n1
Hedges, Chris, ix n1
Herod, 44, 46–47, 48, 124
Herod Antipas, 48, 49
Herodias, 48
Hezekiah, 3
Hicks, L. W., 128nn65-66
Hillel (rabbi), 13n31, 17, 66, 100, 108–109, 117, 119, 123, 123n55, 167–168
Holdheim, Samuel, 204n6
Homer, 56, 57n5
Horgan, Maurya P., 126n62
Horsley, Richard A., 48n27, 49n30
Hosea, 151–152, 196–197

I

Irenaeus, 39, 40, 131n75
Isaac, 78–80, 128–129, 174, 193
Isaiah, 118, 148–150
Isbell, Charles David, 2n4, 3n7, 10n24, 33n78, 42n14, 59n13, 86n82, 154n20, 167n43, 175n6, 176n7, 177n12, 185n29, 187n34
Ishmael (member of Judaic royal family), 149n12
Ishmael (son of Abraham), 193–5
Ishmael ben Elisha`, 18, 66–80, 205
Isserles, Moses, 34

J

Jacob, 192n46
Jacobs, Louis, 64n33
Jacobson, Israel, 97
James, 49, 52, 126
Jehoiakim, 150
Jehu (king of Israel), 3n6, 151–152
Jereboan II, 151
Jeremiah, 6, 114, 149–151, 190
Jeremias, Joachim, 134m93
Jeroboam II, 151
Jesus, 37–38, 39, 40–44, 46–49, 50, 51, 52–53, 103, 104–119, 123–129, 131, 134–135, 174–180, 183–186, 189–190, 193, 195–196

names index   229

Job, 6, 153
Johanan (high priest), 92n91
John (apostle), 49, 126
John the Baptist, 48, 185–187
Joseph (Mary's husband), 117, 124, 175, 176
Joseph (son of Jacob), 59, 164, 166
Joseph of Arimathea, 50
Josephus, Flavius, 47, 49, 58–59, 112, 129, 173, 185–186, 186n31
Josiah, 3
Judah (rabbi), 164
Judas Iscariot, 49n29

K

Kaplan, Mordecai, xxi
Karo, Joseph, 34, 55
Kittel, Gerhard, 194n48
Kolatch, Yonatan, 8n21, 61n17, 64n31, 82n73, 84n80, 89n85
Krueger, Friedhelm, 140n111
Kugel, James L., 39n5

L

Lamberton, Robert, 57n5
Langford, Jerome L., 141n115, 142nn116-119, 143n121
Lazarus, 49, 179n15
Lemuel, 6
Levenson, John D., 129n70
Levine, Baruch, 163n31
Lot, 165, 194
Lot's daughters, 194
Lot's wife, 200n2
Luther, Martin, 137–139, 140

M

Mahler, Refael, 93n95
Maimonides, 32–34, 55, 61n17, 84n79, 86–90
Malter, Henry, 82n75
Manasseh, 166
Mangan, J. J., 141nn113-114
Marcion, 37–38
Marius, Richard, 131n77, 138n102, 138n104, 140n110
Martin-Achard, Robert, 128n65

Mary (mother of Jesus), 52–53, 117, 124, 175–176, 186
Mary (woman at Jesus's tomb), 53
Maslin, Simeon J., 100nn117-118
Mason, Steve, 58nn7-8
Matthew, 104–119, 123, 123–128
Mendelssohn, Moses, 95–97
Micah, 196–197
Mielziner, Moses, 64n33, 67n41, 68n42, 83n78
Milgrom, Jacob, 171
Milgrom. Jacob, 196n55
Miriam, 176
Moab, 194
Montanus, 38–39
Moses, 4–6, 58, 59, 60, 63, 87, 124, 125, 126, 147, 170, 192n46, 194, 196, 205n7
Moses ben Maimon. *See* Maimonides
Mowry, L., 57n6

N

Napoleon Bonaparte, 94, 97
Nathan, 133, 149, 151
Nebuchadnezzar, 114, 127
Nehemiah, 6, 9, 61n21
Neusner, Jacob, 64n33, 102–103
Newton, Isaac, 143
Nicodemus, 50, 183

O

O'Keefe, John, 39n4, 56n4
Omri (king of Israel), 3, 151
Origen, 130, 141
Ozick, Cynthia, 181n23

P

Papias, 40
Paul, 45, 46, 51–54, 103, 119–123, 130–131, 132, 136, 175, 178, 180, 190–196, 206–207
Pelagius, 140n108
Peter, 40, 45, 46, 49, 103, 115–116, 126, 134, 175
Pharaoh, 63
Philip, 189–190

names index

Philo of Alexandria, 56–58, 111, 112, 129, 130, 131, 173
Pius XII (pope), 143
Plato, 85, 118, 121n49
Pontius Pilate, 48, 50
Pope, M. H., 112n21
Potiphar, 164
Proten, Gary, 64n33

Q

Quirinius, 44

R

Raitt, Thomas M., 151n17
Rashi, 29, 84–85, 164
Rehoboam, 114n25
Reno, R. R., 39n4, 56n4
Rivkin, Ellis, 49
Roth, Cecil, 82n77

S

Saadia Gaon, 82–83, 91–93
Saldarini, Anthony J., 103n1
Samaritan woman, 183
Samet, Moshe Shraga, 96n102, 98n110, 99n112
Samson, 59, 62n25
Samuel, 127, 174
de Santilla, G., 143n120
Sarna, Nahum M., xix, 32, 63n27, 163n32, 170n52
Saul (king of the Jews), 59, 127
Saul (Paul), 116
Schniedewind, William M., 81n72
Sermoneta-Gertel, Shmuel, 93n95
Shammai (rabbi), 13n31, 17, 108–110, 117n34
Shimon ben Gamliel I, 18, 159, 160
Shulman, Yaacov Dovid, 91n88, 92n90, 93n92, 96n102, 97nn103-105, 98n111, 98nn106-108, 99nn113-116
Sigal, Phillip, 104n4
Silberman, Neil Asher, 48n27, 49n30
Silvanus, 46

Simpson, D. P., 162n29
Sofer, Moshe (rabbi), 96–99
Solomon (king of Jews), 3, 6, 59
Solomon ben Isaac, 84–85
Sonsino, Rifat, 34n80, 92n89
Sorkin, David, 95n98
Spinoza, Baruch, 94–95
Steinsaltz, Adin, 25n52, 26n54, 26n57, 27n59, 27n61, 28n62, 31n73, 52n39, 64n33, 66n37, 67n39, 67n41, 104n4
Strack, Hermann L., 64n33

T

Tarfon (rabbi), 18, 120n45, 159, 160
Telushkin, Joseph, 24n50, 169n47
Tertius, 45–46
Thoma, C., xixn7
Thomas (apostle), 53, 179
Thomas Aquinas, Saint, 85, 141–142
Tigay, Jeffrey H., 56n2, 170n49
Trepp, Leo, 9n22, 22n47, 64n33, 89n83

U

Uriah, 111–112

V

Vermes, Geza, 129n69

W

Wyschogrod, M., xixn7

Y

Yehudah ha-Nasi,' 18, 62
Yohanan ben Zakkai, 16, 18, 170
Yose ben Elazar, 2n4

Z

Zedekiah, 114, 149
Zevi, Shabbetay, 92n89

Subject Index

A

Abraham
    Biblical link to Moses, 194
    binding (sacrifice) of Isaac, 78–80, 128–129
    debate with God, 5
    family of, 131
    God's promise to, 193
    hospitality of, 165, 167
    Josephus on, 59
    means of obtaining righteousness, 52, 192
    name for God, 5
    parable about centrality of, 134
    Philo's interpretation of, 57
accidents, 71–72
Acts, 45, 46–50
addenda (additions)
    Biblical interpretation in struggle with science, 141–144
    by rabbis of the Diaspora, 90–101
    rabbis on the Pharisees, 196–199
    by *Tanna'im*, 14n34
adultery
    Jesus's teaching on, 106–110
    of Lot's daughters, 194n50
    punishment for, 158, 204
    related to homosexuality in Jeremiah, 165
    rules for in Mishnah, 14, 76, 108–109

adverse selection, 42–43, 103–104, 136
agriculture (section of Talmud), 14
Akiva
    death of, 24n49
    objection to Ishmael's hermeneutic rules, 205
    opinions cited in Mishnah, 18
    ruling on death penalty, 159, 160
    ruling on divorce, 108–109, 110
    theory on language of Torah, 66, 80
allegory
    early Christians' use of, 38, 90, 130–131
    Greek philosophers use of, 56–57
    Luther's use of, 138–139
American Revolution, 94
Amoraic period, 30–31
'Amoraim
    addition of *haggadah* in *Gemara*, 22, 83–84
    application of Ishmael's rules, 71n49, 74
    development of *Gemara*, 19–20, 83–84, 94, 177
    discussions of issues
        corporal punishment, 161, 162
        homosexuality, 164, 166
        law of *prozbol*, 169–170
        witness qualifications, 65–66
    formula for introduction of Scripture, 105n6
    opening question, 122

anagogical interpretation, 132
analogy, 68–70, 113
angels, 60
animals, treatment of, 73, 75
Antioch, 37
Antitheses (Marcion), 38
Apocalypse, 40
apocalypticism, 60, 153–157, 156
Apocrypha, 36, 134
apostles, 50. *See also specific apostle*
appropriation, x–xi
'Aqedah, 78–80, 128–129
archaeological recoveries, 143–144
argument from prophecy, 38, 123–128
'asham (guilt offering), 188–189
Assyrians, 9, 148–149
authorship
    determined by modern scholarship, 60
    of Jewish Bible, 63
    of Latter Prophets, 3–4
    of New Testament books, 36, 38, 42n13, 44, 45, 46
    of Pentateuch, 4–6, 60, 87, 205n7
    of Psalms, 59
    of Pseudepigrapha, 59

B

Babylonia
    exile of Jews in, 9, 10, 17, 149, 154, 187, 189
    fall of, 154
    Jewish centers of learning in, 32
    Jewish return from exile in, 9, 10, 61, 187
    production of *Gemara* in, 18–19
    siege and destruction of Jerusalem, 149–151
Babylonian Talmud (TB), 19, 19n42, 198. *See also* Scripture and Other Sources Index
baptism, 48, 130, 186
Baraitot, 26n53, 26n56
betrothal, 14, 109, 194n50
binding (sacrifice) of Isaac, 78–80, 128–129

Binyan 'Av (formation of leading rule), 70–72, 164
biur (comments), 95
blessings, 14
burnt offering, 187–188
business, 14

C

canonical Scriptures
    development of Christian Bible, xix, 37–43, 46, 103, 135
    development of Jewish Bible, 6–7
    finalization of, 10
    Luther's reduction of, 137–138
    reaffirmation by Council of Trent, 138, 139
capital crimes, 68, 76–77, 105, 204
capital punishment. *See* death penalty
capitalism, 94
Catholic Bible, 2n1, 36n1
Catholic Church
    acceptance of Copernicus's theory, 142
    Biblical interpretation after Vatican II, 143
    clash with science, 142–143
    Council of Carthage (394 CE), 136n95
    Council of Florence (1441 CE), 138
    Council of Trent (1545-1563 CE), 137–140, 142
    penance, 138n103
    transvaluation of Ten Commandments, 181
children
    in Crusades, xx
    Essenes's adoption of, 111
    Jewish education of, 20–31, 118, 154
    names of Hosea's, 152
    punishment for disobedience, 65–66, 170, 204, 206
Christian Bible
    acceptance of New Testament, 131
    acceptance of Old Testament, 136, 200

development and canonization of, xix, 36–43, 46, 103, 135
finalization of, 10
Luther's reduction of, 137–138
reaffirmation by Council of Trent, 138, 139
translations of, 206
transvaluation of
  by Church fathers, 136, 138–139
  influences on, 173
  by Luther, 138–139
  in present, 144
Christianity
  acceptance of oral tradition, 136–137, 140
  adoption of Jewish Bible, 136, 200
  center of early church, 37
  Council of Carthage (394 CE), 136n95
  Council of Florence (1441 CE), 138
  Council of Trent (1545-1563 CE), 137–140
  development of faith system, 13, 36–37, 203
  divisions over issues, ix
  effects of holocaust, xx, 203–204
  failure to define difference between principle and practice, xviii
  formation of denominations, 140
  generation of interfaith tolerance, xxi
  Maimonides's creed vs., 86–88
  Maimonides's position on, 34
  methodology of interpretation
    after Vatican II, 143–144
    allegory, 130–131
    anagogical interpretation, 132
    argument from prophecy, 123–128
    ecclesiastical political effects, 135–141
    effects of ecclesiastical politics, 135–141
    of Jesus in Matthew, 104–119, 123
    parables, 133–135
    Paul's methodology, 119–123, 190–191
  rabbinic influence, 100–101, 102–104, 132–133
  tropology, 132
  typology, 128–130
  Vatican II, 143–144
  places of worship, 37
  rationalism of, 85
  sacred texts
    Acts, 45
    apocalyptic literature, 46
    canonization of, 37–43
    epistles, 45–46
    gospels, 43–45
    Old Testament, 36–40
    split between Rome and Luther, 137–140
  struggle with science, 34, 141–143
  transvaluation of Scripture
    concerning resurrection of Jesus, 178–179
    concerning Virgin Birth, 174–177
    influential writings, 173–174
    Jesus's teachings on eye for an eye, 184–185
    on manna, 182–184
    purpose of, xviii–xix
    on Ten Commandments, 179–182
    treatment of Isaiah 40:3, 185–187
  See also Catholic Church; Protestantism
Christians
  freedom of interpretation of Scriptures, xviii–xx, 27–28, 144, 173–174, 177, 180, 182
  Jewish believers' interpretation of Scripture, 102, 105–119
  requirements for non-Jewish converts, 52, 130
  survival of destruction of Judea, 13
church
  Biblical interpretation after Vatican II, 143–144
  creation and acceptance of oral tradition, 136–137

church (Cont.)
  creation and interpretation of canon, xix, 36–43, 46, 103, 135, 135–136
  idea of penance, 138n103
  as new creation of God, 129
  split between Rome and Luther, 137–140
  struggle with science, 141–143
  See also Catholic Church; Christianity; Protestantism
circumcision, 59, 130, 154
cities of refuge, 71–72
Codex Neofiti, 61
context
  effect on interpretation, 148–151, 152–157, 167–168, 171–172, 174, 177, 181–182, 193
  effect on Scripture, 153–157
  interpretation of Midrash and Talmudim within, 103
  interpretation of Scripture within, xix, 65, 68, 76–77, 148, 168, 200–201, 206–207
  interpretation without considering, xi, xii, xix
contradictory Scriptural statements, 77–81
corporal punishment. *See* capital punishment; eye for an eye rule
Council of Carthage (394 CE), 136n95
Council of Florence (1441 CE), 138
Council of Trent (1545-1563 CE), 137–140, 142
covetousness, 106
creation story, 4–5
crucifixion, 47, 48–49, 50

D

damages, 14
David
  authorship of Psalms, 59
  God's promise to, 149, 151
  Josephus's view of, 59
  means of reconciliation, 192n46
  reduction of precepts, 118
death penalty
  Christian transvaluation of, 105
  current thinking on, 201, 206
  rabbinic transvaluation of, 68, 157–160, 164
"Declaration of the Rights of Man" (1789), 94n96
deductive reasoning, 67
derash (Talmudic use of Midrashic forms), 132n83
deutero-canonical books, 36, 137
Diaspora, 10–11, 91
di-theism, 37
divine justice, 152–153, 170–171
divorce, 14, 107–110, 125
drash (detailed examination), 65–66. *See also* Gemara; hermeneutics of the rabbis; Midrash; Mishnah (oral Torah); *responsa*; Talmud; *tosephta* (additions)
dualism, 45

E

ecclesiastical canon law, 201
ecclesiastical politics, 135–141
education of Jews
  organization of, 25–28
  role of the synagogue, 30–31
  role of the teacher, 28–30
  subjects of inquiry, 20–25
Egypt, 32, 124–125, 149n11
'Ein mikra' yotze' mi-ydei peshuto (Scripture verse never loses its plain meaning), 81
'Ein mukdam u-me'uḥar ba-Torah (there is neither early nor late in the Torah), 80–81
Elijah (prophet), 126, 151, 186
empiricism, 94
Enlightenment (European), xxi, 93–94
Enlightenment (*Haskalah*), 93–94
epistles, 40, 45–50, 135–136, 138. *See also* specific epistle in Scripture and Other Sources Index
equivalency. *See* eye for an eye rule; monetary compensation

subject index 235

Erasmus, Desiderius (1466-1536 CE), 140–141
Essenes, 12, 81n72, 110–112
evangelion. *See* gospels
exclusion rule, 80
exegesis
    Christian methodology
        allegory, 130–131
        anagogical interpretation, 132–133
        argument from prophecy, 123–128
        of Jesus in Matthew, 104–119
        parables, 133–135
        of Paul, 119–123
        tropology, 132
        typology, 128–130
    defined, 64
    development of, xix
    development of Reform Judaism, 90–91
    'Ein mikra' yotze' mi-ydei peshuto (Scripture verse never loses its plain meaning), 81
    'Ein mukdam u-me'uḥar ba-Torah (there is neither early nor late in the Torah), 80–81
    of Erasmus and Luther, 141
    inclusion and exclusion rules, 80
    Ishmael's rules applied
        Binyan 'Av (formation of leading rule), 70–72, 164
        general and particular rules, 72–76, 168, 184
        gezerah shavah (analogy), 68–70
        Qal va-ḥomer (lenient to stringent), 67–68
        reconciliation of contradictory verses, 77–81
        thing is taught by context, 76
    of Jesus, 104–119
    of Mendelssohn, 95–96
    modern agenda, 100–101
    necessity of, 63, 64, 201
    post-rabbinic Jewish hermeneutics, 81–90
    rabbinic compared to Christian, xvii, xvii–xviii, 41, 132–133, 135, 139–140, 190, 192–193, 200–201, 201, 204
    rise of *Haskalah*, Reform, and Orthodoxy, 93–99
    See also interpretation of Scriptures; methodology
extra-canonical gospels, 41–43
extremist Christians, xx
extremist Jews, xx
eye for an eye rule
    Jesus's transvaluation of, 112–113, 184–185
    Jewish transvaluation of, 68, 160–164, 181, 184, 206

F

false witness, 147
family life, 14. *See also* adultery; divorce; marriage
fasting, 69–70
fasts, 14
feasts, 14, 17, 31, 197
festivals, 17n37, 31, 94
Former Prophets, 2–3, 10, 41. *See also specific prophetic writing in Scripture and Other Sources Index*
free-will offering, 188
French Revolution, 94
fundamentalist Christians, ix
fusion
    of Aristotle's ethics and Jewish tradition, 33, 83, 85–90
    of Hellenistic philosophy and Christianity, 45
    of Hellenistic philosophy and Judaism, 56–57

G

Gamaliel (Hebrew scholar)
    Paul's study under, 119, 123
    recital of Shema on wedding night, 24, 114–115
    ruling on law of *prozbol*, 169

garments, 72, 75
Gemara
  addition of *haggadah*, 22
  discussion of
    corporal punishment, 162
    Genesis 13:13, 166
    homosexuality, 164, 166
    law of prozbol, 169–170
    male-female relationships, 107
    manumission, 70
    witness examination in capital trials, 159n24
  importance in Jewish life, 95
  as justification of repetition, 83
  list of types of Pharisees, 197–198
  majority and opposing opinions in, 20
  opening question of '*Amoraim*, 122
  publication of, 31
  rejection of, 81–82
  study of in Yeshiva, 25–26
  transvaluation of scripture, 63
  writing of, 18–20
  See also Mishnah (oral Torah); Scripture and Other Sources Index; Talmud
Gemara period (ca. 200-500 CE), 21n44
general and particular rules, 72–76, 106, 168, 184
gezerah shavah (analogy), 68–70, 113
gnosticism, 45, 130
God
  acknowledgement of Jesus as His Son, 126
  binding (sacrifice) of Isaac, 78–80, 128–129
  commission of Moses, 63
  conversations with Moses and prophets, 58, 170
  guidelines for acceptability to, 196–197
  Jewish vs. Christian and Islamic view of, 86–87, 88
  Maimonides on nature of, 89, 90
  Marcion's view of, 37
  mercy and retribution of, 152–153, 170–171
  proof of existence of, 85
  rest on seventh day of creation, 146–147
  as source of wisdom, 60
  sovereignty of, 153
gospels
  canonization of, 40–43, 135–136
  extra-canonical gospels, 41–43
  historical context, 46–50
  John (110 CE, Ephesus, Asia Minor), 45
  Luke (85-95 CE, Achaia, Greece), 44–45
  Mark (70-75 CE, Rome), 43–45
  Matthew (80-90 CE, Antioch, Syria), 44
  teachings of, 40–41
  See also Scripture and Other Sources Index
graven images, 181, 182
great commandment, 43, 118–119, 127–128
Great Midrash. *See* Midrash Rabbah
Greek philosophy
  analogy used, 68–69
  inference *a fortiori* used, 67
  influence on Christianity, 38
  influence on Judaic interpretation, 56–57, 83, 85–90
guilt offering, 188–189

H

haggadah (stories), 22–23, 24, 31, 107, 132
halakhah (life path or law)
  defined, 21–22
  development of rulings, 26, 64
  Essenes' agreement with Pharisees on, 111
  as ideological weapon against Torah, 97–98
  of Jesus, 112, 115–116
  New Testament view of, 197
  relationship to Scripture, 65, 125n58
  Shuḥan Arukh, 34–35, 55
  on significance of *Shema*, 24

subject index 237

source of, 83
taking yoke of the kingdom and, 114
teaching of, 31
haraz (argumentation method), 122
Ḥasidim, 91–93, 100
Haskalah (Enlightenment), 93–94
Hasmoneans, 110–111
hatred, 106
ḥaver (study partner), 27, 29, 30n71
Hazal (scholars), 19n40
Hebrew Bible
   Christian adoption of, 38–39, 136, 200
   cited in *Gemara*, 19
   divisions of, 1–2
   language of, 7–8, 66, 80, 205
   Marcion's rejection of, 37
   miraculous birth narratives of, 174–175
   parables of, 133
   reduction of written traditions, xvii, 118, 137–138
   significance to Christianity, 39
   translations of
      in era of Joshua, 8
      Jerusalem Targum, 31
      by Mendelssohn into German, 95, 96–97
      Septuagint, 36–39, 58, 108, 137n99, 147, 173, 186, 189, 191
      Targum Onkelos, 30, 61n17, 62, 89n85
      Targumim, 61–63
   transvaluation by, 157
   wording of ninth commandment, 147
   See also Old Testament; Scripture and Other Sources Index; transvaluation: of Jewish Bible
Hebrew language, 7
hermeneutics. *See* hermeneutics of the New Testament in early church; hermeneutics of the rabbis; methodology; post-Biblical preludes to rabbinic interpretation; post-rabbinic Jewish hermeneutics
hermeneutics of the New Testament in early church
   allegory, 130–131
   anagogical interpretation, 132
   argument from prophecy, 123–128
   context of, 102–103
   effects of ecclesiastical politics, 135–141
   of Jesus in Matthew, 104–119
   Matthew's arguments from prophecy, 123–128
   methodology of Paul, 119–123
   parables, 133–135
   Paul's methodology, 119–123
   tropology, 132
   typology, 128–130
hermeneutics of the rabbis
   defined, 64
   'Ein mikra' yotze' mi-ydei peshuto (Scripture verse never loses its plain meaning), 81
   'Ein mukdam u-me'uḥar ba-Torah (there is neither early nor late in the Torah), 80–81
   Elazar's principles, 2n4
   Hillel and Akiva's principles, 66, 80
   inclusion and exclusion rules, 80
   influence on Christian hermeneutics, 102–106
   Ishmael's rules
      Binyan 'Av (formation of leading rule), 70–72, 164
      freedom of interpretation illustrated by, 171–172
      general and particular rules, 72–76, 106, 168, 184
      gezerah shavah (analogy), 68–70, 113
      Jesus's application of, 106–107
      Qal va-ḥomer (lenient to stringent), 67–68, 135, 162
      reconciliation of contradictory verses, 77–81
      thing is taught by context, 76–77, 148, 168
   modern agenda, 100–101

hermeneutics of the rabbis (Cont.)
   rise of *Haskalah,* Reform, and
      Orthodoxy, 93–99
   switch from to Reform Judaism,
      90–91
high priest, 50n32
Hillel
   establishment of law of *prozbol,*
      167–168
   on fulfilling the law, 123
   influence by, 17, 119
   as liberal rabbi, 13n31
   personal life of, 117
   position on divorce, 108–109, 110
   principles of interpretation, 66
   reconstruction of Biblical
      principles, 100
   on study of Torah, 123n55
   on two Torahs, 17
Hillel school, 17, 108–109, 119
Historical Books. *See* Former Prophets
historical influences
   conditions in Palestine, 46–50
   Crusades, xx–xxi
   destruction of Temple, 12–13, 14,
      17–18, 36, 37, 58, 63, 89–90,
      102, 149
   Diasporic life, 91
   Holocaust, xx–xxi
   on Philo, 56–57
   revolutions, 94
   Roman conquest, xx–xxi, 63
   Roman occupation of Judea, xxi,
      10, 46–47, 102, 159, 185, 203
   suffering of Jews, 9–10, 17,
      152–157
history
   in Acts, 45
   in Former Prophets, 2–3, 41, 42
   in gospels, 42
   predetermination of, 155–157
holocaust, xx, 203–204
holy of holies, 18
holy things, 15
homicide, 71–72
homosexuality, 164–167, 204, 206
hospitality, 111, 165–167
house of scholars, 26

ḥaṭa 't (sin offering), 188
Humash. See Torah

I

ideological influences, xx–xxi, 11, 15–
   16, 17–18, 93–94, 172, 200
illness, treatment of, 15
imperialism, 94
incest, 158, 194
inclusion rule, 80
individualism, 93–94
inerrancy, x–xi, 58–59
inference *a fortiori,* 67
Infinitive Absolute, 80
injury, 15, 160–164, 184–185
inner-Biblical transvaluation
   of Elijah, Elisha, and Hosea,
      151–152
   of Isaiah and Jeremiah, 148–151
   of Job and Ecclesiastes, 152–153
   of prophecy and apocalypticism,
      153–157
   of Ten Commandments, 145–148
innovation, 98–99, 100–101
insult, 160–161, 184
inter-faith dialogue, 203–204
interpersonal relationships, 14
interpretation of Scriptures
   Akiva's principles, 68
   by Catholic Church, 136–137,
      139–140, 141–142
   Christians' freedom of, xviii–xx,
      27–28, 144, 173–174, 177, 180,
      182
   current methods, 143–144
   freedom of modern interpreters,
      206–207
   future directions, 200–207
   Hillel's principles, 68
   historical influences, xx–xxi, 9–10,
      12–13, 17–18, 37, 46–50, 56–
      57, 63, 91, 94, 152–157
   ideological influences, xx–xxi, 11,
      15–16, 17–18, 94, 172, 200
   as integral to Judaism, 55–56
   Jesus's freedom and authority,
      105–106, 109–110, 180

by Luther, 137–139
modern interpreters' freedom of, 200–204
Paul's freedom and authority, 121, 180
post-Biblical preludes to rabbinic interpretation
    Josephus, 58–59
    Philo of Alexandria, 56–58
    Pseudepigrapha, 59–63
post-rabbinic Jewish hermeneutics
    Maimonides, 85–90
    Rashi, 84–85
potential for disater, 202–203
by Protestants, 140–141, 142
rabbinic compared to Christian, xvii, 41, 132–133, 135, 139–140, 190, 192–193, 200–201, 204
rabbis' freedom and authority, xviii–xx, 16–17, 24–25, 27–28, 76–77, 164, 167, 171–172, 179
by radical and fundamentalist adherents, ix, 203
by Sadducees, 11
See also hermeneutics of the New Testament in early church; hermeneutics of the rabbis; methodology; post-Biblical preludes to rabbinic interpretation; post-rabbinic Jewish hermeneutics; transvaluation
Isaac, 78–80, 128–129, 174, 193
Isaiah, 118, 148–150
Ishmael's rules of hermeneutics
    Binyan 'Av (formation of leading rule), 70–72, 164
    general and particular rules, 72–76, 168, 184
    gezerah shavah (analogy), 68–70, 113
    Jesus's application of, 106–107
    Qal va-ḥomer (lenient to stringent), 67–68, 135, 162
    thing is taught by context, 76–77, 148, 168
Islam, 34, 82, 86–88

Israel, 9, 153–154

J

Jeremiah, 6, 149–151, 190
Jerusalem
    ban on Jews in, 13
    as center of rabbinic Judaism, 37
    Roman siege and destruction of, 12–13, 17, 106
Jerusalem Gemara, 19nn41-42
Jerusalem Talmud, 19, 198
Jerusalem Targum, 30–31
Jesus
    affiliation with John the Baptist, 48
    application of Old Testament to life of, 131
    baptism of and by, 48, 186
    compared to Paul, 51
    conception and birth, 44, 52–53, 174–177
    crucifixion of, 47, 48–49
    eye for an eye teaching, 184–185
    flight to Egypt, 124–125
    as fulfillment of law, 128, 195
    as goal of Torah, 195
    gospel accounts of, 40–42
    healing of leper, 125
    hermeneutics of, 104–119, 123
    metaphorical teachings, 183
    Moses's relationship to, 124–126
    parables of, 134–135
    prophecy related to, 123–128, 189–190
    questions asked by religious leaders, 43, 117, 118, 125
    raising of the dead, 179
    recording of teachings of, 103
    references to Pentateuch, 125
    relationship with Pharisees and Sadducees, 50, 117–118
    on requirements for eternal life, 180
    resurrection of, 53, 178–179
    as rock in the wilderness, 195–196
    as seed of Abraham, 193
    teachings of, 37–38, 39

Jesus (Cont.)
   teachings on
     adultery and lust, 106–107
     divorce, 107–110, 125
     eye for an eye rule, 112–113
     greatest commandment, 118
     hate and murder, 105–106
     his *halakah*, 114–116
     love for enemies, 112–113
     oaths, 110, 112
   transfiguration of, 126
   types of in Old Testament, 128–129
   use of parables, 134–135
   view of scribes and Pharisees, 116–117
Jewish creed (Maimonides), 86–89
Jewish principles of interpretation. *See* hermeneutics of the rabbis; post-Biblical preludes to rabbinic interpretation; post-rabbinic Jewish hermeneutics
Jewish sacred writings. *See* sacred texts and instruction
Jewish scholarship, ix–x. *See also* '*Amoraim*; hermeneutics of the rabbis; Maimonides; post-Biblical preludes to rabbinic interpretation; post-rabbinic Jewish hermeneutics; Spinoza, Baruch; *Tanna'im*
Jews
   Antiochus Epiphanes's persecution of, 154
   Diaspora, 10–11, 91
   education of children, 20–31, 118, 154
   exile in Babylonia, 9, 10, 149, 154, 187, 189
   explanations for suffering of, 9, 17
   in German army, 97
   holocaust, xx, 203–204
   requirement for converts, 114n29
   return from Babylonia, 9, 61, 187
   Roman persecution of, 18
   See also Essenes; Orthodox Judaism; Pharisees; rabbis; Reform Judaism; Sadducees
Job, 153

John, Gospel of (110 CE), 45. *See also* Scripture and Other Sources Index
John the Baptist, 48, 185–186, 186, 186–187
Josephus, 47, 49, 58–59, 112, 129, 173
Judah (kingdom of), 10, 148–151, 153, 154
Judahism, 10
Judahite preference, 3
Judaism
   Antiochus Epiphanes's persecution, 154
   center of, 37
   conflict within, 81–83, 90–101
   development of faith system, 13, 17–18, 36, 203
   failure to define difference between principle and practice, xviii
   generation of interfaith tolerance, xxi
   hermeneutics of. *See* hermeneutics of the rabbis; post-Biblical preludes to rabbinic interpretation; post-rabbinic Jewish hermeneutics
   origins of, 10–11
   place of worship, 37
   replacement of Temple sacrifices, 17, 36
   struggle with science, 34
   texts of
     Bible, 1–8
     Gemara, 18–19
     Mishnah (oral Torah), 8–18
     responsa, 32
     Shulhan Arukh, 34–35
     teaching of, 20–31
     works of Maimonides, 32–35
Judea
   administration of, 11
   Roman conquest of, 58
   Roman occupation of, xxi, 10, 46–47, 102, 159, 185, 203
   Roman siege and destruction of Jerusalem, 12–13, 17, 106
   war against Rome, xx, 58

K

Karaism, 81–83
Karaites, 81–83, 91, 100
kashrut (kosher preparation), 75, 94, 130, 206
kelal (general) law, 72–81
ketubbot (marital agreement), 109–110
Ketuvim (Writings), xvii, 1–2, 4, 104
kidnapping, 76–77
kingdom of God (heaven)
    gospel of, 41
    Jesus as way into, 193
    Jesus's references to, 48–49
    parables about, 134–135
    requirements for entry into, 18, 178
    yoke of, 24, 113–115
kosher preparation, 75, 94, 130, 206

L

Latter Prophets, 2, 3–4. *See also specific prophetic writing in Scripture and Other Sources Index*
law, 52, 119–123, 180, 190–195. *See also* halakhah (life path or law); Torah
leading rule, 70–72, 164
"Lekha Dodi," 146n4
lex talionis. *See* eye for an eye rule
liability, 73–74
literal interpretation of holy books
    alteration in Pseudepigrapha, 60
    of capital punishment, 158–159
    historical influences on, xx, 10–11
    ideological influences on, xx–xxi, 11
    inerrancy compared to, x–xi, xii
    Jewish and early Christian interpretation vs., 204–207
    rabbinical view of, 58–59
    by radical and fundamentalist adherents, ix, 203
    by Sadducees, 11
    See also pesha ṭ (plain sense)
liturgy, 170–171, 197
loans, 70, 167–170
Luke, Gospel of (85-95 CE, Achaia, Greece), 44–45. *See also* Scripture and Other Sources Index
Luther, Martin, 137–139, 140–141, 142, 181n23
LXX. *See* Septuagint

M

Maimonides (1135-1204 CE)
    creed of, 86–89
    fusion of Greek philosophy with Scripture, 86–90
    on *Targum Onkelos*, 61n17
    teachings on magic, 33
    transvaluation of Scripture, 55
    works of. *See* Scripture and Other Sources Index
manna, 182–184
manumission, 70–71
Mark, Gospel of (70-75 CE, Rome), 43. *See also* Scripture and Other Sources Index
marriage
    betrothal, 14, 109, 194n50
    between Christians and unbelievers, 122
    divorce, 14, 107–110, 125
    Essene prohibition of, 111
    evading procreation in, 164–165
    between Ḥasidim and Orthodox Jews, 92n91
    Jesus's teachings on, 106–110, 125
    remarriage, 109–110
    rules for in Mishnah, 14
    See also adultery
Mary (mother of Jesus), 52–53, 117, 124–125, 175–176, 186
masal (proverb), 134
Matthew (apostle)
    arguments from prophecy, 123–128
    presentation of teachings of Jesus, 104–119
    transvaluation of Biblical texts, 177
Matthew, Gospel of (80-90 CE, Antioch, Syria), 44, 104–119. *See also* Scripture and Other Sources Index
Mendelssohn, Moses, 95–96, 97
messiah, 60n16, 88, 175, 186, 187–190

242 *subject index*

methodology
    after Vatican II, 143–144
    allegory, 56–57, 90, 130–131
    anagogical interpretation, 132
    argument from prophecy, 123–128
    of Jesus in Matthew, 104–119
    of Jewish scholars, 32
    of Paul, 119–123
    of Pharisees, 12
    rabbinic compared to Christian, xvii–xviii, 200–201, 206
    of rabbis, 20
    of Sadducees, 11
    study of, x, xvii–xx
    of *Tanna'im* and ⊠*Amoraim*, 15–20
    tropology, 132
    typology, 128–130
    See also hermeneutics of the rabbis; post-Biblical preludes to rabbinic interpretation; post-rabbinic Jewish hermeneutics
middat Sedom (acting like Sodom), 166
Midrash
    content of, 62, 63
    criteria for examination of, 103
    defined, 24–25
    on Ishmael, 194
    rabbinic use of, 132
    Sofer's adherence to, 96–97
    use of *haggadic* material in, 31
    See also Scripture and Other Sources Index
Midrash Rabbah, 31
miracles, 89
Mishnah (oral Torah)
    authorship of, 60
    criteria for examination of, 102
    development of, 8–15, 64–81, 94, 102, 103–104, 203
    discussion of homosexuality, 164, 166
    discussions of issues
        corporal punishment, 161
        divorce, 108
        form of, 15–17
        oaths, 110
        slave treatment, 70
        types of issues dealt with, 13–14
        witness qualifications, 65–66
        yoke of the kingdom of heaven, 114
    establishment of law of *prozbol*, 168–169
    explanations for suffering of Jews, 9, 17
    as *halakhah*, 22
    importance in Jewish life, 95
    Maimonides's commentary on, 33, 86–88
    paucity of citations of Bible, 15, 132n79
    publication of, 18–20, 31, 103–104
    rejection of, 81–82
    as repetition of Scripture, 83
    teaching of, 25, 26
    title of, 200
    transvaluation of scripture, 63
    See also Gemara; Scripture and Other Sources Index; Talmud
Mishnaic period (ca. 100 BCE - 200 CE), 21n44
mishpaṭ (custom become law), 77n65
missionaries, 37
modern Jewish agenda, 100–101
monetary compensation, 68, 160–163, 184, 185
Moses
    as author of Pentateuch, 4–6, 60, 205n7
    authorship of Psalms, 59
    Biblical link of Abraham to, 194
    commission of, 63
    conversations with God, 58, 170
    giving of commandments, 147
    Jesus's relationship to, 124–126
    Jewish vs. Christian and Islamic view of, 87
    means of reconciliation, 192n46
    production of water in wilderness, 196
    at transfiguration of Jesus, 126

Moses ben Maimon. *See* Maimonides (1135-1204 CE)
murder, 76, 105–106, 158, 181

N

nedavah (free-will offering), 188
Neder (sacrifice ratifying vow), 188
neo-Platonism, 38, 57–58
Nev'im (History), 1–4, 104
New Testament
    acceptance as Scripture, 131, 173
    Acts, 45
    apocalyptic literature, 46
    canonization of, xix, 10, 37–43, 46, 103, 135
    citing of Ten Commandments, 180
    as continuation of Old Testament, xvii–xviii
    epistles, 45–46
    gospels, 43–45
    historical context, 46–50, 102–103
    language of, 37, 40, 205–206
    Luther's excision of books of, 137–138
    methodology of interpretation
        allegory, 130–131
        analogical interpretation, 132–133
        argument from prophecy, 123–128
        hermeneutics of Jesus in Matthew, 104–119
        methodology of Paul, 119–123
        tropology, 132
        typology, 128–130
    parables of, 134–135
    transvaluation of Old Testament texts
        concerning resurrection of Jesus, 178–179
        concerning Virgin Birth, 174–177
        on manna, 182–184
        on Ten Commandments, 179–180
        treatment of Isaiah 40:3, 185–187
    words of Jesus, 205
    writing of, 43–46, 102, 103–104, 135
    See also Scripture and Other Sources Index
non-denominational congregations, ix
non-Jewish Christian converts, 52, 115–116

O

oath-taking, 110, 112
offerings, 17n37, 73, 77–79, 89, 187–188
'olah (burnt offering), 187–188
Old Testament
    application to Jesus, 131
    canonization of, 36–39
    Christian adoption of, 136, 200
    Luther's reduction of, 137
    New Testament interpretation of, 104–119
    parables of, 133, 134
    reduction of written traditions, xvii–xviii, 118, 137–138
    references to in Matthew, 123–128
    translations of, 157
    See also Hebrew Bible; Scripture and Other Sources Index; Septuagint
opening question of argument, 19, 122–123
oral Torah, 13–14. *See also* Mishnah (oral Torah)
oral tradition
    of Catholic Church, 136–137, 139
    of Judaism. *See* Mishnah (oral Torah)
Orthodox Judaism
    authority of rabbinate, 98
    foundation of, 84n80
    fundamental doctrines of, 96n102
    opposition to Reform Judaism, 96–99, 100
    position on Jewishness, x

P

pais (child), 189
Palestine, 13, 32, 46–50
papal fiat, 201
parables, 133–135
pardes, 132n83
Passover meal preparation, 77–78
Paul
    compared to Jesus, 51
    contradiction of Virgin Birth, 175
    correlation of water in the wilderness with Jesus, 195–196
    death of, 46n24
    dispute with Peter, 115–116
    as founder of Christianity, 51–54
    on marriage between Christians and unbelievers, 122
    methodology of, 119–123, 131
    position on law, 119, 121–123, 190–195
    position on repentance, 121
    reference to Ten Commandments, 180
    teaching on lawsuits, 185
    treatment of resurrection of Jesus, 178, 179
    use of his own judgment, 206–207
    writing of Scripture, 103, 136
peace offerings, 188
penance, 138n103
Pentateuch. *See* Torah
pera ṭ (particular) law, 72–81
Persian Empire, 10
pesha ṭ (plain sense), 65–66, 68, 77, 81, 132n83, 168
Peter
    dispute with Paul, 51, 115–116
    epistles of, 40, 45, 46
    as foundation of church, 134
    lack of reference to Virgin Birth, 175
    at transfiguration of Jesus, 126
    writing of Scripture, 103
    as Zealot, 49
Pharisees
    actions against Jesus, 43, 50
    on authoritative Scriptures, 12
    interpretation of Scriptures, 11, 12
    involvement in politics, 110
    Jesus's attack on, 44, 116–117
    questions asked of Jesus, 43, 117, 118
    rabbis on, 196–199
    reduction of written traditions, xvii
    survival of destruction of Judea, 13
    types of, 198
Philo of Alexandria
    interpretation of Scripture, 56–58
    on practices of Essenes, 111, 112
    use of allegory, 130, 131
    use of Septuagint, 58, 173
    view of binding of Isaac, 129
philosophical thought, 94. *See also* Greek philosophy
Plato's body/soul dualism, 118, 121n49
plerein (fulfillment), 126
political independence, 18
post-Biblical preludes to rabbinic interpretation
    Josephus, 58–59
    Philo of Alexandria, 56–58
    Pseudepigrapha, 59–63
    view of Israel's suffering, 9
post-rabbinic Jewish hermeneutics
    challenges to oral-Torah, 81–84
    Maimonides, 85–90
    Rashi, 84–85
post-Talmudic era, 32
prayer, 17, 25
pre-canonical gospels, 103
property rights, 68, 73–74
prophecy
    compared to apocalypticism, 156
    Matthew's argument from, 123–128
    transvaluation of, 153–157
prophets (men), 10, 118, 196–197
Prophets (Old Testament books), 2–4, 6, 12, 61. *See also* Scripture and Other Sources Index
Protestant English Bible, 2n1
Protestantism
    Luther's break with Catholicism, 137–139
    rise of denomination, 140

transvaluation of Ten
    Commandments, 181
proto-orthodox Christianity, 38
proverbs, 134
prozbol law, 167–170, 182
Pseudepigrapha, 137, 157, 173
Pseudo-Jonathan, 61
purification, 188
purities, 15

Q

"Q," 44, 103
Qal va-ḥomer (lenient to stringent),
    67–68, 135, 162
Qal va-ḥomer sylogism, 67
Qumran community, 81n72, 111,
    124n57, 126

R

rabbi shopping, 17, 32n75
rabbinic era (ca. 100 BCE-100 CE), 10
Rabbinic Judaism, 13, 82–83. See also
    Judaism; rabbis
rabbinic rulings, 13. See also Gemara;
    Mishnah (oral Torah); Talmud
rabbinic texts. See Gemara; Midrash;
    Mishnah (oral Torah); Other
    Rabbinic Works in Scripture
    Index; *responsa*; Talmud
rabbis
    authority of Orthodox rabbis, 98
    development of, 12
    development of faith system, 36,
        64–81, 203
    development of *responsa*, 84–85
    evidence of idea of interpretation,
        56–63
    freedom and authority to interpret
        scripture, xviii-xx, 16–17,
        24–25, 27–28, 76–77, 164, 167,
        171–172, 179
    hermeneutics of, 64–81
    influence on early Christian
        hermeneutics, 102–104
    interpretation of Jeremiah 1:5, 190
    interpretation of Torah, 2n4, 84,
        132–133
    on Ishmael, 194–195
    movement to Babylonia, 18
    organization against Reform
        movement, 96n102
    on Pharisees, 196–199
    position on adultery, 106
    position on resurrection and
        judgment, 179
    problem facing, 9, 17
    production of Septuagint, 58n10
    requirements for, 8–9
    response to Ḥasidim, 91–93, 100
    response to Karaite stance, 82–83
    response to Reform Judaism, 91
    role in synagogue, 30–31
    succession, 98
    as teachers, 20–30
    transvaluation of Biblical texts on
        on capital punishment,
            157–160
        on divine mercy and
            retribution, 170–171
        on eye for an eye rule, 160–164
        on homosexuality, 164–167
        institution of law of prozbol,
            167–170
    transvaluation of Scripture, xvii–
        xix, 200–201
    use of parables, 134, 135
    uses of *haggadah* and Midrash,
        24, 132
    view of God, 85
    view of Pharisees, 197
    See also Akiva; '/yo/yoAmoraim;
        Gamaliel (Hebrew scholar);
        Hillel; Shammai; *Tanna'im*;
        Zugot
Rashi (1040-1105 CE), 84–85
rationalism, 85–90
reconciliation, 192
reductionism, xvii, 118, 137–138
Reform Judaism
    clash with Orthodoxy, 96–99, 100
    foundation of, 84n80
    founding of, xxi, 90–91, 93–95
    interpretation of Scriptures, 204n6
    view of Yeshiva, 98–99
remarriage, 109–110

remez (allegorical), 132n83
reparation, 160–164
repentance
    Paul's position on, 121
    prophetic call for, 155, 157
    rabbinic view of, 120–121, 192
    sin offerings and, 188
responsa, 32, 63, 84–85
restitution, 68, 73–74, 160–164, 184–185
resurrection
    of Jesus, 53, 175, 178–179
    Pauline doctrine, 53–54
    Pseudepigrapha's emphasis on, 60
    Sadducees' rejection of, 11
    as trap question, 43
retribution, 170–171
Revelation of John, 46
righteousness
    Paul's concept of, 52
    Paul's position on, 192
    reward for, 153, 154–155
    as right thing to do, 156–157
Roman era, 11–12
Rome
    capital punishment decisions, 159
    as center of Christianity, 37
    Christianization of (313 CE), 19n42
    conquest of Judea, 58
    crucifixion of criminals, 47
    Jewish war against, xx, 58
    laws on reparation, 162n29
    occupation of Judea, xxi, 10, 46–47, 102, 159, 185, 203
    persecution of Jews, 18
    Sadducees' partnership with, 11, 47, 110
    siege and destruction of Jerusalem, 12–13, 17, 106

S

sacred texts and instruction
    of Christianity
        Acts, 45
        apocalyptic literature, 46
        Apocrypha, 36
        context of, 46–50
        epistles, 45–46
        gospels, 40–45
        Old Testament, 36–40
        Septuagint, 36–39
        teaching of, 37
    of Judaism
        Babylonian Talmud, 19
        Gemara, 18–19, 63, 95
        Jewish Bible, 1–8, 60
        Midrashim, 24–25
        Mishnah (oral Torah), 8–18, 60, 63, 95
        Palestinian/Jerusalem Talmud, 19
        responsa, 32, 63, 84–85
        Shulḥan Arukh, 34–35
        teaching of, 20–31, 37
        works of Maimonides, 32–35
    reshaping for intolerance and violent purposes, xix–xxi
    See also exegesis; hermeneutics of the New Testament in early church; hermeneutics of the rabbis; interpretation of Scriptures; methodology; post-Biblical preludes to rabbinic interpretation; post-rabbinic Jewish hermeneutics; Scripture and Other Sources Index; transvaluation; *specific text*
sacrifices
    categories of, 187–188
    Christian doctrine concerning, 37
    Maimonides view of, 89
    Mishnah on laying hands on, 17n37
    replacement of, 17, 36
    validity of, 197
Sadducees
    on authoritative Scriptures, 11, 81, 83
    as opponents of Jesus, 50
    partnership with Romans, 11, 47, 110
    questions asked of Jesus, 43, 125

sages, 56, 118, 159. *See also* '*Amoraim*; Pharisees; rabbis; Sadducees; *Tanna'im*; Zugot
Sanhedrin
  legislative authority of, 56
  members' actions at trial and death of Jesus, 50
  vote for death penalty, 159
  Zugots as members of, 13n31, 16, 18
science, 34, 141–143
scribes, 116–117, 125
seeds (section of Talmud), 14
Septuagint
  changes to Hebrew text, 58
  as Greek translation of Jewish Bible, 36–39
  influence on Christian interpretation, 173
  Josephus and Philo's use of, 58
  Luther's view of, 137n99
  Paul's use of, 191
  rendering of '*eved* YHWH, 189
  rendering of '*evat davar*, 108
  rendering of Isaiah 40:3, 186
  wording of sixth commandment, 147
Sermon on the Mount, 105, 179–182
Seven Commandments of the Sons of Noah, 164
sexual activity
  adultery, 14, 76, 106–110, 158, 165, 194n50, 204
  Essenes restriction of, 111–112
  homosexuality, 164–167
  between humans and divine beings, 175–177
  incest, 158, 194
  punishment for incest, rape, adultery, 158
Shabbat
  ceremony of, 30
  Christian Sunday replacing, 181, 182, 206
  commandment to remember and celebrate, 146–148
  prohibition of work during, 67–68, 148

  punishment for violation of, 158
Shahadah, 86–88
Shammai, 13n31, 17, 108–110, 117
Shammai school, 108–110
Shema, 24, 105n6, 114–115
Shoah, xx, 203–204
Shulḥan Arukh (Karo), 34–35, 55
Sidra, 31
sin
  Paul's position on, 121
  penance for post-baptismal sin, 138n103
  punishment of, 153–157. *See also* corporal punishment; death penalty; monetary compensation
  rabbinic view of, 120–121, 191–192
sin offering, 188
slave treatment, 69, 70–71, 147
sod (mystical meaning), 132n83
Sodom, 165–167
Sofer, Moshe (rabbi), 96–99
sola scriptura (theological method), 138
Spinoza, Baruch, 94–95
study, 17, 20
succession of rabbis, 98
superstition, 33
synagogue, 17, 25, 30–31, 37

T

Talmud
  Babylonian Talmud (TB), 19, 198
  biur in, 95
  criteria for examination of, 103
  defense of, 82–83
  discussion of unacceptable people, 197
  Maimonides's teachings on, 33–35
  Mishnah (oral Torah), 8–18, 63
  on original number of precepts, 118
  Palestinian/Jerusalem Talmud, 19, 198
  Paul's view of, 52
  publication of, 31

Talmud (Cont.)
  rejection of, 81–82
  Sofer's adherence to, 96–97
  subjects of inquiry, 20–25
  teaching of, 25
  view of homosexuality, 164–167
  See also Gemara; Mishnah (oral Torah); Scripture and Other Sources Index
Talmudic reasoning, 21
Tanakh. See Hebrew Bible
Tanna'im
  application of Ishmael's rules, 70–71, 74
  classification of learners, 29
  development of Mishnah, 13, 15–17, 83, 132n79, 177
  discussion of
    corporal punishment, 161
    death penalty, 159
    divorce, 125
    establishment of law of *prozbol*, 167–168, 169
    Pharisees, 197
    witness qualifications, 65
    yoke, 114
  formula for introduction of Scripture, 105n6
  interpretation of Proverbs, 29
  Josephus's view of rulings of, 59
  known as Hazal, 19n40
  perspective on Biblical language, 205
  positions of, 13n31, 16–17
  privacy of discussions, 93n94
  use of parables, 135
  See also Akiva; Gamaliel (Hebrew scholar); Hillel; Shammai; Zugot
Targum Jonathan, 61
Targum Neofiti, 63
Targum Onkelos, 30, 61n17, 62, 89n85
Targum Onqelos, 61, 63
Targum Yerushalmi, 62
Targum Yonatan, 62
Targumim, 30–31, 61–63, 89n85
taxation, 43, 44, 47
teaching. See education of Jews

Temple
  destruction of, xxi, 12–13, 14, 17–18, 36, 37, 58, 63, 89–90, 102, 106, 149
  Herod's expansion, 47
  Mishnah's rules for worship, 15
  rebuilding of, 10, 187
  replacement of, 17–18, 36, 37
Temple authorities, 43, 117
Ten Commandments
  Christian transvaluation of, 105–106, 179–182
  Jewish transvaluation of, 76, 145–148
thank offering, 188
theft, 73–74, 76–77, 158
theodicy, 152–153, 170–171
Theological-Political Treatise (Mendelssohn), 95n97
Tôdah (thank offering), 188
Torah
  authorship of, 4–6, 60, 87, 205n7
  chronicles of actions of Moses, 196
  commandments in, 164n39
  completion of, 9
  halakah as weapon against, 97
  Matthew's arguments from prophecy, 123–128
  Midrash covering, 31
  as only authoritative Scripture, 11, 81–83
  order of, 80–81
  Paul's citing of, 122, 123
  Paul's transvaluation of, 190–195
  Paul's view of, 52, 119, 121–123, 191
  precepts of, 118, 127–128
  procedure for healed lepers, 125
  provision for failure, 119–120, 192
  rabbinic view of rejection of, 119–120, 194–195
  reading of in Shabbat service, 30
  Sadducees' interpretation of, 11
  subdivisions of, 1–2
  as a translation, 205n7
  translations of, 8, 31, 61
  See also Law
tosephta (additions), 14n34

subject index   249

tradition, 138-139
translations of Christian Bible, 206
translations of Hebrew Bible
   into Arabic by Rashi, 82
   into German, 95
   impossibility of literal translation, 205
   purpose of early translations, 8
   Targumim
      Codex Neofiti, 61
      explanatory comments in, 61
      Jerusalem Targum, 31
      Pseudo-Jonathan, 61
      Targum Neofiti, 63
      Targum Onkelos, 30, 61n17, 62, 89n85
      Targum Onqelos, 61, 63
      Targum Yerushalmi, 62
      Targum Yonatan, 62
   of Torah, 6, 31, 61
   transvaluation by, 58, 61-63, 96-97, 157
   See also Septuagint
transvaluation
   of Christian Bible
      by Church fathers, 136, 138-139
      influences on, 173
      by Luther, 138-139
      in present, 144
   defined, xi, xii, xix
   historical influences, xx-xxi, 9-10, 9-11, 12-13, 17-18, 37, 46-50, 56-57, 63, 91, 94, 152-157
   ideological influences, xx-xxi, 11, 15-16, 17-18, 94, 172, 200
   of Jewish Bible by
      Christians, 13, 38-40, 102, 131, 136, 138-139, 174-199, 200-201
      Jesus in Gospel of Matthew, 105-119
      Josephus, 58-59
      Maimonides, 85-90
      Matthew, 123-128
      Mendelssohn, 95-96
      Paul, 52, 190-196
      Philo, 58
      post-Biblical preludes to rabbinic interpretation, 55-63
      post-rabbinic Jewish hermeneutics, 81-90
      rabbis, 64-81, 157-171
      Rashi, 84-85
      Reform Jews, 91
      Tanna'im and *'Amoraim*, 8-16, 20, 55
      translations, 58, 61-63, 95-97, 157
      Yeshiva students, 25-27
   of Jewish Bible on
      capital punishment, 157-160
      divine mercy and retribution, 170-171
      eye for an eye rule, 160-164
      homosexuality, 164-167
      Isaiah 40:3, 185-187
      Isaiah and Jeremiah, 148-151
      loan repayment, 167-170
      manna, 182-184
      resurrection of Jesus, 178-179
      Ten Commandments, 145-148, 179-182
      Virgin Birth, 174-177
   potential for disaster, 202-203
   in Pseudepigrapha, 59-63, 157
   purpose of, 100, 102, 144, 157, 164, 167, 171-172
   rabbinic compared to Christian, 173-174, 190, 192-193
   validity of, 151, 152, 171-172
tropology, 132
Twelve Tables of Canonized Law (Rome), 162n29
typology, 38, 128-130, 138-139

U

universal flood, 129-130

V

Vatican II, 136n96, 143-144
Virgin Birth, 174-177
vows, 110, 112

W

water in the wilderness, 196
Westphalian rabbinical council, 97
witnesses, 65, 110, 147
women, 14
work, 148
Writings
    authorship of, 6
    early use of, 10
    Pharisees' interpretation of, 12
    subdivisions of, 4
    translations of, 61
    See also Scripture and Other Sources Index

Y

Yehuda ha-Nasi,' 18
Yeshivah, 25–27, 98–99
YHWH. *See* God
yoke, 24, 113–116
Yom Kippur, 69–70, 112

Z

Zealots, 12, 49
zera' (offering), 189
zevaḥ, 187–188
Zugot, 13n31, 16–17, 18, 37. *See also* Akiva; Gamaliel (Hebrew scholar); Hillel; Shammai; *Tanna'im*
Zugot era (ca. 174 BCE - 10 CE), 13, 16–17

www.ingramcontent.com/pod-product-compliance
Lightning Source LLC
Chambersburg PA
CBHW050344230426
43663CB00010B/1985